THE WISDOM OF FRUGALITY

THE WISDOM
OF FRUGALITY

Why Less Is More—More or Less

Emrys Westacott

PRINCETON UNIVERSITY PRESS

Princeton and Oxford

Published by Princeton University Press, 41 William Street,
Princeton, New Jersey 08540

In the United Kingdom: Princeton University Press, 6 Oxford
Street, Woodstock, Oxfordshire OX20 1TR

press.princeton.edu

Jacket art: Diogenes of Sinope. Detail from Raphael's
The School of Athens (1509–1511)

Library of Congress Cataloging-in-Publication Data

Names: Westacott, Emrys, author.
Title: The wisdom of frugality : why less is more—more or
    less / Emrys Westacott.
Description: Princeton, NJ : Princeton University Press, 2016.
    | Includes bibliographical references and index.
Identifiers: LCCN 2016002388 | ISBN 9780691155081 (hard-
    cover : alk. paper)
Subjects: LCSH: Simplicity. | Thriftiness.
Classification: LCC BJ1496 .W47 2016 | DDC 179/.9—dc23
    LC record available at https://lccn.loc.gov/2016002388

British Library Cataloging-in-Publication Data is available

This book has been composed in Minion Pro and Goudy Sans Std

Printed on acid-free paper. ∞

Printed in the United States of America

10 9 8 7 6 5 4 3 2 1

For Sophie and Emily

Contents

THE WISDOM OF FRUGALITY

Introduction

For well over two thousand years frugality and simple living have been recommended and praised by people with a reputation for wisdom. Philosophers, prophets, saints, poets, culture critics, and just about anyone else with a claim to the title of "sage" seem generally to agree about this. Frugality and simplicity are praiseworthy; extravagance and luxury are suspect.

This view is still widely promoted today. Each year new books appear urging us to live more economically, advising us how to spend less and save more, critiquing consumerism, or extolling the pleasures and benefits of the simple life.[1] Websites and blogs devoted to frugality, simple living, downsizing, downshifting, or living slow are legion.[2] The magazine *Simple Living* can be found at thousands of supermarket checkout counters.

All these books, magazines, e-zines, websites, and blogs are full of good ideas and sound precepts. Some mainly offer advice regarding personal finance along with ingenious and useful money-saving tips. (The advice is usually excellent; the tips vary in value. I learned from

Amy Dacyczyn's *The Tightwad Gazette* how to make a toilet-brush holder out of an empty milk carton, and I have never bought a toilet-brush holder since! On the other hand, her claim that one can mix real and fake maple syrup with no significant loss in quality failed a rudimentary family taste test.) But while a few treat frugality as primarily a method for becoming rich, or at least for achieving financial independence, most are concerned with more than cutting coupons, balancing checkbooks, and making good use of overripe bananas. They are fundamentally about lifestyle choices and values. And although they are not works of philosophy, they are nonetheless connected to and even undergirded by a venerable philosophical tradition that in the West goes back at least as far as Socrates. This tradition constitutes a moral outlook—or, perhaps more accurately, a family of overlapping moral perspectives—that associates frugality and simplicity with virtue, wisdom, and happiness. Its representatives typically critique luxury, extravagance, materialism, consumerism, workaholism, competitiveness, and various other related features of the way many people live. And they offer alternative ideals connected to values such as moral purity, spiritual health, community, self-sufficiency, and the appreciation of nature.

One could view the plethora of publications advocating frugal simplicity as evidence of a sea change regarding values and lifestyles that is currently under way or at least beginning. But the fact that philosophers have been pushing the same message for millennia without it becoming the way of the world should give us pause. Many people pay lip service to the ideals of frugality and simplicity, but you still don't see many politicians trying to get elected on a platform of policies shaped by the principle that the good life is the simple life. On the contrary, politicians promise and governments strive to raise their society's levels of production and consumption. The value of continual economic growth is a given. The majority of individuals everywhere, judging by their behavior, and in spite of all the aforementioned literature, seem to associate happiness more with extravagance than with frugality.

One way of understanding this paradox is to see it as a paradigm case of good old-fashioned human hypocrisy. But that is too simple, and not just because many people live consistently thrifty or exuberantly extravagant unhypocritical lives. The gap between what is preached and what is practiced, between the received wisdom we respect and the character of our culture, reflects a deeper tension between two competing conceptions of the good life, both of which are firmly grounded in our intellectual and cultural traditions. Events like the recession that began in 2008 heighten this tension and make us more aware of it. Hard times spur renewed interest in the theory and practice of thrift while intensifying people's desire to see—and enjoy—a return to getting and spending.

Most books and articles about frugality and simple living are polemical: their aim is both to criticize materialistic beliefs, values, and practices and to advocate an alternative way of thinking and being. Although I am

decidedly sympathetic to the outlook they recommend
(and my family can vouch for my being certifiably tight-
wadish), this book is not a polemic. Readers expecting
a searing critique of consumerism will be disappointed.
Although in places, particularly in the final two chapters, I
defend some of the tenets of the "philosophy of frugality"
against possible criticisms, the purpose of the work is not
to tell the reader: You must change your life! Rather, the
book is a philosophical essay, an extended reflection on
a set of questions relating to the notions of frugality and
simplicity, a reflection that begins by referencing certain
strains in the history of ideas in order to elucidate issues
and to provide a springboard for discussing whether the
wisdom of the past still holds today.

The book began as a study of frugality, but I soon realized
that it was hard to discuss frugality without also discussing
the idea of simplicity, or simple living. From ancient times
to the present, the notions have very often been run together
and discussed as an entire package of virtues and values. To
a large extent I do the same. For brevity's sake I use labels
like "the frugal sages," "the philosophy of frugality," or "the
frugal tradition," but in all such cases I am referring to the
philosophical tradition that associates both frugality and
simplicity with wisdom, virtue, and happiness.

The question I began with seemed straightforward
enough: Should frugality be considered a moral virtue?
Almost every canonical philosopher with whose work
I was familiar seemed to think that it should be. But
why? These questions quickly led to a host of others.
For instance:

- Why have so many philosophers identified living well (the good life) with living simply?
- Why is simple living so often associated with wisdom?
- Should extravagance and indulgence in luxury be viewed as moral failings? If so, why?
- Is it foolish or morally reprehensible to be extravagant even if one has the means to be a spendthrift?
- Are there social arguments for or against frugal simplicity quite apart from its consequences for the individual?
- Is it possible that frugality, like chasteness, or silent obedience in children, is an outmoded value, a trait that most people no longer consider an important moral virtue?

Chapter 1 examines what is meant by the terms "frugality" and "simplicity," identifying what I take to be their most important senses, and fleshing out the explication of these by using as illustrative examples specific figures from the philosophical tradition I am mining. After a preliminary discussion of the distinction between moral and prudential reasoning, chapter 2 examines the main arguments that have been given for thinking that living simply promotes moral virtue. This is one of the main lines of argument advanced by the frugal sages. Chapter 3 looks at their other main line of argument, that living simply leads to happiness.

It is rather striking that although there is a consensus among the sages that living simply is better than living luxuriously, and that frugality is better than extravagance, hardly any of them take the trouble to consider seriously arguments that might be mustered against this view. Chapters 4 and 5 seek to correct this deficiency. Chapter 4 discusses the dangers of frugality along with the positive side of wealth and acquisitiveness. Chapter 5 considers what can be said in favor of extravagance.

The Epicureans, the Stoics, and many of the other well-known sages belonging to the frugal tradition in philosophy wrote long ago. Given the dramatic transformation of the world since the Industrial Revolution, it is reasonable to ask to what extent their wisdom is still relevant today. Two changes in particular need to be taken into account: the vast increase in the size, complexity, and productivity of modern economies; and the threat to the natural environment posed by the activities and lifestyles that accompany all this economic growth. Chapter 6 examines the idea that the philosophy of frugality is basically obsolete in the modern world since in a consumer society the general happiness depends on most people not being especially frugal. Chapter 7 lays out the argument that a general shift toward frugal simplicity is exactly what we need to protect our environment from further damage, and considers several objections to this proposition.

A good deal of contemporary academic philosophy consists of sophisticated discussion, often couched in technical jargon, of narrowly defined theoretical issues. Papers at a recent meeting of the American Philosophical Association with titles like "Quantifier Variance and Ontological Deflationism" or "Modally Plenitudinous Endurantism," are of this sort. Scholarship in the history of philosophy typically offers subtle interpretations of thinkers and texts, backed by impressive erudition showing, perhaps, how Kant's moral philosophy does not, as some critics claim, inconsistently make use of utilitarian arguments, or uncovering ways in which Sartre's account of "the other" is indebted to Augustine's conception of God. It is not my concern here to criticize these ways of contributing to our understanding of philosophical issues. But philosophy has always been conceived more broadly than this. From the beginning, it has also included a general reflection on life, and this reflection does not have to be terribly complicated or use lots of specialized terminology. This is the sense in which figures like Seneca, Marcus Aurelius, More, Montaigne, Rousseau, Voltaire, Johnson, Emerson, or Thoreau can legitimately be called philosophers. Many of these are not much studied in Anglophone philosophy departments these days. To some extent this is a historical accident, but it also reflects the interests, both intellectual and vested, of academic philosophers, who generally prefer to tackle challenging theoretical or hermeneutic problems that offer opportunities for them to exercise their particular skills.

What I refer to as the "philosophy of frugality" is an example of philosophizing in the broader sense. Unlike the more specialized and professionalized kinds of philosophy, it often finds expression in literature and popular culture, and I have occasionally referenced these to bring out this connection. One book that was especially instrumental in directing my attention to this tradition of philosophy as reflection on life, and is itself a fine contribution to that tradition, is William Irvine's *A Guide to the Good Life:*

The Ancient Art of Stoic Joy.[3] Irvine argues that the ancient Stoics offer insights into human nature and sound advice on how to achieve happiness that we would be well advised to listen to today. I agreed with much of what I read in Irvine's book, but found myself wondering why, in spite of its seeming cogency, a mass revival of Stoicism is unlikely. This led me to try to set out and appreciate some of the plausible arguments that can be made in favor of the quite different outlook on life that prevails today.

Again, the book is not a polemic. My general outlook is sympathetic to those who advocate frugal simplicity, but I do not think all the good arguments are on one side of the ledger. I have tried to do justice to some of the objections that might be leveled against the philosophy of frugality, and on some questions my final position is to come down firmly on both sides of the fence. Rather than making the strongest possible case for a particular conclusion, my main purpose has been to clarify the concepts, values, assumptions, and arguments related to the sort of questions posed above. My hope is that by bringing these into sharper focus, the book will help readers to reflect on such questions for themselves. For the issues are both inherently interesting and important, concerning as they do how we choose to live, what ends are worth pursuing in life, and what goals we should seek to realize as a society.

CHAPTER 1

What Is Simplicity?

The concept of simple living is complex. It encompasses a cluster of overlapping ideas, so our first task must be to identify and clarify the most important of these. One useful way of achieving an initial orientation is to consider some of the synonyms for terms like "frugal," "thrifty," and "simple." Here is a partial list.

mean	ascetic	serious	frugal	wholesome
miserly	self-denying	simple	thrifty	salubrious
closefisted	abstemious	prosaic	economical	unpretentious
cheeseparing	austere	stodgy	temperate	unaffected
stingy	severe	plain	moderate	unassuming
ungenerous	Spartan	homespun	continent	honest
illiberal	puritanical	dry	self-controlled	natural
parsimonious	unpampered	measured		pure
penny-	poor	careful		
pinching	hardy	sparing		
	unadorned	prudent		
	undecorated	provident		
	modest	scrimping		
		skimping		

The attentive reader will notice that the columns have been strategically arranged to bring out the fact that the terms form a spectrum of implicit or associated value judgments from mean and miserly (bad) to pure and natural (good). As one would expect, though, the champions of frugal simplicity like to accentuate the positive; and positive associations are also provided by the etymology of words like "frugality" and "thrift." "Thrift" has a common root with "thrive"; both derive from the Old Norse *thrifa*, meaning to grasp or get hold of. In Chaucer's Middle English of the late fourteenth century, "thrifti" meant thriving, prosperous, fortunate, respectable. And in his eighteenth-century dictionary, Samuel Johnson defines "thrift" as "profit; gain; riches gotten; state of prospering." "Frugal" comes from the Latin term *frugalis*, meaning economical or useful, which is itself derived from *frux*, meaning fruit, profit, or value.

Today, most people are favorably disposed toward the idea of simple living, at least in theory. When a person is described as practicing frugality or having simple tastes, this is usually understood as a form of praise, especially if he or she could easily live otherwise. Celebrities who live in modest homes and ride the bus are not just applauded for remaining in touch with the common people; their lifestyle is also thought to bespeak nonmaterialistic values and hence a certain moral health or purity. But even when viewed in this positive light, the notions of thrift, frugality, and simple living carry a number of meanings. Here we will consider the most important of these, in some cases fleshing out the idea by identifying exemplary figures who serve to represent and articulate the senses of frugality or simplicity in question. Making use of particular sages in this way should also lend a little color to the idea of a long-standing tradition of philosophical reflection on the nature and virtues of simple living.

ECONOMIC PRUDENCE

This is probably the most familiar and uncomplicated sense of thrift. It finds expression in many well-worn adages:

> Waste not, want not.
> A penny saved is a penny earned.
> Willful waste makes woeful want.
> Take care of the pennies and the pounds will take care of themselves.

One frugal sage particularly associated with this idea of fiscal prudence is Benjamin Franklin. Franklin was the archetypical self-made man. At seventeen he arrived in Philadelphia a penniless fugitive, having left without permission an apprenticeship at his brother's printing house in Boston. By the age of forty he was a best-selling author and comfortably off. When he died at eighty-four, he was celebrated as one of greatest men of his time for his achievements as an entrepreneur, writer, politician, diplomat, scientist, inventor, and philanthropist. An interesting and rather endearing section of his autobiography is his account of how he sought to cultivate within himself thirteen specific virtues. The fifth in his list of virtues was frugality, which he defined for himself in this way: "Make no Expence but to do good to others or yourself; i.e. Waste nothing."[1] Although Franklin was surprised by and lamented his failure to perfect within himself many of the qualities on the list, frugality seems to have been one that gave him little trouble. One reason for this, according to his own account, was that his wife Deborah was

> as much dispos'd to Industry and Frugality as my self. . . . We kept no idle Servants, our Table was plain & simple, our Furniture of the cheapest. For instance, my Breakfast was for a long time Bread and Milk, (no Tea,) and I ate it out of a twopenny earthen Porringer with a Pewter Spoon.[2]

Franklin amusingly goes on to note "how luxury will enter families . . . in spite of principle"; in his case, Deborah one day served him breakfast with fine tableware that she had bought simply because she thought "*her* Husband deserv'd a Silver Spoon & China Bowl as well as any of his Neighbors."[3] But by then, and for the rest of his life, he could easily afford such luxuries, a circumstance he repeatedly ascribes to his early habits of frugality and industry.

Franklin's essay "The Way to Wealth" contains many of his best-known maxims on frugality, most advising us to live within our means and to beware of waste and luxuries. For example:

> A fat kitchen makes a lean will.
> Who dainties love, shall beggars prove.
> Fools make feasts, and wise men eat them.
>
> Fond pride of dress, is sure a very curse;
> E'er fancy you consult, consult your purse.

Get what you can, and what you get hold;

'Tis the stone that will turn all your lead into gold.[4]

Franklin is especially concerned to warn against the dangers of debt, since "he that goes a-borrowing goes a-sorrowing." Debt, he says, "exposes a man to confinement, and a species of slavery to his creditors." Debt is still spreading much misery, of course, usually in the form of credit card balances, student loans, and underwater mortgages. But in the eighteenth and nineteenth centuries, the consequences of going into debt could be even more ruinous than today. In Dickens's London, the debtor's prison and the workhouse cast long shadows over many lives. And Victorian novels are stuffed with edifying examples of characters who illustrate the folly of living beyond one's means, from Mr. Micawber in Dickens's *David Copperfield* to Felix Carbury in Trollope's *The Way We Live Now*.[5]

Partly because it is so familiar, however, this sense of frugality—exercising fiscal prudence and living within one's means—is one of its less interesting meanings. Practicing thrift is obviously sensible for those of us who haven't inherited a fortune, who don't posses some highly marketable talent, or who lack the extraordinary salary-negotiating skills of a Kenneth Chenault (CEO of American Express, who in 2011 received a pay increase of 38 percent, taking his weekly wage to around half a million dollars). There can, of course, be circumstances where going into debt temporarily makes sense: for instance, to buy a house, pay for education, take advantage of a business opportunity, or deal with a pressing hardship such as eviction or a medical emergency. But for most of us, most of the time, Ben Franklin's advice is clearly sound. "Beware of little expenses," he says; "a small leak will sink a great ship." And who would disagree? Well, there is always Oscar Wilde, according to whom, "the only thing that can console one for being poor is extravagance," and who, according to one account, lived and died true to his philosophy. Impoverished and on his deathbed in a seedy hotel in Paris, Oscar supposedly raised a glass of champagne and declared, "I die as I have lived—beyond my means." But few aspire to that sort of end.

My main concern in this chapter and throughout is not primarily with frugality understood as Franklinesque fiscal prudence. That notion is relatively uncomplicated, and the reasons for practicing it are fairly obvious. Rather more interesting are some of the other meanings attached to the notion of simple living as championed by the philosophers of frugality.

LIVING CHEAPLY

Living cheaply means adopting a lifestyle that requires relatively little money and uses relatively few resources. One point on which most frugal sages are agreed is that such a lifestyle is not difficult to achieve, since the necessities of life are few and easily obtained. What are these bare necessities? Strictly speaking, they consist of nothing more than food and drink adequate for survival and protection from the elements in the form of basic clothing and shelter. But one might also throw in a few tools and implements to be used in the securing of these necessities, along with some companions in deference to Epicurus's claim that friendship is indispensable to human happiness.

Many of us like to believe we live cheaply, or at least that we know how to. Even people with three-car garages, summer homes, and sailboats enjoy telling stories of how earlier in life they lived in a shoebox and got by on oatmeal and the smell of an oily rag. But before we get too smug, we should perhaps recall and compare ourselves with Diogenes of Sinope, beside whom Ben and Deborah Franklin look like a pair of decadents wallowing in luxury.

Diogenes (c. 404–323 BCE) is the best known of the Cynic philosophers. The label "Cynic" is derived from the Greek *kynikos*, meaning doglike, and it was probably first applied to the Cynics as a term of abuse that likened their way of life to that of dogs. The stories told about Diogenes indicate that he had an acerbic wit, loved to buck convention, was contemptuous of abstract theorizing (Plato's in particular), and rigorously practiced what he preached. They also suggest that he found it amusing to see how he might live on less and with less.

Although he is usually depicted as using a barrel or large earthenware jar as a shelter, this may have been during his more decadent period. The sight of a mouse running around without any concern for finding a bed or protective shelter is supposed to have inspired him to accept cheerfully even greater poverty. Thereupon he doubled up his cloak to make a bed, kept his food in a bag, and ate, slept, and did whatever else he felt like doing wherever he felt like doing it. Reproached for eating in the marketplace, he said, "I did it, for it was in the market place I felt hungry"—a classic example of criticizing conventions in the name of what is natural. Yet he found he could still make do with even less. Seeing a child drinking out of his hands, he threw away the one cup he owned, saying, "That child has beaten me in simplicity." On another occasion he threw away his spoon, after seeing a boy whose bowl had broken eat his lentils using a crust of bread.[6]

Like Socrates, Diogenes seems to have had no problem accepting things from others. Asked what wine he most liked to drink, he answered, "That which belongs to another." But he did not see this as incurring an obligation to the giver, since he viewed material goods as having little or no value, especially when compared to simple, easily obtained pleasures. This is the moral of the famous story about the meeting of Diogenes and Alexander. When the ruler of the world was taken to see the philosopher, he found him sitting contentedly in the sun. Asked to name a favor he would like Alexander to do for him, Diogenes merely asked him to stop blocking the sunlight. He argued that since the gods lacked nothing, to want nothing was to be like the gods, and to come closer to this state Diogenes would toughen himself to put up with any hardship by rolling in the hot sand in summer and embracing snow-covered statues in winter. To be sure, he once asked the Athenians to erect a statue in his honor, which looks like a fairly grand desire; but when asked his reason for making this request, he said, "I am practicing for disappointment"—in other words, he was toughening himself up mentally as well. Were he a philosophy professor today, he would probably ask for regular pay raises.

Not surprisingly, Diogenes was considered pretty eccentric in his time, but he was understood to be putting a philosophy into practice. Anyone emulating him today, though, would probably be viewed by most people as mentally ill. This brings out the obvious point that what people consider "cheap" or "basic" or "necessary" varies according to time, place, and social class. These concepts are relative. A normal lifestyle for an Athenian citizen in Diogenes's day required far fewer accoutrements than are needed by a twenty-first-century New Yorker, whose "basic needs" might include electricity, running water, a flush toilet, central heating, air-conditioning, an equipped kitchen, a smartphone, an Internet connection, and a nearby Starbucks.

Scores of books and an unending stream of magazine articles are devoted to the topic of how to live cheaply by cutting costs, although the basic strategies are hardly mysterious: buy used items rather than new; where possible, do things for yourself rather than pay someone else; stock up on staple groceries when they're on sale; use discount coupons; grow some of your own food; don't eat out much; and in general follow the old formula "Use it up, wear it out, make it do, or do without." Some of this advice is timeless, but some can be rendered less relevant, less sensible, or less appealing by social and technological change. There was a time when it almost always made economic sense to repair an item rather than replace it, so people would darn socks, patch sheets, and take their defective video recorder in for repair. But when half a dozen socks cost what a minimum-wage worker can earn in less than an hour, and when the cost of repairing a machine may easily be more than the price of a new one, some of the old ways can seem outdated. Treating things as disposable used to be an attitude associated with the rich. When Russian aristocrats hurled their wineglasses into the fireplace after drinking from them, they were flaunting their wealth. Today, though, using disposable items, or treating things as disposable, is often more economical in terms of both money and time. So while the guiding idea of living cheaply remains central to the notion of frugal simplicity, the methods of achieving this goal have to take into account changing times.

SELF-SUFFICIENCY

Taken literally, to be self-sufficient is to not be dependent on anything other than oneself. No living things can be perfectly self-sufficient in this literal sense since all depend on their environment to provide them with the means of life. But they can be more or less independent of others. Self-sufficiency is thus always a matter of degree.

The frugal sages regularly praise self-sufficiency, but they do not all have exactly the same thing in mind. Self-sufficiency contrasts with dependence, of which there are two main kinds: dependence on another's patronage, and dependence on someone else's skills or services, either directly, as when one hires a plumber, or indirectly through technology produced by others. When Greek and Roman thinkers like Epicurus and Seneca talk about self-sufficiency, they typically contrast it with the first sort of dependency since they worry a good deal about the dangers of patronage. For them, being self-sufficient means, above all else, not being dependent on another person's favor or good opinion. For much of human history, enjoying the favor of one's social superiors has been a major avenue to success and an important defense against poverty and oppression. But of course one usually pays a price for such favor. Ideally, favor would be bestowed purely on the basis of merit, but everyone knows that the world does not typically work that way. Dependents must often flatter and fawn; they are expected to endorse their patron's words and approve of his or her actions. This is true whether one is a courtier complimenting a king, a politician currying favor with the crowd, or an employee hoping to impress a supervisor. Dependency of this sort thus inhibits one's ability to think, speak, and act as one sees fit. Being independent of such constraints is liberating, which is why Epicurus says that "the greatest fruit of self-sufficiency is freedom."[7]

There are interesting lines of connection between this classical conception of self-sufficiency and Emerson's famous essay on self-reliance, which urges the importance of thinking for oneself. But in the modern world, especially in America, the more practical notion of self-sufficiency has come to the fore. Being self-sufficient in this second sense means being able and willing to do things for oneself as opposed to relying on the labor of others. Romantics like Thoreau particularly stress the value of this sort of self-sufficiency, and some extend it to include reducing our dependence on technology. Those who advocate self-sufficiency in this sense seek to counter the alienating effects of modernity, which, by increasing the division of labor and mechanizing so many tasks, has distanced us from nature and from the elementary activities that underpin our lives.

As already noted, self-sufficiency is a matter of degree. Very few human beings are capable of surviving outside a community, and within every community there are cooperative enterprises and some division of labor. Perhaps this is why one of the best-known exemplars of and meditators on this particular frugal virtue is a fictional character. Robinson Crusoe, one of modernity's first great literary heroes, exemplifies almost perfect self-sufficiency, at least in the years before he encounters Friday and makes him his servant. He is not completely self-sufficient since he makes use of tools and materials salvaged from the ship on which he was voyaging before he was shipwrecked, but he comes as close to it as any product of Western civilization is likely to come. In fact Robinson Crusoe celebrates literal independence and self-sufficiency as an important virtue just when it is starting to decline (Defoe's novel was published in 1719). Crusoe himself, as he sets about making bread, is struck by how ignorant he is of the process.

> I neither knew how to grind or make Meal of my corn, or indeed how to clean it and part it, nor if made into Meal, how to make Bread of it, and if how to make it, yet I knew not how to bake it . . . 'tis a little wonderful,

and what I believe few People have thought much upon, (viz.) the strange multitude of little Things necessary in the Providing, Producing, Curing, Dressing, Making and Finishing this one Article of Bread.[8]

In effect, Crusoe's struggle to survive—and eventually thrive—purely by his own wits and labor becomes a metaphor for a different kind of self-sufficiency, the sort that allows individuals to make their own fortune through ingenuity and hard work. The comprehensiveness of his skills and activities—he becomes, among other things, a hunter, a farmer, an animal breeder, a builder, a carpenter, a boat maker, a weaver, a soldier, and a writer—also offers a striking contrast to the specialization and division of labor characteristic of emerging capitalism. For these reasons Crusoe has long been an inspiration to others. In *Emile*, Jean-Jacques Rousseau's seminal work on education, the only novel that Emile is allowed to read before the age of twelve is *Robinson Crusoe*, specifically on the grounds that it will help inculcate the virtue of self-sufficiency.[9] And Thoreau's experiment at Walden can plausibly be viewed as an attempt to re-create for himself, a few miles from home, the conditions of a castaway.

Self-sufficiency is obviously linked to living cheaply, since when you do something for yourself, you don't pay someone else to do it. Consequently, frugality self-help books have always been full of advice on how to brew your own beer, mend your own clothes, extract your own teeth, and so on. But the obvious truth is that most of us living in modernized societies are a million miles from self-sufficiency. Yes, we might cultivate a vegetable garden, learn how to bake bread, and build a bookcase or two. Such activities are not to be despised; apart from saving money they can be intrinsically rewarding. But unless they add up to a definite lifestyle, we should not kid ourselves that we are doing more than playing at self-sufficiency. Most of us depend on others to build and equip our houses, grow and distribute our food, make our clothes, and provide our entertainment. We rely on a complex infrastructure for energy, transport, communication, and education. And we are hopelessly lost without our cars, phones, computers, stoves, and refrigerators. A new generation is now literally lost without a GPS navigation device.

Some communities, such as the Amish, clearly do achieve a significantly greater degree of self-sufficiency. This is partly in virtue of their general preference for forgoing the use of modern technology. But it is also because, as in kibbutzim, monasteries, and other collectives, the Amish work toward communal rather than individual self-sufficiency. Indeed, one reason they are able to manage so well, even farming without tractors or chain saws, and building houses without power tools, is that they can rely on one another to provide the necessary additional labor power. For all that, their horse and buggies may still be seen at times parked outside Walmart.

One further complication in the link between self-sufficiency and simplicity is worth noting. Self-sufficiency may be part of the traditional notion and the Romantic ideal of simple living, but in fairly obvious ways using technology can simplify our lives considerably. Which is simpler, washing all your clothes and sheets by hand, or using a washing machine? Collecting and chopping wood to make a fire to cook over, or turning on the gas burner and pushing the electric ignition button? Walking across town and back to deliver a message, or making a phone call? The point here is that the concept of simple living contains crosscurrents. Reducing our dependence on infrastructure and technology may bring us closer to simple living in one sense—we are more self-sufficient—but takes us away from it in other ways since it makes basic tasks much more difficult, arduous, and time-consuming. And in some ways technology can even help us to be more self-sufficient, as when we use a washing machine to do our own laundry instead of using servants or sending it out.

BEING CLOSE TO NATURE

Some of the sages who advocate simple living have been resolutely urban, living their entire lives within cities and showing little interest in bonding with nature. But a connection between simplicity and the natural is a long-standing idea affirmed by many philosophers of frugality. The link can be made in several ways, though, depending on how the idea of being close to nature is conceived.

Diogenes the Cynic was one of the first to urge that whatever is natural cannot be bad and so should not be a source of shame. According to some reports he thought nothing of urinating or defecating in public.[10] The Stoics also prized the natural: according to Marcus Aurelius, "the natural can never be inferior to the artificial."[11] They particularly stressed the importance of living in harmony with nature, of trying to cultivate a state of mind and a way of being that are attuned to the cosmos rather than at odds with it. That is a rather abstract formula, of course, but it can be cashed out, at least in part, as encouraging us to accept rather than oppose or lament the natural order of things. Aging and death, for instance, should be seen as necessary aspects of life, no more to be regretted than the succession of the seasons or the alternation of day and night. The Stoics also pointed out that contemplating and studying nature can be one of life's greatest pleasures. It is also, happily, the most readily available, open to everyone at all times, even those like Seneca or his fellow Stoic Musonius who found themselves stripped of their wealth and exiled to remote islands.

Contemporary notions of what being close to nature involves have been heavily influenced by the Romantic movement, triggered by the advent of industrialization and increasing urbanization in the eighteenth and nineteenth centuries. In response to these trends, the Romantics stressed the importance of remaining in touch both physically and spiritually with the natural world. As Wordsworth succinctly put it:

One impulse from a vernal wood
Can teach you more of man,
Of moral evil, and of good,
Than all the sages can.[12]

But probably the best-known modern example of an individual choosing to live in rustic simplicity, away from the artificiality and sophistication of urban society (and its accompanying expenses), in order to be closer to nature is Henry David Thoreau. In 1845 Thoreau built a small cabin on land owned by his friend Ralph Waldo Emerson close to Walden Pond near Concord, Massachusetts, and lived there for a little over two years. The literary fruit of this experiment in living was *Walden; or, Life in the Woods*, a strange combination in one book of memoir, naturalist observations, philosophical reflections, and social commentary. Thoreau's detractors like to point out that his experiment was slightly less radical than readers of *Walden* might think, since he maintained contact with family and friends throughout his sojourn, often enjoying meals at their houses. But Thoreau does not hide this fact, and just because his experiment in living was not more extreme does not mean it has less interest or value. He was, after all, living more economically, more self-sufficiently, and closer to nature than any of his critics.

One of the things that makes *Walden* memorable and important is Thoreau's ability to illustrate and articulate— to both show and tell—exactly why living close to nature is a cardinal value for people like himself, and, by implication, why a healthy connection to the natural world would ideally be a feature of every human life. In Thoreau's view, it is not simply one among many optional sources of pleasure to be chosen from the hedonic buffet counter. To be close to nature is necessary if one is, in Thoreau's phrase, "to live deep . . . and suck out all the marrow of life."[13] *Walden* is punctuated with prose-poetic passages expressing various shades of contentment, pleasure, delight, gratitude, and awe awakened by the sights and sounds of nature, from the rising of the sun to the buzzing of a mosquito. This passage is typical:

> Sometimes, in a summer morning, having taken my accustomed bath, I sat in my sunny doorway from sunrise til noon, rapt in a revery, amidst the pines and hickories and sumachs, in undisturbed solitude and stillness, while the birds sang around or flitted noiseless through the house, until by the sun falling in at my west window, or the noise of some traveller's wagon on the distant highway, I was reminded of the lapse of time. I grew in those seasons like corn in the night, and they were far better than any work of the hands would have been.[14]

Elsewhere Thoreau explicitly affirms the indispensability of this relationship with the natural world to his own happiness:

> I experienced sometimes that the most sweet and tender, the most innocent and encouraging society may be found in any natural object, even for the poor misanthrope and most melancholy man. There can be no very black melancholy to him who lives in the midst of Nature and has his senses still. There was never yet such a storm but it was Æolian music to a healthy and innocent ear.[15]

Thoreau conducted his experiment for only a short period of his life, returning after a sojourn of two years, two months, and two days to spend the rest of his life living with friends in the town of Concord. The reason he gives is that he "had several more lives to live, and could not spare any more time for that one."[16] In other words, he had other experiments in living to conduct. But until his death in 1862 he remained an avid naturalist. Working as a land surveyor, he continued to extend and deepen his knowledge of the natural environment around Concord, communicating his observations and reflections through lectures and essays.

Few of us try to emulate Thoreau. But a yearning to be in some way in touch with a natural environment runs deep and expresses itself in many ways. It is one reason why people who live in perfectly comfortable homes choose to go camping. It helps explain the popularity among people who can afford them of second homes or cabins in the country, bucolic retreats where life is simple, clean, and quiet, and of backyard gardening for those whose budgets don't extend quite far enough for a country estate. At the very least, most people will include in their domestic ornamentations a few house plants, or some landscape reproductions, or a Sierra Club calendar.

BEING CONTENT WITH SIMPLE PLEASURES

Not every advocate of frugal simplicity values pleasure. Ascetics and puritans have seen pleasure as a worldly distraction from more important spiritual concerns. The ancient Spartans distrusted its potentially softening influence on the character of warriors in training. But the enjoyment of simple pleasures, and their sufficiency for happiness, has long been central to many philosophers' conception of simple living.

The first and still one of the finest champions of simple pleasures is Epicurus. Born in 341 BCE, Epicurus grew up on Samos, although he was an Athenian citizen. After studying philosophy for several years, he began to teach his own doctrines and develop his own school. In his thirties he bought a piece of land on the outskirts of Athens and lived there contentedly with a group of friends and a few servants for the rest of his life. Unlike Plato and a host of other philosophers, Epicurus and his followers unabashedly affirmed the value of pleasure. Ancient Athenian gossips and scandalmongers thus had a field day spreading rumors about the kinky goings-on at the Epicurean compound, and some of this dirt stuck. The term "epicure" for a long time meant someone devoted to sensual pleasures. Today its primary sense is that of a person of refined gastronomic tastes. Yet both senses misrepresent Epicurus's philosophy. He does indeed say that life is good because it affords the opportunity for pleasure:

> I know not how I can conceive the good, if I with-
> draw the pleasures of taste . . . of love . . . of hear-
> ing . . . and the pleasurable emotions caused to sight
> by beautiful forms.[17]

Moreover, Epicurus is no prude: pleasures of the flesh are included in the list of things that make life worth living. So although he is all in favor of simplicity, if he were with us today he would not be ordering a year's supply of Soylent, the "meal replacement" drink created by software engineer Rob Rhinehart, which contains all the nutrients a person needs but which is more or less tasteless. But Epicurus does place some important constraints on the pursuit of plea-sures, and generally prefers those that are easily obtained. Like Socrates, he is convinced that only good people can be truly happy, so whatever pleasures we pursue must be compatible with virtue. He also warns against short-term pleasures like gluttony and sexual license that lead eventu-ally to long-term pains.

The simple pleasures that Epicurus especially praises are such things as plain but good food, satisfying work, the contemplation of nature, and friendship. Naturally, different sages rank these differently. As we just saw, Tho-reau, living in isolation at Walden, places less store on relationships than on the delight he takes in his natural surroundings. Epicurus, on the other hand, sharing his liv-ing quarters and large garden with friends and disciples, holds that "of all the things which wisdom provides for the happiness of the whole life, by far the most important is the acquisition of friendship."[18]

For someone devoted to pleasure Epicurus seems to have been remarkably hardworking. He wrote a prolific number of works, including a treatise on nature that ran to thirty-seven papyrus rolls, although, sadly, few of his writings have survived. But the paradox is only apparent. Philosophical reflection is itself a simple pleasure for those who find it pleasurable, since it requires few resources and can be practiced by anyone at any time.

Epicurus died aged seventy-two, cheerful to the last, even though he spent his final days in considerable pain from kidney stones and dysentery. According to his philosophy, pain is generally bad, but it is not to be feared, since if mild it is bearable, and if severe it is usually short-lived, as it was in his case. Nor is death to be feared: it is simply a return to nonexistence, a trouble-free condition. Underlying Epicurus's outlook on life is a strong sentiment of gratitude, both for life itself, which provides opportunities for pleasure, and for the fact that the best pleasures—the simple ones—are so easily obtained. His character and his philosophy are captured rather nicely in a surviving fragment from one of his letters. "Send me some preserved cheese," he writes to a friend, "that when I like I may have a feast."[19]

ASCETICISM

Asceticism is simple living taken seriously, often for moral or religious reasons. Ascetics deny themselves worldly comforts and physical pleasures. The word comes from the Greek *askesis*, which means exercise or training, and was used to describe the regime practiced by athletes getting ready for a competition. Since ancient times asceticism has been one significant form of simple living, and many religious groups have embraced asceticism to varying degrees. Jains, for instance, traditionally possess very little, wear few clothes, and sleep without blankets. Asceticism has been integral to many strains of Hinduism and Buddhism throughout their history, and has also been taught and practiced by various Christian sects and monastic communities.[20] Carthusian monks, for instance, occupy simple rooms where they spend most of their time in solitude, forgoing even the pleasures of conversation. Judaism and Islam, however, have generally viewed the more extreme forms of asceticism negatively on the grounds that they express a rejection of God's gifts, even though both religions warn against materialism, and revered figures like Muhammad and Baal Shem Tov, the founder of Hasidic Judaism, are admired for their simple lifestyles.

Sometimes ascetics go beyond merely renouncing worldly pleasures like sex, fine food, or cultural entertainments, and deliberately induce discomfort through measures such as fasting, wearing hair shirts, or attaching heavy chains to their legs. Here the purpose is usually to help direct one's attention away from the world and toward more spiritual concerns (although there is always the danger that one might fall into a sort of competitive asceticism, where the extent of one's renunciation becomes a matter of pride). Self-denial has also been viewed and used as a form of penance, a path to enlightenment, and a method of cultivating particular virtues such as hardiness and resilience.

Famous ascetics include the Jainist reformer Mahavira, Siddhartha Gautama (Buddha), John the Baptist, Francis of Assisi, Gandhi, and Tolstoy (in his later years). Few modern Western philosophers have taught or practiced serious asceticism, but quite a few have exhibited decidedly ascetic tendencies, among them Spinoza, Nietzsche, and Wittgenstein. The latter inherited a vast fortune but gave it away to his siblings, from whom he then refused financial assistance, and favored rigorously austere accommodations, partly, it seems, from an innate puritanical streak and partly because he felt this was most conducive to intensely focused thinking. Nietzsche, retiring in his thirties from a professorship at Basel owing to ill health, had no inheritance to fall back on. He eked out a humble existence on a meager pension, renting sparsely furnished rooms in small boardinghouses, during which time he wrote about "ascetic ideals," by which he meant modes of living and evaluating that in some way renounce this world and its joys. His conclusion that philosophers tend to embrace ascetic ideals because they recognize in them conditions that favor their own flourishing was presumably based, to some degree, on self-observation.[21]

In particular times and places asceticism has been surprising popular—among the Puritans, for instance—and occasionally its promotion has even been state policy, as in ancient Sparta. Today, in modernized societies, severe asceticism is practiced only here and there by small groups or by isolated individuals. But we can perceive surviving traces of an ethic of self-denial in our everyday world, as when we describe some luxury or gastronomic delight as "sinful," or enjoy humor that rests on the premise that pleasures like sex or drinking alcohol are matters to be spoken of guiltily in whispers and euphemisms. For the most part, though, asceticism is thoroughly out of fashion nowadays. Vast amounts are spent by advertisers selling comfort, luxury, and sensory enjoyment, and the market for these items appears robust.

PHYSICAL OR SPIRITUAL PURITY

The idea of adopting a lifestyle that one considers clean or pure may sometimes be the motive behind asceticism, but it is nevertheless a distinct notion. The purity in question can be moral/spiritual, involving, say, the avoidance of certain sins or temptations such as covetousness, envy, pride, sexual license, or causing injury to others. Or it might be a more physically grounded notion, satisfied, perhaps, by wearing simple garb, eschewing ornamentation, shaving one's head, and avoiding foods thought to be unclean. Very often, of course, these physical measures symbolically express an inner purity that is typically taken to be more important. This idea comes through in the well-known hymn "Simple Gifts," in which lines like

> When true simplicity is gained
> To bow and to bend we shan't be ashamed

link simplicity of lifestyle with unconcern for the opinions of the world (which tended to mock the Shakers' dancing).

While the idea of clean or pure living may overlap with some of the other senses of simple living, it can also be at odds with them, just as the project of trying to be self-sufficient by eschewing technology can in one sense simplify and in another sense complicate one's lifestyle. Thus the ancient Pythagoreans, who aspired after purity, supposedly would not eat beans, or certain kinds of fish, or food that had fallen on the floor. Yet growing your own beans is so cheap, easy, and beneficial that it has become almost emblematic of the simple life. It is what W. B. Yeats imagines himself doing after he has arisen and gone to Innisfree to live in a cabin "of clay and wattles made."[22] It is what Thoreau actually spent much of his time doing at Walden. As for not eating what has fallen from the table—that particular commandment will be positively shocking to tightwads everywhere who typically operate with a "five-second rule" rather than see good food go to waste.

LIVING ACCORDING TO A FIXED ROUTINE

Obviously, following a strict routine is compatible with a luxurious lifestyle. One could begin each day with a caviar breakfast, run through a fixed schedule of expensive pleasures, and retire each evening after bathing in warmed goat's milk. But quite often, when people describe themselves as living simply, or when they say they would prefer a lifestyle simpler than the one they have, at least part of what they have in mind is the simplicity of order and regularity. It is the felt absence of these that can sometimes

make parenting and traveling stressful—doubly so when   ha!
these are combined!

A strict regimen is, of course, a noteworthy feature of life
in a monastery, where it helps serve the general purpose of
allowing the monks to focus their minds on what they
believe matters most. No mental energy is expended on
deliberations about what to wear, what to eat, where to go,
what to do, or when to do it. The benefits can be significant,
and go beyond just clearing one's day of distractions. As
recent research in psychology suggests, the stress of making
decisions, even small ones, can drain our willpower, while
putting things on autopilot helps conserve it.[23]

Of course, there are institutions other than monasteries
that also impose on the inmates a strict regimen: military
barracks and prisons, for instance. Most people would not
embrace the sort of lifestyle simplification such environments
enforce, just as most people do not join monastic orders. We
value the freedoms that life on the outside permits us, even
if these bring anxieties too. Yet we recognize the advantages
of routine, especially those of us fortunate enough to enjoy
a reasonable amount of leisure. The nineteenth-century
German philosopher Arthur Schopenhauer goes so far as
to claim that "the greatest possible simplicity in our relations and even monotony in our way of living will make
us happy, as long as they do not produce boredom."[24] By
all accounts Schopenhauer practiced what he preached.
After settling in Frankfurt in 1833, where he lived for the
last twenty-seven years of his life, he emulated his hero
Kant in following a strict daily regimen: breakfast; write
for three hours; play the flute for one hour; lunch at the

Englischer Hof; coffee and conversation; afternoons in the reading room of the Casino Society, followed by constitutional walk with poodle; evening spent at home reading.[25] It is not clear that this made Schopenhauer happy. He was, after all, a card-carrying philosophical pessimist with curmudgeonly tendencies. But it probably made him happier than he would otherwise have been. Many of us willingly submit to routines, or impose them on ourselves, and being buffeted out of them by the busyness of events can be stressful enough to produce a longing for the attractions of order and regularity, even where these are purchased by sacrificing freedom and choice.

AESTHETIC SIMPLICITY

For some people simplicity is an aesthetic value, so one further sense that might be attached to the notion of simple living is a preference for an uncomplicated, uncluttered living environment. Imagine, for instance, an apartment with white walls, white trim, bare wood floors, simple wooden furniture, plain white kitchenware, white towels in the bathroom, and white blankets on the simple wooden beds. Or a house where the brick walls and overhead beams are left exposed, the furniture is rustic, and any artwork on display is clearly local and amateurish. Or a study containing nothing but a desk and a chair. All these are interiors that people deliberately create for themselves.

Simplicity of this sort is not necessarily frugal. The uncluttered apartment could be in the center of Paris; the plain wooden furniture might be custom-made. Wittgenstein

designed a house in Vienna for his sister Margaret characterized by austere, almost minimalist aesthetic lines, yet
built with no concern for cost. But although such setups
may not be cheap, they make no exhibition of expense.
And the styles have symbolic significance. They bespeak
sympathy with the plain, the unpretentious, the unosten-
tatious. They connote honesty, purity, and a mind focused
on essentials. In the case of country retreats, closeness to
nature may also be sought and expressed. Fallingwater,
the famous country home in Pennsylvania that Frank
Lloyd Wright designed for the Kaufmann family, beautifully illustrates some of these notions, including the point
that aesthetic simplicity can be pricey: the house cost
the Kaufmanns $155,000 in 1937, which translates to over
$2.3 million in 2010 dollars.

Fiscal prudence, living cheaply, self-sufficiency, being
close to nature, contenting oneself with simple pleasures,
asceticism, routine, and aesthetic austerity: these are the
main senses and associations attached to the concept of
simple living. Some are obviously more closely linked
than others to the idea of frugality: living cheaply is an
essential part of the notion, while aesthetic simplicity is
connected to it in a more marginal way. These different
senses can be separated out, but they are naturally associated and in many cases overlap with or imply one another.
Home vegetable gardeners eat more cheaply by increasing
their self-sufficiency in a way that yields the simpler pleasures attendant on being more in touch with nature.
Religiously oriented communities have sought spiritual

purity by embracing an ascetic lifestyle, following strict daily routines, and working to make themselves largely self-sufficient in an aesthetically austere environment. Sometimes, though, forms of simplicity can conflict. Diogenes may have lived cheaply, but as a beggar he hardly exemplifies self-sufficiency.

Simplicity has additional associations, of course. In his essay "On Simplicity," Ben Franklin is especially interested in praising unaffectedness in speech and manners; and he takes it for granted that these qualities are fostered by a simple lifestyle.

In the first Ages of the World, when Men had no Wants but what were purely natural, before they had refin'd upon their Necessities, and Luxury and Ambition had introduced a Thousand fantastik Forms of Happiness, Simplicity was the Dress and Language of the World, as Nature was its Law.[26]

Although Franklin himself was from first to last an urbanite, he strongly linked affectation with the city and honesty with the countryside. "What Relief do we find," he writes, "in the simple and unaffected Dialogues of uncorrupted Peasants, after the tiresome Grimace of the Town!"[27] Many others, though, have conceived of peasant life less flatteringly as characterized by ignorance, crudeness, and even simplemindedness—all decidedly negative associations.

Because the notion of simple living has multiple meanings, it is not possible to make any straight comparative assessment of how simply anyone is living compared to someone else. We always have to specify what senses of the term are intended, and, as we noted earlier, the concept is relative to time, place, and culture. Montaigne observes that when the general practice among Romans was to bathe before dinner in water and perfume, to say one lived simply meant that one bathed in just water.[28] Yet for some people, even bathing in water would be viewed as luxurious.

The various sages mentioned in passing serve not only to exemplify one or more forms of frugal or simple living but also to illustrate the fact that this idea has occupied an important place in intellectual history. It has been explicitly discussed and defended by philosophers, moralists, and religious teachers since ancient times, and to this day remains linked in many people's minds with virtue and wisdom. In the next two chapters we will examine in more detail the main arguments that have been given for favoring the life of frugal simplicity. We will then be in a better position to consider to what extent these arguments still hold good today or have been rendered obsolete by the great social and technological revolutions that have transformed the world in the modern era.

CHAPTER 2

Why Simple Living Is Supposed to Improve Us

Why praise simple living? The main reasons that have been given fall under four general headings:

1. Moral reasons: living simply is inherently good, or it fosters certain virtues, or it fulfills social obligations.
2. Prudential reasons: living simply leads to or promotes happiness (understood broadly as well-being, not narrowly as just feeling good).
3. Aesthetic reasons: the simple life presents a more satisfying spectacle as an example of a human life well lived.
4. Religious reasons: living simply is in accord with the divine will.

Of these the first two dominate the literature, and I propose to focus on them almost exclusively. Both the religious and the aesthetic considerations generally reduce, in the end, to moral or prudential arguments. It is easy enough to find passages in scripture praising simplicity and exhorting us to eschew the pursuit of riches. But if God urges us to live simply, that is presumably because he knows that this will be in our interests; if it were not, why would he command it, and why should we listen? The aesthetic perspective is encountered less often, but it is how I would characterize the thinking of Nietzsche at times, as well as some of those influenced by him. It is a way of asserting that something has value without appearing moralistic or utilitarian. But if the spectacle of simple living is satisfying to ourselves or to other human beings, then that is essentially a prudential argument. If, on the other hand, it is aesthetically pleasing to some other party—the gods, say—it is hard to see why that consideration by itself would ever motivate us to live one way rather than another.

PRELIMINARIES: THE DISTINCTION BETWEEN MORAL AND PRUDENTIAL REASONS FOR PRAISING SOMETHING

It is easy to distinguish the moral and the prudential in the abstract, as labels for kinds of argument. For instance, if we tell a child to share her toys because it is *right* to share, or that she has a *duty* to share, our reasoning is essentially moral. If we tell her to share because this will make her playmates like her and will prompt them to share their toys with her, consequences that will make her happy, then our thinking is primarily prudential. But although the distinction between moral and prudential reasoning is familiar, it is far from clear-cut. In the next two chapters I employ the distinction in order to separate out two general lines of argument in support of simple living. Proceeding this way helps to clarify the nature and strength of these arguments. But before we examine particular arguments of either sort in detail, a brief preliminary discussion of this distinction is in order to clarify both why they have often been so difficult to separate clearly and how I propose to understand the relation between them.

Suppose we praise frugal living because it makes one tough. The obvious next question is this: why is toughness a good thing? A prudential reason is that if you are tough, you will suffer less when misfortune strikes; a moral reason is that toughness is a virtue. But why should we consider toughness a virtue? One answer is that it is an inherently good quality to possess. But although some people might try to defend this way of thinking, it is hard to fathom. Why call a quality good except for the reason that possessing it is likely to bring some benefit to someone? One could, perhaps, argue that the spectacle of someone being strong in adversity is pleasing in something like the way the sight of a beautiful figure is pleasing. But then the value of the virtue lies in its giving pleasure to someone. Or one could argue that the spectacle offers an inspiring example to others. But then we have to ask why it is good that these others are inspired to cultivate toughness in themselves.

If we give up trying to justify the claim that toughness is an intrinsically valuable quality, we seem to be thrown back on viewing it as instrumentally valuable in some way. As originally suggested, it could help one suffer less in

adversity. It might also be useful in fending off adversity.
And of course tough individuals are also an asset to their
community; they can help others who are suffering, and
they can help the group overcome difficulties. Each of these
reasons for praising toughness is essentially prudential: it
is a quality useful to oneself or to others, by which is meant
a quality likely to promote the happiness of oneself or of
others.[1] But the argument that toughness should be cultivated because those who have this virtue will be more useful to their community is also a moral argument. For while
the individual obviously stands to benefit from belonging
to a happier community, neither the value of the virtue
nor the motivation for cultivating it reduces to a matter of
self-interest.

The general point illustrated by this example is that the
distinction between moral and prudential motivations,
judgments, or arguments can often be useful, but it is neither sharp nor absolute. In the rest of this chapter we will
examine moral arguments for praising simple living, and
in the following chapter we will consider prudential reasons for doing so. The distinction between moral and prudential reasons for praising simple living here serves as an
initial classification made for expository purposes. Most
arguments clearly fall on one side or the other. But it is to
be expected that, on analysis, they will be found to spill
over onto the other ground.[2]

Most of the moral arguments in support of simple living
connect it to individual virtue. The basic idea underlying
the arguments discussed here is that living in a certain way
helps people cultivate certain desirable qualities (virtues)

and makes it less likely that they will develop undesirable qualities (vices). This emphasis on lifestyle and character is characteristic of the philosophical tradition known as virtue ethics. Instead of seeing morality as a set of general rules that it is right to obey and wrong to break—a view that until recently dominated much modern moral philosophy—virtue ethics emphasizes the way that moral behavior flows naturally from a virtuous disposition just as, to use one of Jesus's metaphors, a sound tree reliably bears good fruit. It thus naturally pays attention to the everyday practices and habits that shape and reflect a person's moral character.

SIMPLE LIVING KEEPS ONE AWAY FROM TEMPTATION AND THE RISK OF CORRUPTION

Call to mind, if you can, a legend, a literary work, a film, or an edifying biography that tells of how a young man, raised in the lap of luxury, finds himself among poor, simple country folk whose company corrodes his virtues and leads him down the rocky road to moral degeneracy. No, I can't either. Perhaps there are such stories, but none come readily to mind. In all the familiar morality tales—Dickens's *Great Expectations* being a paradigmatic example—the corrupting influence flows the other way: the country mouse is led astray by the wicked ways of the city as he leaves his humble origins behind and fills his head with dreams of wealth and status.

This is perhaps the simplest moral argument for simple living: it removes one from the thousand temptations mortal flesh is heir to. The argument crops up in a variety of

contexts. It is one of the reasons Plato insists that the ruling caste in a well-governed society should be required to
eschew wealth and luxuries[3]—a suggestion that has found
favor with numerous idealists and utopians, but which
sadly seems no more likely to be implemented today than
when it was first proposed. It is a reason why so many who
seek holiness or spiritual improvement impose on themselves a strict austerity. And it is why schools and colleges
used to emulate the ways of monasteries.

The first Christian hermits and monastics who practiced extreme austerity in the desert saw themselves as
emulating Jesus during his sojourn in the wilderness.
Once monastic life became institutionalized, removing
oneself from carnal temptation was a major reason why
religiously minded individuals would choose to take vows.
The Rule of St. Benedict, set down around the year 530,
included commitments to poverty, humility, chastity,
and obedience, and this became the paradigm for most
Christian monastic orders. The vow of poverty generally
involved renouncing all individual property, although the
monastic community was allowed to hold property, and of
course some monasteries eventually became quite wealthy.
But the lifestyle of most monks in the Middle Ages was
kept deliberately austere. Here is how Aelred of Rievaulx,
writing in the twelfth century, describes it:

> Our food is scanty, our garments rough, our drink
> is from the streams and our sleep upon our book.
> Under our tired limbs there is a hard mat; when
> sleep is sweetest we must rise at a bell's bidding. . . .

self-will has no scope; there is no moment for idleness or dissipation.[4]

Strict precautions to eliminate the possibility of sexual encounters, regular searches of dormitories to ensure
that no one was hoarding personal property, a rigid and
arduous daily routine to occupy to the full one's physical and mental energy: by means of this sort monasteries
and convents did their best to provide a temptation-free
environment.

More than a trace of the same thinking lay behind the
preference for isolated rural locations among those who
sought to establish colleges in nineteenth-century America. Sometimes the argument might be conveyed subtly by
a brochure picturing the college surrounded by nothing
but fields, woods, and hills, an image that also appealed
to the deeply rooted idea that the land was a source of virtue.[5] But it was also put forward explicitly. The town of
North Yarmouth sought to persuade the founders of Bow-
doin College of its advantageous location by pointing out
that it was "not so much exposed to many Temptations
to Dissipation, Extravagance, Vanity and Various Vices as
great seaport towns frequently are."[6] And the 1847 catalog of Tusculum College, Tennessee, noted that its rural
situation "guards it from all the ensnaring and demoral-
izing influences of a town."[7] Needless to say, reassurances
of this sort were directed more at the fee-paying parents
than at the prospective students. One should also add
that not everyone took such a positive view of the rural
campus. Some complained that life far away from urban

civilization fostered vulgarity, depravity, licentiousness, and hypocrisy.[8]

What sort of temptations to ruin does a life of frugal simplicity, preferably away from the trappings of the city, keep at bay? The most obvious one is the temptation to live beyond one's means, the tried and tested path to financial ruin. This consideration is perhaps more prudential than moral, although going into unnecessary debt has long been frowned on by moralists both because it can adversely affect other people (for instance, one's creditors, or one's family) and because it can prove a slippery slope to other failings. More interesting temptations are those that offer the shorter road to what conventional morality views as moral ruin: namely, debauchery, prostitution, drink, drugs, and gambling. In addition, there is the danger that a worldly lifestyle in which wealth, luxury, status, and power figure prominently may gradually corrupt one's moral character, inducing traits such as acquisitiveness, covetousness, pride, conceit, and hard-heartedness—and, not least, cowardice (since the covetous will feel they have most to lose).

This last argument is the one most often advanced by the philosophers of frugality. In modern America and in many other societies, the desire to accumulate wealth and then to keep accumulating is respected as an engine of progress and prosperity. But since ancient times philosophers have generally regarded it with suspicion. Naturally, those who have made their millions are likely to see this as just sour grapes on the part of the philosophers, who, they will point out, have rarely found a lucrative market for their ideas or their

services. To this snide observation philosophers have traditionally responded by pointing to the example of Thales
of Miletus, who flourished around 600 BCE and is commonly identified as the first Western philosopher. Thales,
so the story goes, realized from his meteorological observations that there would be a bumper crop of olives later
in the year. So he shrewdly bought up all the olive presses
in the region where he lived, and when harvesting season
arrived, he rented them out at a great profit. The moral
of the story, of course, is that if we philosophers chose to
apply our mighty intellects to moneymaking, we could do
as well as anyone, but we prefer to keep our minds focused
on higher things. It is, admittedly, a little suspicious that we
are still citing a case from over twenty-five hundred years
ago to make the point; but then a single example is all one
needs to demonstrate that something is *possible*.[9]

A few philosophers do find something positive to say
about wealth, but most spend much more time calling
attention to its dangers. One concern, voiced by Epicurus, is that it is hard to acquire wealth without adopting a servile attitude toward someone: toward a superior
if one seeks patronage, toward the mob if one seeks popular approval.[10] This was presumably more true in ancient
times than today, since in prosperous modern societies
the opportunities for ordinary working people to build a
decent-sized nest egg are far greater than in the past. Yet
Epicurus's observation is not entirely outdated. Employees
in any organization, if they wish to advance their careers
or even just keep their jobs, usually have to make nice to
their superiors. And a concern for money, even if not in

the form of an individual's lust for wealth, often underlies the quest for public approval, whether it is politicians
seeking votes, entrepreneurs selling goods or services, college presidents seeking to boost admissions, TV producers
with their eyes on ratings, or writers hoping to sell books.
All will find themselves drawn toward trying to gratify
their audience's desires.

Wealth carries other moral dangers, as pointed out by
sages of many schools. The desire for riches, it is feared,
once aroused can never be fully satisfied. Like the dog who
has tasted blood, those who have come to enjoy making
money will find it difficult to say, "Enough!" Because the
wealthy have much to lose, they are likely to be less brave,
fearing adversity and death more than most. If they feel
the need to exhibit their wealth, as many do, they will
start to indulge in various luxuries and extravagances that
make them increasingly dependent on others—both those
who are the source of wealth (patrons, bosses, clients) and
those who provide services (servants, chauffeurs, beauti-
cians). And this concern for expensive superfluities will
lead to their wasting both their resources and, much more
importantly, their time. Tom Wolfe's 1987 novel *The Bon-
fire of the Vanities*, set in the world of New York's financial
wheelers and dealers, offers a memorable portrayal of all
these failings in a modern context.

Claims of this sort regarding the effects of wealth
on an individual are obviously neither necessary nor
universal. Some who become rich, far from becoming
extravagant, grow increasingly parsimonious. Hetty
Green, the "Witch of Wall Street," who when she died

in 1916 was one of the richest women in the world, was famous for her miserliness: according to one story, she insisted that her laundress wash only the hems of her dresses—the most soiled parts—in order to save on soap. Some make or inherit their pile and then sit contentedly on it, enjoying the leisure and independence it brings. Some become philanthropists and in so doing deepen their awareness of other people's needs and their own desire to do good.

Aware of this, the Stoics and like-minded thinkers do not see material wealth as *intrinsically* bad and therefore to be scrupulously avoided; everything depends on one's attitude toward it. Marcus Aurelius, who as emperor of Rome was fabulously wealthy, regarded his adoptive father's outlook as exemplary:

> The way he handled the material comforts that fortune had supplied him in such abundance—without arrogance and without apology. If they were there, he took advantage of them. If not, he didn't miss them.[11]

For the Stoics, who place a premium on peace of mind, more or less identifying happiness with tranquillity, the crucial thing is to be free from the fear of loss. Seneca writes to a friend:

> I do not interdict the possession of wealth, but my aim is for you to possess it fearlessly, and this attitude you can achieve only if you are convinced that you can live happily even without wealth.[12]

Seneca, as it happens, was one of the wealthiest men of his day, so it would have been a bit rich for him to tell others to eschew wealth entirely. Yet he was very aware, perhaps from self-observation, of how the prospect or the possession of riches can lure people away from the Socratic principle, embraced by the Stoics, that no real harm can befall a good person. "That poverty is no disaster," he writes, "is understood by everyone who has not yet succumbed to the madness of greed and luxury which turns everything topsy-turvy."[13]

The pernicious influence of riches and of the desire to acquire them is a commonplace in folk wisdom, religious scripture, philosophy, and literature. The Hebrew Bible, for instance, tells us: "Do not toil to acquire wealth,"[14] for "he who loves money never has enough,"[15] and "the covetous man provokes many disputes."[16] We should be content to live simply, therefore, since "there is no happiness for man but to eat and drink and to be content with his work."[17] The apostle Paul is uncompromising, bluntly asserting that "the love of money is the root of all evil."[18]

Yet these venerable founts of wisdom also point out that wealth can exert a positive moral influence while poverty can lead one astray. The same book of Proverbs that advises us not to toil for wealth also tells us that "a rich man's wealth is his strong city, and like a high wall protecting him." When, at the beginning of Plato's *Republic*, Socrates asks the wealthy Cephalus to name the greatest advantage that wealth brings, Cephalus answers that, at least for one who is already an honest person, the best thing about wealth is that it removes any temptation to be dishonest.[19]

The qualification *for someone who is already honest* is obviously important. Fabulously wealthy individuals are regularly found guilty of criminal wrongdoing in their efforts to multiply their millions. But a lack of resources undoubtedly can provoke desperate remedies, including actions a person would not countenance in better times.

SIMPLE LIVING BUILDS GOOD CHARACTER

The idea that living simply and frugally helps build good moral character is as familiar as it is old. This is presumably one reason why politicians running for office, if they can get away with it, will tout their humble origins, their struggle to make ends meet, and their simple recreational tastes. And if they can't plausibly spin that yarn, they will describe the humble origins and character-building struggles of their parents, or their grandparents, or some other distant forebear, hoping to claim virtue by association.

How is simple living thought to be edifying? In various ways. Practicing frugality fosters prudence, temperance, and self-control. The need to work produces a strong work ethic (whereas "idle hands are the devil's tools"). Doing things for yourself leads to self-sufficiency and a proper pride in your independence as opposed to the false pride of looking down on those who serve your needs. While luxury makes one soft, living closer to the bone makes one physically and mentally tougher, better able to cope with adversity and stronger in a crisis. And a modest, simple lifestyle will naturally be mirrored in character traits such as modesty, humility, and honesty, along with a corresponding absence of traits associated with high status such as pride, arrogance, and vanity. This last idea, that simplicity of life will produce simplicity of heart, is an assumption underlying a number of monastic orders, most notably the Franciscans.

Perhaps no society was ever more committed to the edifying benefits of the simple lifestyle than the ancient Spartans. If the accounts that have come down to us are to be believed, they made this idea a guiding principle of their entire way of life. According to Plutarch, Lycurgus, the legendary lawgiver of Sparta, instituted a set of regulations and practices that were consciously designed to promote a particular set of virtues in the citizenry, notably courage, physical fitness, hardiness, self-control, patriotism, indifference to wealth, an absence of envy, and straightforwardness. The measures regulated all aspects of day-to-day life. Meals were eaten by the male citizens communally, and diners, if they were not so concerned about appearing tough, could certainly have echoed the Woody Allen–esque complaint that the food was lousy and the servings too small. The rations were meager to keep the young men lean and supple and accustomed to functioning on an empty stomach; the food was kept plain in order to foster a willingness to eat whatever was at hand, no matter how unappetizing. In fact, the most popular, or at least the most common, dish was a notorious black broth made of pork, blood, vinegar, and salt, which by all accounts was judged pretty repulsive by non-Spartans. One traveler who tasted it is said to have commented, "Now I know why the Spartans don't fear death." Boys, who also ate at the communal mess, were given especially small servings so that they would be prompted to try to steal additional food. Not that the Spartans thought thieving a virtuous activity. Their idea was that if the punishments for anyone caught stealing were sufficiently severe, those driven to steal would naturally develop great daring and ingenuity.

The cult of simplicity spread into every aspect of Spartan life. Lycurgus is said to have prohibited the use of any tools other than an axe in the building and furnishing of a house in order to discourage luxurious fixtures and superfluous decoration. The Spartans prided themselves on their pithy way of speaking (the term "laconic" is derived from Laconia, the region containing Sparta).[20] Spartan music, too, was kept rigorously simple. According to Plutarch, one of their finest harp players, Terpander, was fined and had his harp confiscated just for adding an extra string to his instrument.

The Spartan way of life appealed to a number of Greek intellectuals. The ideal city that Socrates describes in Plato's *Republic* has many features borrowed from the Spartan model. Plato seems to express genuine admiration for Spartan ways, even if at times, as when he outlaws instruments with more than one string, he may be speaking tongue in cheek. But overall Plato wholeheartedly embraces the idea that simplicity in housing, dress, food, music, and literature is morally beneficial. And many of his philosophical heirs sound the same refrain. Here is how Jean-Jacques Rousseau describes Sparta: "that city as renowned for its happy ignorance as for the wisdom of its laws, that republic of demi-gods rather than men, so superior did their virtues seem to human nature."[21]

Few today endorse Rousseau's admiration of Spartan ways, and as a matter of historical fact, the Spartans were not able to maintain their system.[22] But the idea that austerity builds character is still with us. It informs the pride with which people relate experiences of past hardship, whether true or exaggerated; the assumption underlying such reports is almost always that such experiences were beneficial rather than harmful. It also underpins the practice among people who are comfortably off of sending their children on wilderness programs or for sojourns abroad in developing countries. The purpose here is not usually to encourage the youngster to embrace an austere lifestyle. On the contrary, well-off people normally like to see their offspring eventually acquire the standard (and expensive) outward signs of success, and most of those who undergo temporary "toughening up" do not in fact emerge with a lasting commitment to frugality or aversion to comfort and luxury. But everyone seems to agree that the experience, in some not very well-defined way, is edifying.

The reverse side of the austerity-builds-character argument, noted earlier, is the claim that wealth, luxury, excess, and extravagance encourage undesirable qualities. Children who have it all are prone to become spoiled brats. Excessive concern for acquiring riches leads one to value possessions over people, and, who knows, eventually to corruption and a life of crime, or at least to Wall Street. Those who have more, say the Stoics, are more afraid of material loss, whereas "if you ain't got nothing, you got nothing to lose," as Bob Dylan sings (although like Seneca the trial lawyer, his experience of empty-handedness is somewhat limited). Love of possessions and fear of their loss tends to make people more selfish, less brave, and less generous. Luxurious living makes one soft, slovenly, indolent, dependent on others, and prone to gout.

These sorts of arguments are commonplace in the literature from Plato to Thoreau. They have a prima facie plausibility. But we should not accept them uncritically. Sometimes the effects of frugal simplicity may be the reverse of what is intended or expected. For instance, although frugality is said to foster humility, some of the ancients who practiced it took pride in their austere lifestyle and came to see themselves as superior to others. Diogenes is a case in point; no one ever accused him of humility. On one occasion at a banquet he supposedly trampled on Plato's rich carpets, saying, "Thus do I trample on the empty pride of Plato," to which Plato responded, "With quite as much pride yourself, O Diogenes."[23] Spartan austerity, monastic self-discipline, bucolic naturalness, and working-class frugality may carry positive associations, but other associations are also possible. Monasteries sometimes became rife with religious narcissism and intrigue. Peasants may live close to nature, but they have also enjoyed a long-standing reputation for being ignorant, greedy, and cunning. Struggling against economic adversity may foster virtues such as resilience, self-sufficiency, and solidarity with one's community, whereas prosperous leafy suburbs may be hotbeds of smug, self-serving complacency; but poverty can also be a breeding ground for crime, alcoholism, drug addiction, child abuse, delinquency, and depression, while a privileged upbringing can sometimes instill moral integrity and an impressive sense of social obligation—the emperor-philosopher Marcus Aurelius being a case in point.

The general point here is that the link between living frugally or simply and practicing the moral virtues is not a *necessary* connection. A frugal lifestyle is no guarantee of a virtuous character. Ebenezer Scrooge in Dickens's *A Christmas Carol* offers a memorable example of how habits of parsimony can shrink one's capacity for sympathy, compassion, and generosity. Cato's famous frugality also had an unpleasant aspect: according to Plutarch he used to sell his slaves just as he sold his horses once they were too old to work, since he did not wish to incur the cost of feeding them if they were no longer useful.

SIMPLE LIVING CULTIVATES SUPERIOR VALUES

This is an extension of the previous argument, but the two can be distinguished. Character is a matter of possessing certain qualities; affirming certain values is not quite the same thing. One can sincerely praise a virtue without possessing it. I might admire courage, for instance, without myself being courageous. Of course, some will say that affirming a value without embodying it is at best empty talk and at worst hypocrisy, but that is simplistic. Sometimes, quite often in fact, our thinking starts to change first and our behavior gradually swings around after it.

A value is simply something we consider good: good to be, to have, to be part of, or to experience. Moralists since Socrates have sought to distinguish between true and false values, urging us to endorse the former and renounce the latter. But although the term "false values" is common currency, describing values as "true" or "false," can be confusing. It suggests that there is a set of values (the "true" ones) that mirrors some paradigm, analogous to the way a map corresponds to a terrain, while "false values" are those that fail to correspond to anything in this ideal. In general, however, what most people really mean by "false values" are values it is a mistake to affirm (even if only privately to oneself) because their realization will not bring about the expected or hoped-for consequences. Thus moralists have long warned us against overvaluing wealth, power, glory, or status, and their main argument is simply that neither the pursuit of these things nor their realization will make us happy; those who think otherwise are mistaken.

According to the sages, simple living naturally leads one to embrace such cardinal values as moral virtue, integrity, friendship, peace of mind, and wisdom. Moreover, these goods can be acquired with few means—a happy circumstance since it means the good life is within everyone's reach. These claims seem unobjectionable. However, some important values are not so obviously tied to simple living or frugality, even if many of the sages claim they are. Two especially problematic examples are truth and pleasure.

Everyone knows that the Puritans, powerful advocates of frugal simplicity, were suspicious of pleasure. But this strain in Christianity had some philosophical pedigree since it echoes a sentiment voiced by Plato. In several dialogues Plato argues against those who view pleasure as the ultimate good for human beings. In the *Gorgias*, for instance, Socrates and Callicles, an aspiring politician, go head-to-head on precisely this question. Callicles identifies the good with pleasure and understands pleasure as the gratification of desire. This is the axiom underlying his defense of oratory, since through oratory one can gain power, and with power one can gratify one's desires. Against this, Socrates defends philosophy, which aims at truth (as opposed to mere persuasion), and likens the person who continually seeks pleasure to someone who is continually trying (and failing) to fill up a leaky pitcher. (Callicles responds by comparing the Socratic ideal of serenity to the experience of a stone.) In other works too, Plato's distrust of pleasure is evident. He sees it as an attractive force that pulls us away from what really matters: namely, truth and virtue. In the *Republic*, Socrates's initial vision of an ideal city is one in which the citizens spend their days sitting around discussing philosophy, undistracted by desires for anything beyond the satisfaction of basic needs.[24] (His interlocutors reject this vision as being insufficiently civilized.) In the *Phaedo* philosophy is famously described as a preparation for death, in part because it helps the soul to detach itself from the body with all its sensual appetites and cravings.

As we have already observed, however, not every advocate of frugal simplicity shares this suspicion of pleasure. Epicurus boldly describes pleasure as "the beginning and end of the blessed life . . . the first good innate within us,"[25] and he is far from alone in this. For while asceticism is certainly an important strand in the frugal tradition, so, too, is the celebration of simple pleasures. Indeed, one argument that is made repeatedly in favor of simple living is that it helps one to appreciate more fully elementary and easily obtained pleasures such as the enjoyment of companionship and natural beauty. This is another example of something we have already noted: the advocates of simple living do not share a unified and consistent notion of what it involves. Different thinkers emphasize different aspects of the idea, and some of these conflict.

Truth, unlike pleasure, has rarely been viewed as morally suspect. Its value is taken for granted by virtually all philosophers. Before Nietzsche, hardly anyone seriously considered as a general proposition the idea that truth may not necessarily be beneficial.[26] There is a difference, though, between the sort of truth the older philosophers had in mind and the way truth is typically conceived of today. Socrates, the Epicureans, the Cynics, the Stoics, and most of the other sages assume that truth is readily available to anyone with a good mind who is willing to think hard. This is because their paradigm of truth—certainly the truth that matters most—is the sort of philosophical truth and enlightenment that can be attained through a conversation with like-minded friends in the agora or the garden. Searching for and finding such truth is entirely compatible with simple living.

But today things are different. We still enjoy refined conversation about philosophy, science, religion, the arts, politics, human nature, and many other areas of theoretical interest. And these conversations do aim at truth, in a sense. As Jürgen Habermas argues, building on Paul Grice's analysis of conversational conventions, regardless of how we actually behave and our actual motivations, our discussions usually proceed on the shared assumption that we are all committed to establishing the truth about the topic under discussion.[27] But a different paradigm of truth now dominates: the paradigm of truth established by science. For the most part this is not something that ordinary people can pursue by themselves through reflection, conversation, or even backyard observation and experiment. Does dark matter exist? Does eating blueberries decrease one's chances of developing cancer? Is global warming producing more hurricanes? Does early involvement with music and dance make one smarter or morally better? Are generous people happier than misers? People may discuss such questions around the table. But in most cases when we talk about such things, we are ultimately prepared to defer to the authority of the experts whose views and findings are continually reported in the media.

Of course, when a reported finding contradicts our cherished notions, we may resist it, perhaps citing anecdotal evidence to justify our skepticism ("I know they say blueberries are good for you, but look at Uncle Seamus who lived on 'em—dead of stomach cancer at fifty-three!"). But on most matters, public opinion sooner or later swings into place behind the opinions of those who have studied the issues in a rigorous way using the tools and methods of science. And these tools and methods, from particle colliders to social scientific studies involving hundreds or thousands of subjects, are not available to most individuals. Pursuing truth using them requires not only the requisite intellectual ability, but also an advanced specialized education, institutional support, and, very

often, considerable funding. Perhaps in some fields—pure
mathematics and philosophy, for instance—one can pursue truth in the traditional way with very few resources;
and here an austere regime devoid of distractions might
aid the quest. Wittgenstein, retreating to a remote Norwe-
gian village to work out the fundamentals of his *Tracta-
tus Logic-Philosophicus* in spartan conditions and relative
isolation, offers an impressive example. But all disciplines
today are primarily cooperative enterprises in which progress depends heavily on global communication, confer-
ences, and individuals enjoying institutional support, all
of which cost money.

For these reasons fewer today share Socrates's belief that
a group of intellectuals sitting around discussing ideas will
suffice to yield a deep understanding of nature, human
nature, or society. Knowledge today is expensive. Consequently, truth, at least the sort pursued and established by
science and specialized scholarship, is no longer a value
one would expect to be realized through a retreat from
the world. Today, if truth is to be associated with frugality,
simplicity, or austerity, it will typically be a different sort of
truth, the kind that is sought by one who pursues enlightenment through religious devotions or meditation.

SIMPLE LIVING IS A SIGN OF INTEGRITY

The wealth of ancient kings, the splendor of their courts,
the prosperity of their estates, and the beauty of their possessions were often celebrated by poets and historians.
These were deemed worthy of admiration and entitled the

aristocrats to the respect naturally shown to the powerful. In the Hebrew Bible earthly prosperity is often taken
to indicate that a person or a people enjoy divine favor on
account of their righteousness. Indirectly, therefore, wealth
can be understood as a reward for, and hence an indicator
of, virtue. In the modern era a similar line of thinking has
informed some strands of Protestantism. The bourgeoisie sought to assuage fears that capitalism is at odds with
Jesus's central teachings by arguing that business success is
a sign of God's approval: God helps those who help themselves, and so on.

For all that, moralists have always taken a simple lifestyle to be a fairly reliable indicator of moral integrity.
Diogenes Laertius's *Lives and Opinions of the Eminent Philosophers* is full of anecdotes that illustrate and applaud
the wise man's indifference to wealth. Solon, Anaxagoras,
Socrates, Menedemus, and Xenocrates are some of the
best-known examples he describes, but there are many
others. At his trial, recounted in Plato's *Apology*, Socrates
calls attention to his poverty as evidence of his honesty;
and although this argument failed to impress the jury,
Plato evidently viewed the simplicity of his teacher's life
as underscoring his emphasis on the importance of virtue
above all other things.

In literature, too, characters whose humble bearings and
preference for plain living symbolize their honest, incorrupt-
ible characters are legion: the parson and the plowman in
Chaucer's *Canterbury Tales*, Jean Valjean in *Les Misérables*,
the Peggottys in *David Copperfield*—the type is familiar to
us and is immediately understood when encountered.

The moral soundness of the person shines forth even more brightly when the simple lifestyle is clearly voluntary, adopted by one who could wallow in pomp and luxury but chooses otherwise. Siddhartha Gautama, the Buddha, who turned his back on life as a royal prince to embrace asceticism, is perhaps the most famous example of this, but there are many others. The biographers of individuals like Spinoza, Tolstoy, Gandhi, Wittgenstein, and Mandela automatically place their subjects' preference for simplicity on the positive side of the moral ledger. Plutarch, writing as both a historian and a moralist, offers numerous descriptions of this type for our edification. Here is how he describes Cato the Elder, for instance:

> a man who observed the ancestral custom of working his own land who was content with a cold breakfast, a frugal dinner, the simplest clothing, and a humble cottage to live in, and who actually thought it more admirable to renounce luxuries than to acquire them—such a person was conspicuous by his rarity.[28]

Apparently Cato was admired more for choosing to live this way than for his eloquence, especially at a time when so many other rich Romans were enjoying the novel luxuries imported from the far reaches of the expanding Roman Empire.

Similar attitudes persist today against the backdrop of our celebrity-obsessed culture. When Cardinal Jorge Bergoglio became Pope Francis in 2013, much was made of the fact that he had eschewed the bishop's palace in Buenos Aires for a simple apartment in which he cooked his own simple meals, and that after moving to the Vatican he preferred to live communally in a guesthouse rather than in the sumptuous Apostolic Palace where previous popes had resided. Profiles of the investment billionaire Warren Buffett, who in 2011 was the third richest person in the world, invariably mention that he likes junk food, drives his own car, and has never moved from the house in Omaha, Nebraska, that he bought in 1958. In general, the rich and famous can pick up a little easy moral credit just by riding the subway or turning their own compost pile.

A connection between simplicity and integrity makes some sense. Choosing to live simply eliminates at least one historically common form of hypocrisy—praising poverty while living luxuriously. Moreover, people who are uninterested in luxurious and extravagant indulgence are presumably less susceptible to corruption since the motive of acquiring wealth should have little purchase on them. Along similar lines, embracing simplicity makes one less dependent on patronage of any sort. And as is made clear by Dr. Johnson's caustic definition of a patron—"commonly a wretch who supports with insolence, and is paid with flattery"—this makes it easier to maintain one's integrity and self-respect.

ACQUISITIVENESS AND EXTRAVAGANCE ARE SIGNS OF SHALLOWNESS

This can be viewed as a moral argument in an extended sense. The objection it raises against acquisitiveness or extravagance is not that these traits cause immediate harm to self or others, but that they reveal, and can perhaps be explained by, a spiritual poverty. Those individuals who seek fulfillment through lavish spending or the piling up of possessions are likely to be poor specimens of humanity who concern themselves with externalities rather than cultivating their moral, intellectual, and aesthetic capacities.

The argument seems to be a combination of the moral, the prudential, and the aesthetic, and different thinkers cast it in different ways. The sixth-century philosopher Boethius presents it primarily as a moral issue but adds a religious twist as well. In *The Consolation of Philosophy* the author imagines himself criticized by Philosophy (who is personified) for his excessive interest in superficialities:

> It seems as if you feel a lack of your own inside you, which is driving you to seek your blessings in things separate and external. And so when a being endowed with a godlike quality in virtue of his rational nature thinks that his only splendor lies in the possession of inanimate goods, it is the overthrow of the natural order. Other creatures are content with what is their own, but you, whose mind is made in the image of God, seek to adorn your superior nature with inferior objects, oblivious of the great wrong you do your Creator.[29]

The idea that one has an obligation to steer away from trivial living is found in most religions, as well as in various modern substitutes for religion from Enlightenment humanism to Heideggerian kabbalism. Boethius here justifies his claim on religious grounds, and his reasoning is fairly straight-forward. But those who seek a secular justification for the moral imperative to avoid shallow living have a more difficult task explaining exactly what wrong is being committed by a person who chooses superficiality.

The Stoics typically emphasize the unsatisfactory character of the supposed happiness attained through external possessions, but this makes the argument essentially prudential. Seneca, for instance, imagines god enlightening him about men who are "adorned with gold and silver and ivory":

> The men you look on as happy, if you could see not their outward appearance but their inward nature, are wretched, squalid, mean, well groomed on the surface, like their own house walls; that is not solid and genuine happiness but only a veneer, and a thin one.[30]

One would think that the miserable ersatz happiness of those obsessed with getting and spending should arouse pity. Often, though, the dominant feeling expressed by the enlightened sage is closer to contempt. Schopenhauer offered this analysis of extravagance:

> The source of the deplorable extravagance, whereby many a son of a wealthy family entering life with a large patrimony often gets through it in an incredibly short time, is really none other than the boredom that springs from the poorness and emptiness of his mind. . . . [a vain endeavor] to make his external wealth compensate for his internal poverty by trying to obtain everything from *without*.[31]

Schopenhauer in fact makes pity central to his ethics and offers a view of the human condition that should evoke sympathy. As he sees it, human beings typically oscillate between pain and boredom. Those who lack what they need struggle to avoid the pains of privation; those who have plenty spend their time fighting off boredom. Nevertheless, Schopenhauer is generally scathing about the mental shallowness of both types: "ordinary men," he writes, "are intent merely on how to *spend* their time; a man with any talent is interested in how to use it."[32] Nietzsche, who was greatly influenced by Schopenhauer, shares his tendency to judge people according to their spiritual wealth or depth, singling out for praise those with a capacity for experiencing and expressing the intellectual and aesthetic aspects of human existence. These are the individuals who in themselves constitute the most interesting and pleasing specimens of humanity; their existence justifies and redeems the rest. Here, I would argue, the thinking is essentially aesthetic. Shallow-minded people living trivial lives devoted to getting and spending offer a displeasing spectacle (Nietzsche's favorite term is "nauseating") to the spiritually refined.

This sort of elitism is fairly extreme, of course. But something like it informs the continuing critique of bourgeois materialism and the philistinism that it is assumed to signify. Like some of the other arguments considered earlier, though, the critique of "shallowness," whether on moral, prudential, or aesthetic grounds, should not be accepted too uncritically. For one thing, terms like "trivial," "shallow," or "spiritually impoverished" are hard to explicate. They clearly express negative evaluations; but it is not so easy to specify exactly what makes one way of living more or less shallow than another. There is always the suspicion that the derogatory terms merely express arbitrary preferences that reflect the speaker's tastes and interests. Another problem is that inferences about the quality of people's inner lives on the basis of their outward behavior are unreliable. It is conceivable that someone who appears to be preoccupied with the external trappings of material prosperity is in fact simply "playing the game," or is able to compartmentalize different aspects of life so that none dominates unduly.

Still, underlying all these disparaging remarks about acquisitiveness and extravagance is the idea that the life of frugal simplicity is just inherently superior to the materialistic alternatives preferred by so many. This may well be believed by the frugal sages mentioned, but it is a difficult proposition to prove. The difficulty is similar to that faced by John Stuart Mill in *Utilitarianism* when he tries to argue that some sorts of pleasure are qualitatively better than others. Mill seeks to go beyond what he saw as the rather crude utilitarianism proposed by Jeremy Bentham. According to Bentham, all pleasures are equally good in themselves; everything else being equal, playing a simple video game is as good as listening to Beethoven. What makes some pleasures better than others, according to this view, are differences that can be quantified (at least in principle), such as their duration, their intensity, or their long-term consequences. Thus hill walking may be judged superior to binge drinking, but only because the pleasure lasts longer, or because the long-term effects on one's health are more positive, or because it causes less pain to others (such as those who have to waste their evening looking after their passed-out friend). Mill is convinced that some pleasures are qualitatively better than others quite apart from such considerations. His famous argument to support this claim involves canvassing the opinions of people who have experienced many and varied pleasures. They are the experts in this area. If these experts generally concur in preferring the "higher" pleasures (such as the enjoyment of learning) over the "lower" pleasures (such as winning a game of pool), this must be because they find the "higher" pleasures more satisfying in some way. And the simplest explanation of this preference is that the experts are right: some pleasures are intrinsically better than others.

Analogously, the advocates of frugal simplicity could argue that a simple lifestyle is inherently superior to other ways of living, and the "proof" of this would be the testimony of those who have experienced different lifestyles, including austerity and luxury, simplicity and extravagance. There are two problems with this reasoning, however. First, the form of Mill's argument is dubious. Appealing to supposedly expert testimony does not prove that one sort of pleasure, or way of living, is better than another; it proves only that certain people prefer it. And their preference provides very weak support for a bold claim about the intrinsic value of things. For it is quite possible that their preference simply reflects their natural constitution. Those drawn to the "higher" pleasures could be precisely those who lack the capacity to fully appreciate the so-called lower pleasures, perhaps because they are by nature cerebral rather than sensual. Similarly, those who testify to the superiority of simple living may be the kind who just are not very good at self-indulgence; they are not competitive, they don't find extravagance exciting, and they are not good at wallowing contentedly in the lap of luxury.

A second objection to the claim that simple living is inherently better than the alternatives is that even if what Mill says about expert testimony on pleasure were true, the corresponding testimony regarding frugality and simplicity does not deliver the hoped-for verdict. Most of those who have sampled both austere and extravagant lifestyles seem to clearly prefer the latter. If they did not, we would witness a constant parade of multimillionaires quitting their mansions, giving away their yachts, and settling down to a modest life of simple pleasures. But in fact this sort of renunciation is rare.

We have looked at some of the main reasons that have been advanced to support the view that simple living is morally desirable: it keeps one away from temptations to moral corruption; it builds good character; it helps cultivate superior values; it bespeaks integrity; and its contrary suggests shallowness and superficiality.[33] While these constitute familiar, plausible, and overlapping lines of thinking, there are plenty of places where doubts can be raised. Frugal habits can sometimes foster (or bespeak) miserliness; poverty can breed unsavory traits and provoke desperate, even criminal, remedies; some important values, like truth or scientific progress, may require considerable expenditures for their realization; and while excessive indulgence in luxury and extravagance may constitute what some would criticize as a "shallower" form of existence, the precise meaning of and justification for this sort of claim is hard to spell out. These criticisms, doubts, reservations, and qualifications certainly don't constitute a refutation of the idea that simplicity is more likely than luxury to foster virtue, but they do indicate that the connections between it and desirable character traits are probabilistic rather than necessary.

CHAPTER 3

Why Simple Living Is Thought to Make Us Happier

As already noted, the distinction between moral and prudential reasons for praising simple living is neither sharp nor essential. Many of the philosophers who advocate simple living belong to the tradition of virtue ethics; in their view, the qualities and practices that make us better people and those that make us happier (in the rich sense of self-realization) will generally be the same. Nevertheless, modern philosophy typically does recognize a distinction here, and we have used it to help distinguish and clarify the precise nature of the arguments in favor of simple living that we are considering.

The prudential arguments to be examined here, like the moral arguments discussed in the previous chapter, are far from new. In Western philosophy most of them were first put forward more than two thousand years ago, particularly by Epicurean and Stoic thinkers; have been regularly endorsed by a host of medieval and modern writers; and continue to be rehearsed today in any number of self-help books advocating frugal simplicity.

A basic premise of all these arguments is that happiness is a good thing, something that virtually every human being naturally desires for its own sake. This is the view defended by Aristotle, by John Stuart Mill, and by countless other philosophers, both ancient and modern. Here and there one encounters dissenting voices, such as Nietzsche or Dostoyevsky, but what they say either applies only to a tiny minority, or confuses "desires happiness" with "desires *only* happiness," or with "desires happiness *above all other things*." The assumption that happiness is valuable is one that most people will readily accept. Our concern here is with the various reasons that philosophers have given for thinking that living simply increases the likelihood that one will be happy.

SIMPLE LIVING PROMOTES VIRTUE, WHICH PROMOTES HAPPINESS

In the previous chapter we looked at several reasons for believing that living simply is morally beneficial. That idea constitutes the first premise of this argument. The second premise, that morally good people will be happier in virtue of their virtue, was also discussed at the beginning of that chapter. Some have supported it by invoking a notion of cosmic justice: the law of karma, or the divine dispensation of rewards and punishments, in either this life or the next. Others have argued that moral virtue in and by itself will naturally bring happiness in its train. Plato, for instance, argues that the moral integrity of the virtuous individual constitutes a sort of inner harmony, which he contrasts with the disharmony exhibited by the wicked. Since a person cannot fail, at some level, to experience this internal condition, the virtuous will be fundamentally content, while those who lack virtue will be unavoidably dissatisfied. Plato's conclusion is endorsed by most of the classical thinkers who came after him. The Stoics in particular insistently emphasize the supreme importance of moral virtue over all other good things. Thus Marcus Aurelius, echoing Socrates, insists that the only real harm one can ever suffer is harm to one's character,[1] while Seneca asserts that "virtue per se is sufficient for a happy life."[2]

Hard-bitten cynics may think it easy to dismiss all this as a kind of wishful thinking. But in fact this view—that good people should nearly always be considered more fortunate than those who lack the moral virtues—is very plausible. Compare two people: Jill, who genuinely feels pleasure at a colleague's success, and Jane, who feels intense pleasure at a colleague's failure. Who would you prefer to be? Most of us will of course opt to be Jill. An obvious reason for this is that we view her as the nicer person. But what if we put aside moral considerations? We grant that Jill is the more admirable person, but who do we think it is pleasanter to be? Plato's thinking suggests that Jill's condition is also the more enviable. One obvious reason is that, being a nicer person, she is likely to have more friends, to have better friends, to be more confident of their affection, and to enjoy relationships not sullied

by resentment. But a subtler reason, not so easy to articulate, is that Jill's generous-spirited pleasure in another person's good fortune is superior to—and not just in moral
terms—the mean-spirited enjoyment of a colleague's
failure. Of course, it is not easy to abstract this sense of
nonmoral superiority from its moral trappings. It is not a
matter of the intensity or duration of the pleasure. But it is
perhaps captured fairly well by Plato's metaphor of inner
harmony, a metaphor that extends beyond any particular
moment of pleasure to take in the person's total experience. Self-centered, cruel, mean-spirited individuals are
never at ease with—in harmony with—themselves or the
world, which is why they can never achieve lasting contentment. Generous spirits, by contrast, experience less
conflict between what they in fact feel and what at least
some part of them thinks they should feel; furthermore,
there is less disharmony between what they experience as
their inner reality and the way they present themselves to
the world.

SIMPLE LIVING ALLOWS ONE TO WORK LESS AND ENJOY MORE LEISURE

The more frugally you live, the less money you will need
and the more you are likely to save. Either way, this will
reduce your need to work, thereby increasing your leisure
time, and hence your happiness. The reasoning is straightforward. It is interesting, though, to consider how work,
leisure, and their relation to happiness have been vari-
ously conceived within the philosophical tradition we are

examining, and worth asking to what extent the critical attitude toward work within that tradition remains relevant today.

The idea of leisure carries more than one sense or association. A leisured life could be thought of as essentially indolent: one rises late and spends the afternoon lounging in the pool sipping margaritas. Or it can suggest more active forms of recreation: "leisure activities" such as sports, games, gardening, participation in the arts, trekking in the Andes, and so on. What these have in common is freedom from work, particularly the work that one does out of the need to make a living. To be sure, we draw a contrast between leisure and work even when a person has sufficient means to live without working, or when the work is precisely what he or she would choose to do anyway. In these cases we are thinking of leisure as recreational time. But the fundamental meaning of leisure, a notion that goes back to the ancient Greeks, is time in which one is free to choose what one does, free from having to do work that is a chore, a mere means to an end. For Aristotle, leisure in this sense is a precondition of the good life, since it is obvious that freely chosen activities engaged in for their own sake—for instance, study, sport, or conversation—are more enjoyable and fulfilling than work we undertake out of necessity or simply to secure something else, such as a paycheck.

While leisure is almost universally viewed positively, attitudes toward work have varied greatly over time and between different cultures. The upper classes in most societies have usually looked down on it. To not have to work for a living is what traditionally distinguished them from the rest of society; so they viewed being compelled to work as a misfortune, and most manual work as somewhat shameful in the sense that one would feel shame at being reduced to it. This is the view that is shared, for instance, by the upper echelons of society in ancient Greece, in pre-revolutionary China, and in nineteenth-century Europe. But it is far from universal. Judaism, Islam, and Christianity all officially respect and encourage honest labor. Work is encouraged as a means to avoid want, since as the Bible tells, "He who tills his land shall have bread and to spare."[3] Even members of the leisured classes may come to endorse a work ethic to some extent and give themselves work to do—supervision of estates, public service, charitable work, or arts and crafts—since "an idle mind is the devil's workshop."

Today we continually and confusingly receive both messages. Hard work is touted in every school as the key to success, supermarkets hail the "employee of the week," and among working people at every social and professional level it is far more common to hear people boasting about how hard they work than about how much free time they enjoy. Yet out of the other side of its mouth our society still holds before us as the ultimate prize the dream of becoming one of the fortunate few who, through luck, daring, intelligence, or toil, no longer need to work but can relax and recreate. Obviously, both messages can be used to serve the economic system. Owners of capital who employ others to produce goods and services that are sold for a profit benefit from people believing both that a hard worker is a good person and that the good life primarily involves making and spending money.

Champions of frugal simplicity typically prize leisure highly. There are some, though, who are suspicious of it. The ancient Greek poet Hesiod, opposing the contempt of the upper classes for labor, declares that it is idleness, not work, that is shameful.[4] The Rule of St. Benedict states that since "idleness is the enemy of the soul," the brethren should occupy themselves with manual labor and devout reading.[5] Ben Franklin, who considers any time spent unproductively as time wasted, warns that "trouble springs from idleness, and grievous toil from needless ease."[6]

At the other extreme are those who positively celebrate pure inactivity.

What is this life if, full of care,
We have no time to stand and stare?[7]

asks the tramp poet, W. H. Davies. Wordsworth defends sitting dreamily alone on a stone for half a day by claiming

That we can feed this mind of ours
In a wise passiveness.[8]

And Thoreau, in a passage cited earlier, positively boasts of doing nothing all day except sitting in the sun and staring at his pond. In fact, though, most advocates of idleness still tend to see it as good *for* something. Even Wordsworth, when sitting on a stone, is "feeding" his mind. Inactivity recharges one's batteries; it makes possible appreciation of the present moment; it helps one be receptive to whatever is interesting, beautiful, or

instructive in one's immediate surroundings. Philosophers, naturally enough, praise inactivity for facilitating
reflection. Seneca, for instance, is scathing about the
"antlike existence" of the majority, whose lives of "restless
indolence" allow no time for reflection. The only people
really at leisure," he argues, "are those who take time for
philosophy."

In modern times the work ethic has had plenty of critics;
indeed, there is a distinguished tradition of writing in this
vein, most of it directed at exposing the folly of overwork
while reestablishing the value of leisure. Paul Lafargue,
writing in the late nineteenth century, criticized the way
that well-intentioned labor movement slogans about "the
right to work" and "the dignity of labor" were effectively
preaching values that ultimately serve the interests of the
bourgeoisie rather than those of the working class. Work,
he says in *The Right to Be Lazy*, should be nothing more
than "a mere condiment to the pleasures of idleness."[9]
Bertrand Russell echoes this sentiment. "The morality of
work is the morality of slaves," he writes, "and the modern
world has no need of slavery."[10] The work ethic is outmoded,
Russell argues, because laborsaving technology should
make it possible for us to satisfy all our needs while greatly
reducing the hours spent performing uninteresting and
unfulfilling tasks. From now on, therefore, "the road to happiness and prosperity lies in an organized diminution of
work." John Maynard Keynes predicted and welcomed this
development, which he thought would naturally come
about as a result of increased productivity and economic
growth. More recently, Bob Black and Alain de Botton

have sounded similar themes in supporting a new revolutionary imperative: "Workers of the world, relax!"[11]

Very often, of course, these critics of work and champions of leisure are themselves highly productive individuals. You don't produce an epic like Wordsworth's *The Prelude* or win the Nobel Prize for literature, as Russell did, or crank out a shelf load of books after the fashion of Lafargue or Botton, without working hard. But this paradox is only apparent. What they criticize is work that one is *forced* to do; their own "work" is simply the worthwhile and fulfilling activity to which they devote their leisure time. Lafargue and his ilk do not insist that everyone use their leisure productively; like Baudelaire, they see loafing as a valid way of living. But others are more judgmental. Schopenhauer, for instance, is fulsome in his praise of leisure, seeing it as one of life's greatest goods since it allows a person "to exercise his pre-eminent quality, whatever it is," and doing this constitutes happiness. Yet he is scathing about "mere idlers" and "contemptible loafers" who have material wealth enough to be leisured but insufficient mental resources to use their free time well; instead of achieving happiness, he sneers, this type will simply be bored.[12]

There are various routes to a life of leisure, understood as freedom from necessary (and therefore oppressive) labor. The most farsighted people take the simplest path and make sure they are born into money. Others, through luck, shrewdness, or both manage to marry money, but this is not always easy; if it were, Jane Austen's novels would be much shorter and less interesting. For the majority, though, there are two main paths to independence. One can accumulate enough to obviate the need to work, or one can practice frugality and thereby reduce the amount of work required to meet one's needs. These are not mutually exclusive, of course. Ben Franklin consistently advocates both, since the less that industrious people spend, the sooner they will accumulate plenty: "a penny saved is a penny earned." But frugal sages generally favor the second option. When Seneca observes that "even poverty can transform itself into wealth by applying thrift,"[13] he means that if we learn to make shift and be content with relatively little, we will not lack anything of real value that the rich enjoy because of their wealth. The first route—accumulate! accumulate!—has the disadvantage that it typically involves a huge initial investment of time spent with one's nose to the grindstone. Moreover, as noted in the previous chapter, it carries the very real danger that one will acquire, in addition to riches, habits of acquisitiveness and covetousness, that one will come to so enjoy the pleasurable sensation of making money, and so cherish the purchasing power money brings, that it becomes hard to step off the treadmill.

There is, though, an obvious third option: find work that both pays the bills and is inherently rewarding. Until recent times this would have seemed a rather remote possibility to most people. Work was what you were forced to do out of necessity; enjoyable and fulfilling activities were what you engaged in, if ever, during your leisure hours, when you were not working. This would have been true for most slaves, serfs, peasants, and servants since ancient times. And with the advent of industrial capitalism, the contrast became even more extreme. Marx, in his 1844 writings on alienated labor, was one of the first to analyze this:

> The worker . . . only feels himself outside his work, and in his work feels outside himself. He is at home when he is not working, and when he is working he is not at home. His labour is therefore not voluntary, but coerced; it is *forced labour*. It is therefore not the satisfaction of a need; it is merely a means to satisfy needs external to it. Its alien character emerges clearly in the fact that as soon as no physical or other compulsion exists, labour is shunned like the plague.[14]

This is still the situation of many workers, especially those doing the most poorly paid jobs. But it is also true that, compared to Marx's time, many more people today expect, seek, and find work that in one way or another is reasonably pleasant and fulfilling.

This last claim will doubtless strike some as Pollyannish. Alain de Botton, for instance, holds that "a few jobs are certainly fulfilling, but the majority are not and never can be." So we should maintain, he urges, "a firm belief in the necessary misery of life [that] was for centuries one of mankind's most important assets, a bulwark against bitterness," and remember that "work is often more bearable when we don't, in addition to money, expect it always to deliver happiness."[15] But Botton exaggerates when he says that only a few jobs are fulfilling. Surely, the truth today is that many are, many are not, and many are fulfilling in some ways and to some extent. Hardly anyone enjoys boring, unskilled, repetitive, poorly paid work that takes place in lousy conditions, is not socially valued, and satisfies no social need. But people can and do derive considerable satisfaction from work in which they exercise skills, help others, and serve purposes they consider important, and through which they make friends, socialize, construct an identity, and feel themselves to be a participant in the world at large. The fact that they would not do it if they were not paid does not mean that their work is properly or adequately described as nothing but an oppressive burden of alienating activity. Since most people have to earn enough to live on, if their work were unpaid then no matter how much they enjoyed it, they would be forced to find some other means of livelihood. Nor does the feeling of relief experienced at the end of the day or the end of the week prove much. We feel relief at the conclusion of freely chosen tasks too: digging a garden, hosting a birthday party, attending a meeting, writing a poem. For many people, the reason work is irksome is not because of its inherent nature but because they have to do it rather more than they would like to: five days a week instead of three; fifty weeks a year instead of thirty.

The opposition between work (what one must do to earn a living) and leisure activities (which are freely chosen because they are inherently satisfying) has always been, and still is, quite sharp for many people. But for a much larger number of people than in the past, especially in affluent societies, the contrast has become less sharp, most obviously where working conditions have improved, hours have been reduced, and the work itself requires skills that make it interesting and enjoyable. Thus, while living frugally can certainly loosen the yoke of necessity that binds one to a job, and while not *having* to work for a living still appeals to almost everyone, the ideal of simply belonging to and recreating with the leisured classes is no longer the primary dream that our culture holds before our eyes. It has been displaced, to a considerable extent, by the ideal of a working life spent immersed in fulfilling activity, where one is paid for doing what one enjoys doing. Graduation speakers never advise the graduating seniors to "get out there, find a way to make a quick buck if you can, and then retire." The message is always, rather, "pursue your passion and make a difference." Today, the people many consider most fortunate are not heirs to millions or lottery winners, but those who have a clear sense of their calling and enthusiastically devote their life to it: the scientist, artist, scholar, artisan, entrepreneur, teacher, entertainer, mechanic, or service-provider—all those whose work is their passion. Botton and others may argue that the ideal of work as a primary source of fulfillment is an unrealistic and sugarcoated myth, just an updated version of the work ethic, peddled so that the workers will come to hear the clank of their chains as music. But that position is hard to justify. It is not very plausible to suppose that most of those who claim to find their work somewhat satisfying are suffering from false consciousness.

Nevertheless, the basic argument that living frugally can reduce the need to work and thereby increase leisure time remains sound. And from the perspective of those who live contentedly in this way, the spectacle of people working frenetically for many years just in order to afford the trappings of affluence—second homes, expensive meals out, exotic vacations, and so on—is puzzling. Often, the puzzlement is appropriate. Exactly what is the point of working round the clock buying and selling credit derivatives in order to add another million dollars to the tens of millions one has already made? Sam Volk, a former hedge-fund trader on Wall Street who eventually quit to start a nonprofit organization devoted to helping the poor, believes that such people are "wealth addicts" whose compulsive behavior, distorted perceptions, and forms of self-deception are comparable to what one observes in people suffering from drug or food addictions.[16]

However, two qualifications to the basic argument are in order. First, we have to recognize that individuals often have little choice about how hard they work. Many, just to make ends meet or in order to work in their preferred field, are forced to work harder and longer than they would like. Frugality is not a silver bullet. When wages are low, even working two jobs may not bring in enough to cover the basic costs of even a modest modern lifestyle. And as Barbara Ehrenreich documents in *Nickel and Dimed*,[17] sometimes being poor makes living cheaply more difficult. People who don't have a month's rent in advance, for instance, may be forced to live in a motel where they will pay more for their accommodation than if they were able to secure an apartment.

A second qualification is that in twenty-first-century industrialized societies, work is much less of a curse for many people than it used to be in the days of Aristotle, or, for that matter, of Marx. To be sure, there are still millions working at jobs they dislike for low pay, and for them the opposition between work and leisure remains absolute. But there are millions more who, instead of scratching out an existence as impoverished peasants, or laboring in dark satanic mills, or toiling as slaves, now have somewhat meaningful, adequately paid work in reasonably pleasant conditions that provides several important benefits apart from the pay—friendships, social engagement, routine, and self-respect—that go quite a long way toward compensating for the loss of leisure. (Housework, too, is far less onerous than it used to be when children were many, appliances few, and husbands who did the dishes nonexistent.) Moreover, the idea of the good life as one spent enthusiastically immersed in work that constitutes one's calling has been widely embraced. The idea is not new, of course, and there have always been a few lucky people whose lives meet this description. What is new, though, is the huge expansion of educational and vocational opportunities, especially since the Second World War, that has made the dream of finding work that is inherently fulfilling less of a fantasy for ordinary people than it used to be.

SATISFYING BASIC NEEDS SUFFICES FOR HAPPINESS

The claim that simple living is the surest path to happiness obviously rests on a certain conception of happiness. At the heart of this conception, at least for most of the frugal sages, is the idea that happiness requires only that we satisfy our basic needs and desires. This view is common to Epicureans and Stoics and to the many influenced by them. As Epicurus says: "Thanks be to blessed Nature, because she has made what is necessary easy to supply, and what is not easy unnecessary."[18] The refrain is picked up by Seneca. Writing to his mother to console her on his being exiled in Corsica, he tells her, "Nature intended that no great equipment should be necessary for happiness; each of us is in a position to make himself happy."[19] Boethius, in prison, awaiting execution, writes:

> If you wish only to satisfy your needs—and that is all Nature requires—there is no need to seek an excess from Fortune. Nature is content with few and little: if you try to press superfluous additions upon what is sufficient for Nature, your bounty will become sickening if not harmful.[20]

Twelve centuries later, Thoreau sounds the same theme in *Walden*. As he puts it, with characteristic charm, "While I enjoy the friendship of the seasons, nothing can make life a burden to me."[21] Indeed, Thoreau's experiment in living is, among other things, an attempt to demonstrate existentially the sufficiency of basic necessities for a fulfilling way of life. But perhaps the core of Epicurus's prescription was given its definitive expression in the twentieth century by the philosopher Baloo in Walt Disney's *The Jungle Book*, when he sang in praise of "the simple bare necessities" provided by "Old Mother Nature's recipes."

Just what counts as "necessary" for a satisfactory life is obviously a matter on which reasonable people can disagree. Jean Kazez, for instance, in her reflections on this question, includes happiness, morality, autonomy, and knowledge, all of which would probably be endorsed by both Epicureans and Stoics, but also throws in self-expression and personal development or progress, which seem to be more modern values, while not including friendship.[22] There is also a possible distinction to be drawn between simply being happy and living a satisfactory or fulfilling life, but pursuing this here would take us too far afield since it is not really one that the ancients made.

The thesis that to be happy we have only to satisfy our basic needs is most appealing. Yet while we may nod approvingly at the wise words of Epicurus and the rest, the way most of us in the modernized world live suggests that we don't really accept their claims, or that we at least have a much-expanded notion of what constitutes our basic needs. Epicurus defends his position, however, with arguments that rest on a fairly sophisticated account of human needs and desires. These are worth examining.

According to Epicurus our natural default condition is pleasurable. Pain is a disturbance of this condition. So to live pleasantly is to be by and large free from physical pains and mental or emotional troubles. The key to such a life is first of all to free oneself from foolish anxieties, such as the fear of death, and second to free oneself from foolish desires, which means those whose satisfaction will not really make us happier.

Epicurus proceeds to distinguish between natural desires (e.g., the desire for food) and nonnatural desires (e.g., the desire to have statues erected in one's honor). This distinction is suspect, though. Why call any desire non-natural, given that it arises within a natural being? It is certainly easy, especially after Darwin, to conceive of the desire for glory (statues in one's honor) as having a natural origin: heroes are hot, so they tend to have more sex and make more babies. The problem with Epicurus's use of the terms "natural" and "nonnatural" is that they seem to be intended as descriptions yet also function as evaluations: it is simply a given that the natural is better than the nonnatural. Having made that dubious distinction, he goes on to make an even more dubious assertion: "All that is natural is easy to be obtained," he says, "but that which is superfluous is hard." Prima facie this statement is patently false. Millions who are victims of famine, war, disease, natural disasters, or political oppressions would not consider obtaining things like food, shelter, or security easy; on the other hand, in societies where huge amounts of stuff is produced, acquired, stored in the basement, then thrown away, anyone can gather unlimited superfluous possessions for little or nothing.

Epicurus's distinction between natural and nonnatural desires is thus best put aside. More defensible and relevant is a further distinction he draws between necessary and unnecessary desires. A desire is necessary if failure to satisfy it leads to pain of some sort. Among necessary desires he identifies those essential for life itself (e.g., the desire to escape danger), those necessary for physical comfort (e.g., the desire for protection from the elements), and those required for happiness (e.g., the desire for companionship). Desires that are not needed for any of these are judged unnecessary.

Epicurus does not despise or repudiate nonnecessary desires such as eating novel foods or listening to music. Satisfying them can diversify our pleasures, and this diversification is itself pleasurable. The original Epicureans in fact held a feast in their garden on the twentieth of each month, showing that they did not confine themselves to enjoying only the bare necessities. Epicurus simply advises us to recognize that pleasures enjoyed through the satisfaction of nonnecessary desires are dispensable; we can be happy without them, so we should avoid being consumed or controlled by a desire for them.

The key idea here, which Epicurus takes from Plato, is to bring our desires under control. Unhappiness results when people become too invested in satisfying nonnecessary desires, especially when, as so often happens, such desires become insatiable. For "nothing satisfies the man who is not satisfied with a little."[23] Exactly how and why desires become insatiable is an interesting question. In *How Much Is Enough?* Robert and Edward Skidelsky hypothesize that a proclivity to always want more is rooted in human nature since it is natural to be always comparing ourselves with others, and we do this by reference to various objects of desire—for instance, wealth, income, power, or honors. In premodern societies this tendency is kept in check by religion and traditional mores. These provide a concept of the good life that sets limits to how much of anything it makes sense for a person to want. But capitalism, they argue, "has inflamed our innate tendency to insatiability by releasing it from the bounds of custom and religion within which it was formerly confined."[24] It has done this in several ways: through advertising; by encouraging everyone, not just the better off, to compete for status through buying stuff; by pushing an ideology that applauds incessant striving for more; and by "monetizing" the economy—that is, translating the value of everything into how much it yields or will sell for—a shift that encourages people to want money for its own sake. The phenomenon of insatiable desire for more is most apparent in those who already have the most, such as CEOs, vice presidents of corporations, and traders in high finance. These people do not need more money, but their salaries and bonuses matter to them as indicators of status and recognized achievement. As one of them remarked, money is "just a way of keeping score."[25] Interestingly, two thousand years before the advent of capitalism, Plato observed that, more than any other desire, the lust for money tends toward insatiability.[26]

According to Epicurus, the way to avoid being plagued by insatiable desires is to cultivate an attitude of gratitude: "We should not spoil what we have by desiring what we have not, but remember that what we have too was the gift of fortune."[27] This certainly sounds sensible, and Epicurus's injunctions have been echoed by countless sages since. But they should not be accepted uncritically. Three problems are worth mentioning.

First, one could argue that insatiable desire, far from being a recipe for unhappiness, is precisely what drives some people to attain higher, more intense, or more expansive forms of happiness. People who seek and secure high political office, great wealth, a Nobel Prize, an Olympic gold medal, or a fabulous art collection may, it is true, never still the inner restlessness that drives them onward and upward. In that sense they remain unsatisfied. But they could also claim to experience levels and kinds of satisfaction (happiness) unknown to those who are "satisfied with a little." Here we once again encounter a clash between two conceptions of happiness reminiscent of the debate between Socrates and Callicles in Plato's *Gorgias* described earlier. One side identifies happiness with the state of being free from troubles; the other side identifies it with the continuous process of striving, getting, and striving for more. Instead of assuming that one of these conditions typically makes a person more happy than the other, we might consider the possibility that there are different kinds of happiness, and individuals would be well advised to pursue the kind that is best suited to their circumstances and personality.

Second, the warning against insatiable desires makes more sense with respect to some desires, less sense with respect to others. It seems most reasonable when the object of desire is something like territorial conquests, wealth, power, fame, glory, influence, sex, expensive art objects, fancy clothes, sports cars, and so on. But what if the object of desire is knowledge, understanding, artistic satisfaction, the eradication of a disease, or the elimination of injustice? Is the fact that these desires cannot be finally satisfied a reason for reining them in? Isaac Newton famously lamented that his quest for insight into the nature of things could be compared to the actions of a boy playing on the seashore "whilst the great ocean of truth lay all undiscovered before me." Would it have been better for him to have kept his desire for understanding in check so as to avoid this abiding feeling of disappointment? The accomplished and acclaimed novelist Zadie Smith offers this advice to fellow writers: "Resign yourself to the lifelong sadness that comes from never being satisfied."[28] Should she, instead, advise her readers never to even try?

This argument can be taken in two ways. One way is to see it as supporting the previous objection: there are kinds of pleasure and happiness that are invariably tied to feelings of dissatisfaction, and the Epicurean guidelines fail to appreciate this. The other way is to see it as placing a question mark against the prioritizing of happiness. The insatiable desire of Newton for understanding, of Beethoven for adequate artistic expression, of Shackleton for adventure, or of Harriet Tubman for justice may not have brought them happiness; it may even have interfered with their capacity to be happy. But such examples remind us that happiness may not always be a rational person's primary goal.

A third problem with Epicurus's thesis that happiness requires only the satisfaction of our basic needs is that the notion of "basic needs" is unstable because it is historically and culturally relative. In premodern times, and in some societies today, a person might well be satisfied with being safe, healthy, comfortable, well fed, and befriended. But in most contemporary societies, and certainly in modernized, industrially developed countries, anyone who had *nothing but* these goods would be classified as seriously impoverished. In a country like the United States, even people of relatively modest means are likely to have much more: car, TV, radio, music system, phone, camera, washer, microwave, running hot water, flush toilet, books, games, toys, pictures, ornaments, pets, kitchen gadgets, jewelry, best clothes, best crockery, sports equipment, plus any amount of unspecified junk that mysteriously accumulates in the garage and which one hopes will eventually go to a better home following the yard sale.

There are, of course, people who are so poor that they have little or none of this sort of stuff. And there are communities like the Amish, as well as individuals who opt to live "off the grid" or who accept blogger Dave Bruno's "100 thing challenge"[29] and deliberately choose to do without the conveniences and accoutrements that others take for granted. But it remains an obvious truth that most of us living in the modern world do not think we would be happy with nothing beyond Epicurus's "bare necessities." We may be wrong about this, of course. As psychologist Daniel Gilbert has persuasively argued, we are often extraordinarily bad at predicting what will make us happy.[30] But there are some plausible reasons for thinking the way we do.

First, as the patterns of social life change, so does our notion of what counts as a necessity. This is obviously related to the point just made about the relativity of "basic needs," but it is important to see that the change is not just in our way of thinking. We now view hot running water as a basic necessity; not so long ago it would have been thought a luxury. But the reason is not simply that we have become used to our creature comforts and have therefore raised the bar on what counts as necessary. Social expectations change too, and those who don't change in accordance with them pay a price. People who, lacking access to hot running water and a washing machine, wash themselves and their clothes with merely medieval frequency, are likely to find themselves short of friends and unemployed. To not have a phone in a modern society is to be cut off from the world just as much as if one were housebound in an earlier time. Many jobs require one to drive, and for people without access to good public transport, a car can also be indispensable for shopping and visiting friends. As Jerome Segal argues in *Graceful Simplicity*:

> Exactly what goods and services are required to meet a given need is not something that is fixed. . . . It is not that new needs are being dreamed up. The needs remain the same, but the commodity specification, the goods and services required to meet long-standing needs, changes rapidly.[31]

Segal supports this claim by considering in detail what is typically required in late twentieth-century America to meet one's basic needs for economic security, housing, transportation, food, health care, clothing, and education. It is precisely because meeting these needs now requires one to spend so much money that simple living after the fashion recommended by Epicurus and co. has become harder to achieve in spite of all our wonderful laborsaving technology.

A second reason most of us now feel we need more than the bare necessities to be happy is that as the world changes, so do our desires, ambitions, and expectations. When Segal says that no new needs are being dreamed up, he exaggerates. His claim suggests that human beings at any time have a basic need to be happy, and all that changes over time is the "goods and services" necessary to meet this need. But this fails to recognize that the *substance* of our conception of happiness is affected by the way the world changes. Large numbers of young people aspire to "get on," to travel, to have exotic or exciting experiences, to achieve something of note, to see the world and make a mark on it. Their dreams may often be unrealistic, but that is not the point. The point is that with the great increase in life expectancy, social mobility, vocational prospects, and recreational opportunities that has occurred over the past two centuries, the Epicurean notion of happiness will strike many as excessively modest, if not downright boring. Moreover, if we see others pursuing more ambitious goals and in some cases enjoying success, this will naturally influence our conception of the good life. It will also make it hard for those who stay at home and tend their garden not to feel dissatisfaction with their situation—the sort of frustration experienced by George Bailey (Jimmy Stewart) in Frank Capra's classic film *It's a Wonderful Life* until an angel teaches him to be grateful for what he has.

The last observation leads to a further reason why we find it hard today to be content with Epicurus's bare necessities: we now need more in order to sustain our self-respect. This matters because self-respect is, by common consent, a necessary condition of happiness. In *A Theory of Justice* the political philosopher John Rawls makes it one of his "primary goods"—that is, one of the things that every rational person can be assumed to want, whatever his or her life plan might be. Rawls in fact suggests that self-respect may be the most important primary good, for without it individuals lose a sense of their own moral worth and are liable to feelings of shame.[32]

Ideally, perhaps, we would be like Diogenes in his barrel, utterly indifferent to our standing in the socioeconomic pecking order. We would repeat to ourselves Epictetus's aphorism that "circumstances don't make the man, they only reveal him to himself," and would have no interest in comparing ourselves to others. This is a central element in Stoic wisdom. On this view, if you cannot maintain your self-respect just because others are better off than you, even though you have the basic necessities of life, the problem lies within yourself, not in your situation. But this is a very difficult teaching for most people to fully internalize. As Marcus Aurelius himself observes, "We all love ourselves more than other people, but care more about their opinion than our own."[33] In reality, most of us cannot avoid allowing the way we compare with and are viewed by others to influence the view we form of ourselves. The society we belong to provides a mirror that is largely responsible for our self-image. This has always been true. But in premodern societies, where one's social standing as citizen or slave, master or serf, was largely fixed by birth, it was easier to be content with one's lot in at least two respects: (a) the great majority would not be much better off; and (b) one's social standing was seen by all as something largely outside one's control. It is less easy in societies like contemporary America where competitive attitudes percolate from the economic system to other areas of social interaction, and where one constantly encounters the pervasive (and highly questionable) idea that the society is essentially meritocratic. So even though in many respects the poor today have a much higher material standard of living than ever before, it probably requires greater independence of spirit today to be "poor and proud of it" than at any previous time.

My point here is not that everyone living under capitalism is hopelessly caught up in a materialistic rat race. Most people have no desperate burning desire to be rich or powerful or famous, and are quite capable of being content with what they consider enough. But to live with nothing but the bare essentials invites pity or contempt. Few enjoy being pitied or looked down upon, and few can be subjected to it continually without this adversely affecting their sense of self-worth.

These critical observations on Epicurus's claim that satisfying one's basic needs suffices for happiness do not mean that his thesis is entirely wrong. It offers a useful perspective, a reminder that prods us into reflecting on the way we live with an eye to identifying wants and habits that are foolish, wasteful, unnecessary, or inauthentic. The truly valuable idea it contains is that the key ingredients for happiness are usually within easy reach for those of us not mired in awful circumstances. When we fail to realize this, we assume that happiness lies in the acquisition of what we do not already have. This is the mistake that leads us to step off the path toward contentment and onto the hedonic treadmill.

SIMPLE LIVING PROMOTES SERENITY THROUGH DETACHMENT

This argument is closely tied to the one just considered; indeed, the two are interdependent. Satisfying one's basic needs will suffice provided one embraces a certain conception of happiness in which peace of mind is given paramount importance. It will not be sufficient if one's notion of the good life has to include such things as country club membership, gourmet dining, paragliding, and round-the-world cruises, or full-blooded involvement in complex and demanding enterprises like political campaigns, business ventures, or large-scale theatrical productions. To those with the latter outlook, the fact that simple living may promote serenity is a weak argument since serenity is not their ultimate goal. Among philosophers, however, the identification of the good life with a life of mental and emotional tranquillity is almost a commonplace. Thomas More's thinking is representative: his recipe to ensure happiness for the citizens of Utopia is to pass laws that eliminate both fear of want and pride in pomp (that is, the sort of glory won by excelling others).[34] Once this is done, he assumes that no one would be so irrational as to want more than he or she needs. Poets, too, often sing the same refrain. The best-known poem of More's contemporary Henry Howard (who, like More, met his end on Henry VIII's scaffold) is "The Means to Attain a Happy Life," which praises whatever produces "the quiet mind" as the key to happiness:

The equal friend, no grudge, no strife;
   No charge of rule, nor governance;
Without disease, the healthful life;
   The household of continuance;

The mean diet, no delicate fare;
   True wisdom join'd with simpleness;
The night discharged of all care,
   Where wine the wit may not impress.[35]

For all their differences on metaphysical issues, Platonists, Epicureans, and Stoics largely agree on this point. True, unlike Plato, Epicurus identifies the good with pleasure rather than with virtue and, in contrast to some of the Stoics, seems to favor a quietistic withdrawal from society as opposed to immersing oneself in civic duties. But their conceptions of happiness are all at bottom quite similar. Epicurus, as noted earlier, considers our normal condition to be pleasurable. The main threat to this condition is the occurrence of negative emotions such as anxiety, fear, envy, jealousy, frustration, anger, or resentment; so, as with the Stoics, one of his chief concerns is to learn how one can avoid these. If this endeavor is successful, the result is something like the internal harmony that Plato holds up as the chief indicator of spiritual heath.

The Buddhist view of the normal human condition is entirely different from the Epicurean view, yet in practical terms the conclusion it leads to is not so different. According to the Buddha, human life typically involves a great deal of suffering, so the goal of life should be the cessation of suffering. These assumptions underlie his advocacy of the "eightfold path" to enlightenment and liberation from suffering. Schopenhauer, who was greatly influenced by Buddhist teachings, holds that life is generally a wretched business in which we oscillate between boredom and pain. Our best hope in his view, therefore, is simply to reduce the pain as best we can. "The prudent man aims at pain-lessness not pleasure," he writes, since "the nature of all pleasure and happiness is negative, whereas that of pain is positive."[36] For this reason he decisively sides with Socrates against Callicles: "The happiest lot is that of the man who has got through life without any great pain, bodily or mental, not that of the man who has experienced the keenest delights or greatest pleasures."[37] This is not to deny that there are thinkers who identify moments of unusual joy as being the primary reason for describing any life as happy, but such a view tends to be more commonly found among poets and artists than among philosophers.

What should we make of the thesis that simplicity is a sure way to secure serenity? The claim has been advanced in two ways.

The Franklinesque argument (named in honor of Ben Franklin) is fairly obvious. If you live simply and frugally, you will stay out of debt; and if you make sure your income always stays ahead of your expenditures, you will accumulate a nice little nest egg over time, which means you will not have to live in fear of the workhouse. This approach is, as one would expect from Ben Franklin, solidly prudential.

The Marleyesque argument (named in honor of Bob Marley) advocates an alternative approach, which is nicely summed up in Marley's song "Three Little Birds":

Don't worry about a thing,

Cause every little thing's gonna be all right.

Marley's advice is hardly novel, of course. It belongs to a venerable tradition whose best-known representative is Jesus:

Therefore I say unto you, Take no thought for your life, what ye shall eat, or what ye shall drink; nor yet for your body, what ye shall put on. Is not the life more than meat, and the body than raiment? Behold the fowls of the air: for they sow not, neither do they reap, nor gather into barns; yet your heavenly Father feedeth them. . . . Which of you by taking thought [i.e., worrying] can add one cubit unto his stature? Consider the lilies of the field, how they grow; they toil not, neither do they spin: And yet I say unto you, That even Solomon in his glory is not arrayed like one of these. . . . Take therefore no thought for the morrow: for the morrow shall take thought for the things of itself.[38]

Marcus Aurelius presents the same idea rather more prosaically: "Forget the future," he says. "When it comes it comes, and you'll have the resources to draw on."[39] In the same vein Seneca observes that "expectancy is the main impediment to living; in anticipation of tomorrow it loses today."[40] The underlying point here is that worrying about the future is not just useless most of the time but actually prevents one from enjoying the present moment, for which peace of mind is a necessary condition.

These two ways of linking simple living to serenity do not sit happily together. Franklin says we should think about the future and utilize our resources so as to protect ourselves against future adversity. Marley and co. urge a more direct route to serenity: just stop worrying about the future, period: everything will work out fine (and in Bob's case, the route would typically be made even more direct by toking a joint). But the others call on us to simply have faith in the future without the use of confidence-enhancing drugs. And on the face of it, one has to admit, this does not seem especially sensible. Sometimes the bad thing happens: people die, fall sick, get injured, lose their jobs, lose their homes, find themselves robbed, betrayed, oppressed, or abused, become depressed, and so on. So why should we believe that "every little thing's gonna be all right" when there is so much evidence to the contrary?

Given this obvious objection, a more nuanced understanding of the seemingly less prudential approach is perhaps in order. The idea behind the words of Jesus and Seneca is presumably not that we should eschew future planning entirely; after all, some of Jesus's best-known parables, which describe activities like manuring a fig tree, or repairing garments to make them durable, seem to applaud forward-looking prudence. The key idea is, rather, that we should cultivate habits of mind which make us less attached to things we may well lose, especially material possessions. We will then be less anxious in the present, and better prepared to deal with adversity when it comes. That is how they connect simplicity to serenity.

This seems sensible, at least with respect to material possessions. (The notion that we guard against becoming excessively attached to family and friends—although it is urged by Stoics, Buddhists, and others—is a hard sell to most people these days, especially since the likelihood of a loved one dying early and unexpectedly is so much less than in the past.) One has to admit, though, that it is Franklin's prudential philosophy rather than blithe unconcern for the future that has now become widely established as common sense. Every article on personal finance and every financial-planning consultant urges us to worry about the future, to put aside a sum to deal with a period of unemployment or an unforeseen emergency, to fund as fully as we can private and company pension plans, to pay into college savings programs, to make sure we have adequate life insurance, health insurance, property insurance, long-term care insurance, pet insurance, and so on. For the real worrywarts, there are extended warrantees of every kind plus travel insurance, cell phone insurance, wedding insurance, car loan gap insurance, and extended insurance against alien abduction (in 2013 the best rate going was a single lifetime premium of twenty-five dollars for ten million dollars' worth of coverage). The government requires us or encourages us through its tax policies to make some of these provisions for the future. And if most people in societies without adequate state pensions are not saving enough to ensure a comfortable retirement, that is not because they are closet Stoics or Buddhists, committed to living in the present, but because they simply don't have sufficient spare income.

The idea that we should not concern ourselves unduly about the future because "expectancy is the main impediment to living" has to be qualified for other reasons too. At the societal level, too much focus on present goods, like lower taxes or gas prices, at the expense of future goods such as a cleaner environment and an adequately funded welfare state, is hardly praiseworthy, and we would do well to worry about the consequences of this shortsightedness. With respect to both individuals and communities, it is hard to make significant plans and engage in long-term projects without worrying about the ways in which they might be derailed. This is true whether one is raising a child, planting crops, running a business, carrying out research, writing a book, building an organization, or working for a cause. Yet immersing ourselves in such projects and bringing them to fruition yields some of our most valuable experiences and accomplishments. It hardly makes sense to eschew long-term enterprises on the grounds that they usually produce anxiety as well as (one hopes) satisfaction. And it is hard to really throw oneself into a project without worrying about its prospects for success.

The advice not to worry unduly about the future thus has to be quite restricted if it is to be reasonable. It amounts to telling us not to spoil the present through excessive anxiety about the future, and not to worry unduly about the loss of things that do not really matter. One of the merits of simple living is that it demonstrates how little we need to possess in order to be content, and how much of what we consider necessary is in fact superfluous. Keeping these points in mind may help us become, in Epicurus's phrase, "fearless of fortune," at least with respect to wealth and possessions. But it is less obvious how living simply helps one to achieve greater detachment from other things one values, such as loved ones, meaningful projects, or political causes.

LIVING FRUGALLY PREPARES ONE FOR TOUGH TIMES

This prudential argument in favor of practicing frugality was especially popular with the Stoics. As Seneca puts it, "poverty must become our familiar so that Fortune may not catch us unprepared."[41] Should adversity strike, it will be less of a shock to the system if one has been living frugally rather than wallowing in the lap of luxury, and this will make it easier to cheerfully keep up one's chin.

Notice that this is slightly different from the argument considered in the previous chapter that accustoming oneself to discomfort builds hardiness, industry, self-control, and other virtues. Here, the claim is that it offers a form of protection against being made miserable by a loss of wealth, income, or status. The arguments overlap, of course. Remaining cheerful in adversity, not being susceptible to discouragement or despair, is a socially valuable trait as well as being a quality beneficial to self. But in keeping with the distinction outlined earlier, the claim that practicing frugality decreases one's chances of misery can be classified as primarily a prudential rather than a moral argument.

Seneca, along with other advocates of frugality, actually advises us to practice systematic deprivation of luxuries:

Set aside a number of days during which you will be content with plain and scanty food and with course and crude dress, and say to yourself, "Is this what frightened me?" It is in time of security that the soul should school itself to hardship, and while Fortune is benign it should gather strength to meet her harshness.[42]

This all makes good sense. Taking cold showers every morning is excellent training for a prolonged power outage; survival courses prepare one for any unexpected breakdown of civilization's normal services. This is why we heartily recommend cold showers, wilderness experiences, and the like to other people, especially youngsters who have enjoyed disturbingly comfortable childhoods and have never had to wrestle with the elements the way we had to. But although the argument makes good sense in theory, it is another of those arguments that is better chewed on than swallowed whole; and as is usually the case with familiar ideas, doing this reveals its limitations.

Whether the experience of deprivation, voluntary or otherwise, makes it more likely that one will avoid the slough of despond in times of future hardship is an empirical question. There is a huge literature on the topic of how people can, do, or should cope with adversity. A lot of the psychological research has tended to focus more on emotional traumas such as the loss of loved ones, disabling accidents, rape, the experience of war, or the onset of serious illness. Often the focus is on the long-term damage done by such traumas and how it can be repaired. Psychological research relating to the sort of material deprivation that accompanies poverty, unemployment, or homelessness has shown that many of the associated problems, such as poor health, substance abuse, and depression, result from the chronic stress experienced by people who are continually forced to make the sort of difficult choices that more comfortably off people rarely face. Some studies even show that everyday stress can have a physiological effect on the brain that makes us less able to cope with adversity.[43] But it would clearly be a mistake to think that this proves Seneca and his fellow Stoics wrong, for the sort of voluntary self-denial he recommends is not the sort of thing that should create stress. On the contrary, one of the main arguments for choosing to live simply—which may include accustoming oneself to occasional deprivation—is precisely to reduce stress.

How well people adapt to material deprivation seems to be most of all a matter of temperament, which while affected by experience does not seem to be determined by it. Some who are accustomed to luxury seem to adjust very easily to a change in circumstances. Boethius is a paradigm example. Born around 480 CE into a noble Roman family, he became a senator at the age of twenty-five and consul at thirty. Thus he lived his first forty years as a member of the privileged elite. Yet when in 522 he was charged with treason, imprisoned, and sentenced to death, his reaction was thoroughly sanguine. Instead of cursing and lamenting his sorry fate, he spent his last days writing *The Consolation of Philosophy*, a classic statement of the view that happiness depends on one's inner state, not on one's external circumstances. On the other hand, we can probably all think of people whose difficult experiences seem to have served mainly to entrench resentful, complaining, or self-pitying attitudes that stand in the way of their ever becoming happy. (Once again, Dickens's *Great Expectations* offers a paradigmatic example in the character of Miss Havisham, whose life froze when she was jilted at the altar.) There are no iron laws of character development, just general probabilities, and particular experiences rarely overwhelm the contribution of native temperament.

One could also argue against Seneca and the cold shower brigade that being steeled to endure poverty and hardship, while no doubt a good thing, is less important for a lot of people today than in the past. In the world's richer countries, many now enjoy a more or less continuously comfortable existence from cradle to grave. Unlike the great blights of earlier times—plague, famine, war— today's disasters usually affect a much smaller percentage of the population. Natural disasters are typically local, and an individual's chances of being caught up in one are quite low. Economic recessions are a much more likely cause of hardship; but even here, most of those who suffer the consequences of unemployment do not go from eating oysters to eating cockroaches; their material standard of living, while low relative to that of their contemporaries, usually remains comfortable compared to the privation the poor faced in the past, provided they have adequate housing and enough to eat. According to this argument, then, preparing for adversity as Seneca recommends is rather like

North Americans today taking out an insurance policy against falling ill from cholera; such precautions mattered more and made more sense when the eventuality being anticipated was more likely to happen.

This criticism makes a good point, but common sense still suggests that some experience of deprivation strengthens our ability to cope with adversity, and that this is a good quality to possess even if we are unlikely to find ourselves destitute. For accustoming oneself to occasional deprivations does more than just prepare one for serious setbacks such as sudden poverty. By injecting a little extra steel into the soul, it can perhaps also help one to cope more cheerfully with the sort of smaller discomforts, disappointments, and setbacks that punctuate the days and weeks of everyone—the car breaking down, getting caught in the rain, missing lunch, and so on. Given how frequent such happenings are, this is not such a small thing.

LIVING SIMPLY ENHANCES ONE'S CAPACITY FOR PLEASURE

Choosing occasional voluntary discomfort or deprivation need not be seen merely as a way of inoculating oneself against being made miserable by future hardships or disappointments. It can also be seen as a way of increasing our capacity for enjoying the pleasures available to us. This argument takes two main forms: (a) we appreciate luxurious and exotic pleasures more when they are relatively rare; (b) simple living leads us to appreciate more fully the richness of the mundane. Let us consider these in turn.

According to Epicurus, "they have the sweetest pleasure in luxury who least need it." By "luxury" we can take
him to mean any departure from the fairly simple satisfaction of ordinary needs and desires. Underlying his claim
is a familiar and plausible idea: continual experience of
the expensive and luxurious can turn what ought to be a
delight into a taken-for-granted requirement, the lack of
which causes annoyance and discomfort. But where such
experiences contrast with what we are accustomed to, the
pleasure we take in them is likely to be much keener. Hot
showers and soft sheets are especially pleasurable after a
sustained period of roughing it. We savor gourmet food
in a fancy restaurant more when eating out is an occasional treat. The deprived child will be more excited by
a fine present than the spoiled brats who are accustomed
to getting whatever they ask for as a matter of course.
Interestingly, one hardly ever encounters a similar but
reversed argument in favor of indulgence—that prolonged experience of luxury heightens one's capacity for
enjoying things of cruder quality. Yet this can sometimes
be the case. People enjoy camping; they establish rustic
log cabin retreats; they relish a return to a biscuits-and-
gravy breakfast at the local greasy spoon. For the most
part, though, enjoyment of the contrast is asymmetric:
most people tend not to enjoy going from high quality
to low quality in most areas, whether it be beds, bands,
beer, or bagels.

This observation is connected to the phenomenon psychologists have labeled "hedonic adaptation." Over time,
people generally get used to changes in their circumstances,

whether positive or negative, and tend to revert to the same level of happiness they had before the change. One of the most remarkable illustrations of this was provided by a study of how lottery winners responded to their new circumstances, as compared with accident victims who had been rendered paraplegic. Although their reactions in the short term were what one would expect, within a year the lottery winners were no happier than the accident victims. Both groups had adjusted to their new circumstances, but while the lottery winners were discovering unforeseen problems, such as unreasonable expectations or envy on the part of family and friends, the accident victims were enjoying unexpected compensations, such as closer bonds with those around them whose devotion gave unequivocal assurance of their love. Hedonic adaptation can also be seen in small matters. We relish the slick new cell phone for a short while, but fairly soon it is simply a tool we take for granted, giving us no more pleasure than our clunky old one. And psychologists have found that underindulgence can be a good strategy for enhancing pleasure; subjects who abstained from eating chocolate for a week found they enjoyed a piece of chocolate far more than did subjects in another group who had been fully indulging their chocolate cravings.[44]

On the whole, this sort of adaptation seems to be a good thing: it means that most of us are not utterly destroyed by traumatic losses, not even by crippling accidents or the deaths of loved ones. It also supports the idea, repeated by frugal sages of almost every stripe, that worldly success will not deliver happiness and therefore is not something we should unduly concern ourselves with. And it explains why Epicurus and the rest are right to think that excessive indulgence in luxury, novelty, variety, or the exotic is likely to blunt our ability to savor the pleasure they offer. It does not follow, though, that we should eschew these pleasures entirely. Opulent luxury may be dispensable; but for most people, occasional novelty and change are important sources of pleasure. Some variety in our pleasures, in what we eat, listen to, watch, read, visit, and do, keeps us from becoming bored through habituation. Yet it is also wise to avoid overindulging a taste for novelty and variety. Psychologist Simon Laham, discussing eating habits, suggests that "variety in food, much like spice, should be used sparingly and wisely,"[45] and this advice can be extended to other sources of pleasure. Travel offers a good example. There are a few people who have permanently "itchy feet" and are restless the moment they settle anywhere. And there are some, probably a larger number, for whom the very idea of leaving their home turf is anxiety inducing. For most of us, though, part of the pleasure of traveling lies in encountering things that are different from what we are used to; the familiarity of home (like our staple diet of familiar dishes) serves as the necessary backdrop against which novelty and variety stand out and are enjoyed.[46]

That all sounds eminently sensible, and for the most part it is. There are complications, though, and two are worth mentioning here. The first concerns the idea that those unused to luxury will appreciate it the most. The problem is that some fine things may best be appreciated by connoisseurs who, almost by definition, experience them regularly rather than rarely. A nice example of the contrast in question is presented by a scene in *Babette's Feast*, Gabriel Axel's film adaptation of an Isak Dinesen short story. Babette, a wonderful Parisian chef, is living in a small village on the bleak coast of Jutland in northern Denmark following the violent suppression of the Paris Commune in 1871. The aging local population practice severe austerity as required by their brand of Protestantism. When Babette comes into a large sum of money, she spends the entire amount putting on a fabulous banquet for the two elderly sisters who took her in and their neighbors. One unexpected guest at the feast is General Löwenhielm who, alone among those sitting around the table, has seen the world, has moved in high society, and is accustomed to luxury. Everyone present enjoys the food, and the locals' ingrained distrust of luxury as sinful is swept away by the sensory pleasures they experience at the table. Yet while they are certainly aware of how the feast before them contrasts with their normal plain fare, only the general can fully appreciate the truly exceptional quality of the dishes and the expensive wines that accompany each course. Indeed, his astonishment at encountering such quality in this remote and humble location is made more amusing by the fact that everyone else around the table—for whom all of this is completely novel—is, if anything, less impressed. They know the meal is much tastier than what they are used to; but they cannot know, as the general does, that it compares favorably to the very best available anywhere: that it is, in fact, the work of a great artist. *Babette's Feast* thus provides some ammunition for the antiausterity school of thought, both through its memorable portrayal of the dreary existence of the small community zealously committed to austerity, and by challenging the idea that those accustomed to luxury appreciate it less.

A second critical point to be made, regarding this argument for keeping one's experience of fine things rare, is that it does not obviously generalize to cover all activities. It may be true that if we only ever watch topflight soccer, we derive less pleasure from watching inferior teams kicking a ball about, and that if we only ever listen to the world's best orchestras, we risk impairing our capacity for enjoying less polished amateur performances (except, of course, when our eleven-year-old has the oboe solo). This is a possible drawback to connoisseurship. While being able to discriminate between different levels of performance bespeaks a more sophisticated level of appreciation, which is presumably good, it may also diminish one's ability to enjoy anything less than the best. Yet hardly anyone argues that we should regularly read pulp fiction in order to enhance our enjoyment of good literature, or watch plenty of dumb and tedious B movies so as to appreciate more fully the rare gems when they come along. In some other spheres—science, for instance, or politics—the argument would make even less sense. Thus the principle that having too much of a good thing may lessen one's appreciation of that thing does not hold universally, and even where it does hold, it does not always provide grounds for eschewing quality. It may be a good reason for not overdosing on haute cuisine, but it is not a good reason to spend a lot of time watching bad television.

The second main argument to support the idea that simple living enhances our capacity for pleasure is that it encourages us to attend to and appreciate the inexhaustible wealth of interesting, beautiful, marvelous, and thought-provoking phenomena continually presented to us by the everyday world that is close at hand. As Emerson says: "Things near are not less beautiful and wondrous than things remote. . . . This perception of the worth of the vulgar is fruitful in discoveries."[47] Here, as elsewhere, Emerson elegantly articulates the theory, but it is his friend Thoreau who really puts it into practice. *Walden* is, among other things, a celebration of the unexotic and a demonstration that the overlooked wonders of the commonplace can be a source of profound pleasure readily available to all.

This idea is hardly unique to Emerson and Thoreau, of course, and, like most of the ideas we are considering, it goes back to ancient times. Marcus Aurelius reflects that "anyone with a feeling for nature—a deeper sensitivity— will find it all gives pleasure," from the jaws of animals to the "distinct beauty of old age in men and women."[48] "Even Nature's inadvertence has its own charms, its own attractiveness," he observes, citing as an example the way loaves split open on top when baking.[49]

With respect to the natural world, celebrating the ordinary has been a staple of literature and art at least since the advent of Romanticism in the late eighteenth century. Wordsworth wrote three separate poems in praise of the lesser celandine, a common wildflower; painters like van Gogh discover whole worlds of beauty and significance in a pair of peasant boots; many of the finest poems crafted by poets like Thomas Hardy, Robert Frost, Elizabeth Bishop, William Carlos Williams, and Seamus Heaney take as their subject the most mundane objects, activities, or events and find in these something worth lingering over and commemorating in verse: a singing thrush, a snowy woods, a fish, some chilled plums, a patch of mint.

Of course, artists have also celebrated the extraordinary, the exotic, and the magnificent. Homer gushes over the splendors of Menelaus's palace; Gauguin left his home country to seek inspiration in the more exotic environment of Tahiti; Handel composed pieces to accompany momentous ceremonial occasions. Yet it is striking that a humble activity like picking blackberries—the subject of well-known poems by, among others, Sylvia Plath, Seamus Heaney, and Richard Wilbur—appears to be more inspirational to modern poets, more charged with interest and significance, than, say, the construction of the world's tallest building, the Oscar ceremonies, the space program, or the discovery of DNA's molecular structure. One might even say that it has now become an established function of art to help us discover the remarkable in the commonplace. This, after all, is one effect of art that uses "found objects," such as Duchamp's sculpture *Bicycle Wheel* in which a bicycle wheel is mounted above a wooden stool. Commodity art, which uses mass-produced objects; trash art, which makes art out of garbage; and pop art, which uses commercial labels and logos—all these also reinforce this idea that everything has the potential to be aesthetically interesting. Musicians and composers who use "found sounds" and ambient noises in their work offer a similar lesson.

But it is not just the aesthetic appreciation of the ordinary that simple living can encourage. Ancient philosophers also pointed out that just about any segment of the natural world, from the starry heavens above one's fields to the spiderweb in the corner of one's prison cell, offers abundant material worthy of close observation and poses innumerable fascinating questions to the naturally curious mind. Moreover, the contemplation of nature is recommended not just as a pleasurable activity but also as a source of spiritual refreshment readily available to everyone regardless of rank or fortune since, as Seneca points out, "from any spot whatever eyes can be raised to heaven equally well"[50]—an attitude that seems to have helped him deal with his own misfortune when he was exiled to Corsica. Once again, there is no reason to assume that the connection being asserted—in this case between a simple lifestyle and a heightened appreciation of the commonplace or the wonders of nature—is universal or inevitable. But prima facie it is plausible to suppose that such appreciation is more likely when we are subjected to fewer exotic and expensive diversions.

FRUGALITY FOSTERS SELF-SUFFICIENCY AND INDEPENDENCE

This is another of those arguments that clearly straddle the distinction between moral and prudential values. The frugal sages are united in their praise of self-sufficiency, from

Epicurus, who describes it as "the greatest of all riches,"[51] to Thoreau, whose sojourn at Walden was, among other things, an experimental demonstration of its value. But how, exactly, is being self-sufficient thought to promote well-being?

We noted earlier that among advocates of frugal simplicity there are two main notions of self-sufficiency: not being excessively dependent on another person's favors or good opinion, and doing things for oneself as opposed to relying too heavily on someone else's services or on technology. When classical thinkers like Epicurus and Seneca praise self-sufficiency, they do not primarily have in mind doing everything for oneself after the fashion of Robinson Crusoe; after all, some of them had servants and slaves. Rather, they conceive of self-sufficiency as meaning, above all else, not being dependent on another person's patronage. One way to achieve this, of course, is to be like Seneca or Marcus Aurelius and hold wealth or power in one's own right; but the more secure way is to follow the example set by the likes of Socrates and Diogenes and become indifferent to the material benefits that patronage promises.

Individual patronage may be less central to the workings of society today than in the past, but its negative aspects will be readily understood by any employees who feel they have to court their boss's good opinion, or by students hoping for a good letter of recommendation from a teacher. When I was in graduate school, I knew a distinguished professor who would ask students writing dissertations under his direction to serve drinks and snacks at his house parties. I am certain that all who agreed to work as temporary unpaid servants were acutely conscious of the fact that their career prospects depended heavily on the sort of reference this professor would be giving them.

People who are dependent on the favor of others will almost inevitably be anxious about how they are viewed by their patrons. This anxiety is unpleasant in itself and constrains what they feel comfortable doing or saying. Ultimately it is likely to affect—one might well say *infect*— their thinking. As Upton Sinclair famously observed, "It is difficult to get a man to understand something, when his salary depends on his not understanding it."[52] Thus when Epicurus says that "the greatest fruit of self-sufficiency is freedom," he primarily has in mind freedom from any such inhibitions or anxieties, a condition he views as both conducive to moral integrity and necessary for peace of mind.

Moral approval of self-sufficiency persists today, but in modified forms. Time was when the upper classes would have viewed most kinds of labor as demeaning; not having to work for a living, and not getting one's hands dirty, were marks of gentility. Capitalism helped to usher in a stronger work ethic that eventually affected most echelons of society, and the rise of a more egalitarian outlook promoted new attitudes toward labor. Members of the higher social strata could demonstrate their enlightened attitudes by taking up activities previously considered beneath them— think of Winston Churchill taking up bricklaying as a hobby—and by becoming less reliant on servants, a shift in attitude that admittedly followed in the wake of servants becoming unaffordable. Over the past century a similar shift has taken place with respect to the division of labor between the sexes. Women are now generally expected and encouraged to achieve economic independence by working outside the home; men, who would once have been ridiculed for doing "women's work," now risk losing respect if they are unwilling to shop, cook, clean, change diapers, and so on.

Self-sufficiency is still generally viewed as a virtue, and excessive dependency on others as a failing; but for many today its most important form is not so much the possession of particular practical skills as being fiscally self-supporting. This latter concept includes supporting oneself through paid employment, which is how most people realize it. Today, individuals who are "self-made" are applauded rather than despised, as they once were, for being nouveau riche, while among the least respected members of society today are those who are seen as the least self-sufficient, the alleged "shirkers" and "scroungers," who are dependent on welfare. The opprobrium thrown their way is usually undeserved, but the fact that they have become such a common object of moral contempt is significant.

These points relate to questions of well-being because, as we have already noted, self-respect is a key ingredient of happiness. Seeing oneself as self-sufficient or self-supporting typically bolsters self-respect; seeing oneself as unhealthily dependent on others can undermine it. This is one reason why there is such a strong correlation between involuntary unemployment and depression. It is worth noting, though, that self-respect does not require that one's self-perception be accurate. The lucky guy who was born on third base and thinks he hit a triple may never be troubled by doubts about how he came by his independence. It takes a very independent mind and strong personality to uncouple one's self-perception from how one is regarded by others. For most of us, the extent to which we and our circumstances are respected by society at large decisively influences how we view ourselves. The concept of fiscal self-sufficiency is especially problematic in this regard. It is often applied inconsistently and tendentiously, and in a way that uncritically reflects prevailing assumptions and values. The hefty pensions enjoyed by some retired public servants are seen as honorable and deserved, while the pittances received from the public coffer by the long-term unemployed or disabled are viewed by many as badges of shame. Most people who find themselves impoverished hate having to accept charity; yet recipients of unearned income from inheritances and trust funds rarely suffer from any analogous sense of inadequacy.

Doing things for oneself—the second kind of self-sufficiency identified above—can also be praised on moral grounds. Capable people are useful to have around: they are better able to assist others and less likely to need help themselves. Contemporary advocates of self-sufficiency, however, tend to emphasize its agreeableness to self more than its usefulness to others. Growing vegetables, preparing and preserving food, making clothes, building furniture, undertaking do-it-yourself home improvement, decorating rooms, and so on have become popular recreational pastimes for many, each with its own set of magazines and how-to websites.

This kind of satisfaction did not get much recognition prior to modern times: if one could afford to pay another to perform a necessary task, one naturally did so. When an aristocrat like Tolstoy worked in the field alongside his peasants in the mid-nineteenth century, he was considered decidedly eccentric. Today, though, there would seem nothing especially odd about a wealthy CEO spending a weekend digging over a vegetable garden, building a boat, or preparing a barbecue. Indeed, a significant difference between the lives of those in the better-off social tiers today and in the not-so-distant past lies in the sort of tasks they might routinely undertake. It is rather remarkable, when one thinks about it, that many of those belonging to the professional or leisured classes a hundred years ago would have had little or no experience of such ordinary matters as, say, cooking a meal, doing laundry, washing dishes, changing a diaper, digging a garden, or painting a room. Even today, an entrenched sexual division of labor continues to limit the experiences of many individuals; but the social transformation that has taken place in this sphere over the past half century is nonetheless huge.

The advocates of self-reliance undoubtedly have a point: doing things for oneself can be immensely satisfying. Apart from the simple pleasure of being immersed in a task—achieving what psychologist Mihaly Csikszentmihalyi calls "flow"[53]—one derives satisfaction from a sense of competence and accomplishment, and with this comes an enhanced and pleasurable feeling of independence. Feelings of dependency, by contrast, easily breed negative emotions such as alienation and resentment. One of the best-known philosophical discussions of patterns of dependency is offered by Hegel in *The Phenomenology of Spirit*. His analysis of the master-slave relationship shows how complicated patterns of dependency between people can become. In Hegel's narrative, the slave's initial dependence on his master (who chose to enslave rather than kill his vanquished enemy) is total. Gradually, however, the balance of dependency shifts. The slave undertakes work that puts him in immediate contact with nature; and as he becomes increasingly competent at practical tasks, his work becomes a form of self-expression. The master, by contrast, becomes alienated from nature, lacks a vehicle for self-expression, and becomes increasingly dependent on the slave. Hegel's account is highly abstract; but it suggests and implicitly endorses a modern view of the satisfaction to be derived from self-sufficiency and engaging work.

A rather different dialectic has been playing out in our relation to technology, however. On the one hand, the general availability of laborsaving technology has meant that we now do for ourselves many tasks that we used to pay others to do. Who now sends laundry out to a washerwoman? How many writers pay someone to type up their manuscript? People buy snowblowers so they can clear their own drives, and lawn mowers to mow their own lawns. It has become increasingly easy for us to print our photos, book our own flights, prepare our own taxes, and so on. So in many ways we have become more self-reliant. Yet at the same time we have become ever more dependent on the technology that supports this form of self-reliance.

Our direct dependency on other people has thus shifted to a dependency on technology, and therefore, of course, to an indirect dependency on those people who produce and service the technology. Computerized technology has simultaneously enhanced both of these opposing trends.

Photography offers a nice example of this. Before the advent of digital cameras, serious amateur photographers working with chemicals in darkrooms produced their own prints, created special effects, and generally understood the process they were using. Other people just had their film developed and printed commercially. Today we can all mess about most creatively with any digital photos we put on our laptop. In that sense we are doing for ourselves what used to be done by others. But at the same time this new form of self-sufficiency, which certainly yields the satisfaction of exercising a competency, yields the satisfaction of being independent in only a qualified way, since it rests heavily on having available sophisticated technology that most of us hardly understand at all. Still, it is largely because laborsaving technology has reduced the amount of time and drudgery involved in many chores that a new appreciation of how mundane work might be enjoyable has emerged, especially, perhaps, among those for whom it is optional. Cooking in a modern kitchen, for instance, is generally much easier and more enjoyable than it would be if all one had were a few blackened pots, an oven that needed constant attention, and a few seasonally available ingredients.

Advocates of self-sufficiency also point out, of course, that as well as being inherently satisfying, doing things for yourself can save money, which reduces the need to spend time earning it. This is a further prudential argument for self-sufficiency, and one that will appeal to anyone committed to living frugally. For the most part it is clearly sound. Over time people can spend a considerable amount of money paying for things that they could make or do themselves as individuals or in groups: dinners out, lunchtime sandwiches, haircuts, house cleaning, lawn mowing, garden vegetables, bread, scarves, oil changes, and the like. The frugal zealot will be alert to all such ways of saving money.[54] One must also admit, though, that many goods and services are so cheap today, measured in terms of the hours of labor required to pay for them, that the economic benefits of doing things for oneself are often considerably less than in the past. A good-sized vegetable garden can yield a few hundred dollars' worth of food each summer. But it is very easy to spend close to this on garden products like seeds, tools, soil enrichments, pest repellants, frames, fencing, and so on. Ditto for clothes. Moreover, economists will argue that we should factor in the time spent on such projects—its value being equal to potential earnings forgone—in which case the savings involved would be further reduced. So if I save ten dollars by changing my own oil, but it takes me half an hour, and I can earn twenty dollars an hour doing other work, doing this particular task for myself does not really save me any money.

SIMPLE LIVING KEEPS ONE CLOSE TO NATURE AND THE NATURAL

We noted in chapter 1 that living naturally and being close to nature are among the various meanings attached to the idea of living a life of frugal simplicity. Advocates of simple living typically extol the benefits of being in close touch with nature; but what are these?

According to the Stoics, those who live simply do not just live close to nature; they typically live, or aspire to live, in harmony with nature. Their conception of the good life is centered on the idea of living in accord with the natural order of the world as opposed to fearing it, resisting it, or complaining about it. Similar ideas can be found in many religions, notably Taoism and Buddhism, and clearly inform the outlook of more recent champions of simplicity. This desire to live more in harmony with nature can find many forms of practical expression: preferring artifacts made of natural materials; growing or buying organic produce; giving birth at home, rather than in a hospital; choosing to breastfeed; going without clothes (the definition of "naturism" set out by the International Naturist Federation describes it as "a way of life in harmony with nature, expressed through social nudity").[55] The popular environmentalist idea of seeking to reduce one's "ecological footprint" can also be seen as falling under this rubric.

Living in harmony with nature is assumed to be intrinsically preferable to the alternative. Awareness of and attention to nature are also seen as preconditions for *understanding* the natural world. This can also be valued for its own sake as well as for the many benefits it brings. Epicurus offers an interesting argument in claiming that an understanding of natural phenomena liberates us from the sort of fear spread by superstition and fables—an early shot across the bows in the long-running conflict between science and religion. In a general sense he has been proved right: as our scientific understanding of nature has advanced, fear of supernatural beings—gods, ghouls, ghosts, goblins, and their like—has diminished. But it is primarily the scientific study of nature that has produced this effect, not simply living close to nature or enjoying it. Indeed, superstition of all sorts has traditionally had a firmer hold in rural communities, so it would be a stretch to claim that liberation from superstitious fear is a consequence of simple, natural living. Philosophers like Heidegger have even argued that our scientific understanding of the world, which is essentially aimed at domination and control, has been bought at the price of a damaged relationship between humanity and nature: in Wordsworth's phrase, "we murder to dissect."

Another ancient argument, and one that remains relevant today, is that the pleasures of appreciating and studying nature are readily available to nearly everyone in almost any circumstances. This consideration also grounds a further subtle argument advanced by Epicurus: studying nature makes us happier because it leads us away from envy, resentment, and dissatisfaction over what we lack compared to others. It does so because it leads us to take pride "in the good things of our own minds rather than in our circumstances."[56] The idea here is that readily available pleasures have a beneficial equalizing function. Ocean-front mansions may be exclusive to the rich, but most facets of nature—trees, wildflowers, birds, insects, beaches, rivers, mountains, stars—are open to all. In an often-cited passage in Albert Camus's *The Stranger*, Meursault reflects, while in prison, that he could be content to spend his time simply looking up through a hollow tree trunk at the clouds and birds passing over-head. His thought captures not just the easy and equal accessibility of the pleasures nature offers but also their inexhaustibility.

Delight in the natural world may be neither universal nor necessarily correlated with a commitment to frugality or simplicity. Some urban frugal zealots get their great-est pleasures from dumpster diving, trash picking, and finding bargains in thrift stores. But it is so common that anyone unable to appreciate nature is generally viewed as strange. And most of those who advocate simplicity certainly see a connection to nature as essential to their physical and mental well-being. The benefits people derive from this connection are not reducible to a simple enjoy-ment of nature's beauty. Our link to nature runs deeper than this, as is indicated by the fact that we find nature beautiful in the first place. And even features that appear bleak, dangerous, or disordered—desert sands, open seas, forest undergrowth, or windswept moorland—still please the eye. Typically, people find nature refreshing. Removed from it, many begin to thirst for its sights, sounds, and smells, for fresh air, greenery, birdsong, moving water, the smell of the earth, and open skies.

Thoreau, as we noted in chapter 1, is especially good at revealing how the value of our connection to the natural world can go beyond just taking pleasure in natural beauty. For him, immersing himself in nature helps him to feel at home in the world. He even claims that proximity to nature is more important to him than human society:

> I was suddenly sensible of such sweet and beneficent society in Nature, in the very patterning of the drops, and in every sound and sight around my house, an infinite and unaccountable friendliness all at once like an atmosphere sustaining me, as made the fancied advantages of human neighborhood insignificant, and I have never thought of them since. Every little pine needle expanded and swelled with sympathy and befriended me. I was so distinctly made aware of the presence of something kindred to me, even in scenes which we are accustomed to call wild and dreary, and also that the nearest of blood to me and humanest was not a person nor a villager, that I thought no place could ever be strange to me again.[57]

More recent reflections on the importance of our link to the natural world have given rise to the "biophilia hypothesis," first suggested by Erich Fromm and later developed by E. O. Wilson in his 1984 work *Biophilia*, according to which human beings have a deep-seated impulse to affiliate with other life-forms.[58] This notion may be a little too speculative for some, but a body of empirical evidence seems to support the more modest hypothesis that human beings benefit from proximity to natural surroundings and are susceptible to what Richard Louv has called "nature-deficit disorder:"[59] Surgery patients experience less pain and recover more quickly if they are given beds next to windows that overlook greenery. Natural light promotes improved cognitive performance among Alzheimer's patients. A 2009 Dutch study of over 345,000 medical records concluded that those who live close to greenery suffer less from anxiety and depression. A study in the United Kingdom indicated that even a five-minute bout of "green exercise," such as walking in a park as opposed to on a treadmill, improves one's mood.[60] Such findings are hardly surprising, given that whole libraries could be filled with books that in one way or another describe, celebrate, praise, or give thanks to nature. For many, a life without the possibility of regular communion with nature would be devastatingly impoverished.[61] Choosing to live simply is one way of making this form of alienation less likely.

SIMPLE LIVING PROMOTES GOOD HEALTH

This is a straightforward prudential argument suggested and even partly covered by some of the preceding arguments. To some extent its plausibility rests on stereotypical associations. If we contrast the life of someone living in the countryside, breathing fresh air, getting vigorous exercise daily, eating fresh homegrown fruit and vegetables, the day organized around nature's rhythms, with the life of the city-dweller, surrounded by noise and pollution, exhaustedly navigating busy roads or teeming crowds during the daily commute, grabbing unhealthy snacks between appointments before collapsing on the sofa at night with a TV dinner after another day in the rat race, we have little doubt which form of life is healthier, both mentally and physically. Historically, these stereotypes have some foundation. Since ancient times, cities have often been viewed with distaste as foul-smelling, disease-ridden, dangerous places. Escape to some bucolic retreat has been a perennial dream of poets from Virgil to Yeats.

On the other hand, for many centuries and in many parts of the world right up to the present day, people have left the countryside for the cities, no matter how crowded, dirty, and dangerous, because rural poverty can be so hopeless and unendurable. Cities typically offer more forms of support for the desperate, and more opportunities for those able to work. And cities today, especially in prosperous countries, are generally much cleaner and safer than at any time in the past, and offer access to all sorts of health-promoting benefits such as well-stocked grocery stores, up-to-date medical services, and useful support groups. The complexities of urban life, including the sort of work it often involves, may certainly be stressful, and studies report that in the United States there is less stress in rural populations. But other studies show that on many other counts, such as life expectancy, obesity, high blood pressure, and incidence of diabetes, stroke, and heart attack, rural residents in the United States are today less healthy than those living in the city or the suburbs.[62] Thus while many aspects of simple living can reasonably be associated with a healthy and less stressful lifestyle, the connection is loose. Simplicity is sometimes necessitated by poverty and accompanied by ignorance; those who live high on the hog may benefit from being able to afford good-quality food and gym fees.

In this chapter we have considered some of the main reasons philosophers have given for thinking that frugal ways and a simple lifestyle will lead to happiness. All of these arguments have merit, but in some cases, when we examine them closely, we find that they involve concepts that turn out to be quite complex or to carry more than one sense. This was the case, for instance, with notions like basic necessities, self-sufficiency, and leisure. Recognizing this naturally complicates one's assessment of the arguments.

The key notions we have been discussing—notions like simplicity, frugality, basic needs, simple pleasures, leisure, serenity, self-sufficiency, living naturally—form a family. They overlap and are interconnected in various ways. But as in any family, there will be conflicts and tensions. It would be naive to think that every imperative or suggestion regarding simplicity or frugality will automatically support or even be consistent with all the others. To take just one example, there are times when what is more natural may be at odds with what is frugal. Organic food is generally more expensive than nonorganic; natural materials like wool, wood, or diamonds are often pricey compared to artificial substitutes. When this occurs, we reveal through our choices what matters most to us.

In reviewing the prudential arguments for frugal simplicity, we can readily see that some of them rest on assumptions that can be reasonably challenged, or invoke values that are not universally accepted. Some people do not seek serenity. Some view a life in which one is content with simple pleasures as boring and unambitious. Some will argue that living simply may result in a failure to cultivate one's capacities for more complex pleasures. In the next two chapters we will look at some of these alternative perspectives more thoroughly.

CHAPTER 4

Why the Philosophy of Frugality Is a Hard Sell

Let us sum up the substance of the preceding chapters. Many philosophers, representing many different traditions and schools, have praised frugality and simple living. They typically see these as virtuous in themselves, as fostering virtue, as being typically associated with other admirable traits, and as paving the path to happiness. The main arguments in favor of frugality and simplicity tend to go hand in hand with arguments critical of their opposites, extravagance and luxury. Wealth itself is also often viewed with suspicion because it so easily encourages acquisitiveness, possessiveness, and other tendencies that signify misguided values. Some frugal sages even extend this suspicion of wealth to private property in general.

It would obviously be misleading to suggest that all major philosophers are of exactly the same mind on these matters, and there are some, like Aristotle, Hume, and

Voltaire, who are more favorably disposed toward luxury. Nevertheless, the general outlook I have labeled the "philosophy of frugality" certainly constitutes a substantial tradition and is endorsed by many canonical figures. In that most canonical of philosophical texts, for instance, Plato's *Republic*, when Socrates is asked to describe an ideal city, he paints a quick sketch of what his interlocutors immediately label the "city of pigs," a community in which once the basic necessities of life are met, the citizens devote themselves to philosophical conversation and other simple pleasures.[1] The state that he later goes on to describe, with its philosopher guardians, standing armies, rigorous censorship, and complex breeding arrangements, he describes as a city "in fever."

It is an interesting fact that philosophers have tended to be so favorably disposed to one side and so critical of the other. It is also somewhat surprising, given how many people obviously desire to be wealthy, readily indulge in extravagance, and positively enjoy luxury. Since many philosophers are moralists of one sort or another, looking to edify people, it is perhaps natural that they should focus on those failings they see as most common. It is also possible, as Nietzsche suggests, that in praising various forms of asceticism they instinctively identify the values and the forms of life that are propitious for the philosophical type. Perhaps philosophers just tend not to have the sort of personalities that enjoy luxury, extravagance, adventure, and risk taking. But this discrepancy between what the sages say and what the people do does throw up this question: Why have all those who preach frugality and simplicity not been more successful in persuading others to live according to these values?

We should not exaggerate this lack of success. Millions embrace the values of frugal simplicity in theory, and a significant subset put these values into practice. Even so, it seems fairly obvious that Socrates, Seneca, and the other frugal sages, were they transported to the twenty-first century, would not think their antimaterialistic ideas had triumphed; Diogones the Cynic would not think the world had come to its senses; Thomas More would not see us as any closer to Utopia; Thoreau would probably be even more scathing about the "quiet desperation" inculcated in people by the consumer society. In the modern world people are, if anything, more interested in making money than ever, more drawn toward what earlier generations would have considered luxurious living, and more willing (and able) to live beyond their means in order to gratify present desires.

According to the Pew Research Center, for instance, in 2007, 64 percent of Americans aged between eighteen and twenty-four said becoming rich is their most important goal in life.[2] A Gallup Poll in 2012 found that the same percentage of Americans said they wanted to be rich, which is perhaps one reason why in 2010 US lottery ticket sales totaled $58 billion.[3] A Gallup Poll conducted in 1999 found that 57 percent of American adults had bought a lottery ticket during the preceding twelve months.[4] (It goes without saying that frugal zealots of almost every stripe view a dollar spent on lottery tickets as a dollar misspent.) So much for fantasies. When it comes to realities, many Americans struggle to live within their means. In July 2012, total revolving credit card debt in the United States was $793 billion dollars; and 56 percent of credit card holders carried unpaid balances during the preceding twelve months.[5] This situation was made even worse by the recession that began in 2008. Obviously, not all credit card debt is the result of extravagance: for some people, a credit card may be the only way to fend off homelessness, keep a job, or pay a medical bill. But a good deal of it undoubtedly stems from an unwillingness to postpone the satisfaction of inessential desires combined with some degree of fiscal mismanagement, tendencies that marketers of commodities and credit cards work around the clock to encourage and exploit. As the newspaper columnist Earl Wilson said, "Today, there are three kinds of people: the haves, the have-nots, and the have-not-paid-for-what-they-haves."

This picture is certainly not unique to the United States. In the United Kingdom, for instance, total credit card debt in February 2012 amounted to £58 billion ($89 billion), with two-thirds of the balances incurring interest.[6] At the end of 2012 outstanding overdraft debt stood at £43 billion. Nor is the desire for much greater wealth than is necessary to meet life's basic needs found only or mainly in advanced capitalist societies. The frugal sages would find plenty to criticize in contemporary China, where the transformation of the economy since 1980 has triggered a wave of materialistic individualism, or in Russia, where the exploits of the gazillionaires created by the selling off of state property after the demise of the Soviet Union offer examples of extravagance to rival those found in any other time or place.

Even if we put to one side flamboyant examples of extravagance or statistical evidence of widespread acquisitiveness or imprudence, it still seems clear that the actual or desired lifestyles and spending habits of most of us today, especially in the wealthier societies, run contrary to the advice of the frugal sages and the advocates of simplicity. Many people embrace stressful, complicated lives in order to make more money or advance their careers. Those of us who can afford it, and many who cannot, often purchase all sorts of unnecessary gadgets and appliances to save ourselves the slight discomfort of a little labor (think leaf blowers, electric can openers, bread makers); we quickly become hopelessly dependent on said gadgets (think smartphones or navigation devices); we easily tire of simple pleasures (the double-page spread of weekend activities and attractions in my local paper is titled "Boredom Busters"); we prize and take pride in our novel and exotic experiences, from sampling new food to holidaying abroad; we welcome the prospect of wallowing in luxury (as every ad for hotels and holiday resorts recognizes); and we allow a desire to minimize any discomfort or ungratified desires to push us further away from nature as we spend our days in climate-controlled environments, our diets unrelated to location or season, our experience of nature largely limited to what we see on a screen or through a car window. All in all, our culture seems to be far removed from the sort of ideals championed by the advocates of frugal simplicity.

So why is the consensus of the sages ignored by so many? One simple answer is, to quote a Samuel Beckett character, that "people are bloody ignorant apes." They do not know what is in their best interest because they are unable or unwilling to think intelligently about what they really want out of life. And this is, in effect, what many of the frugal sages say. In dialogues like the *Gorgias* and the *Republic*, Plato argues that people who are ambitious for wealth and power are making a serious mistake about what will make them happy. Jesus says the same about those who, because they are too concerned with laying up treasures for themselves here on earth "where moth and rust corrupt," fail to achieve the kingdom of heaven (i.e., the happiness they seek). Buddhists, Cynics, Epicureans, and Stoics, both ancient and modern, repeat the refrain: people eschew simplicity because they have mistaken ideas about what will make them happy.

A variation on the ignorant ape hypothesis is that people are hypocrites. We hear the message that chasing after wealth, coveting our neighbor's ass, living extravagantly, and wallowing in luxury are misguided, nod in solemn agreement, say "amen," and then head off to chase after wealth and acquire unneeded luxuries on credit. Morality literature offers many examples, from the friar and the monk in Chaucer's *The Canterbury Tales* to Mr. Brocklehurst, the headmaster in Charlotte Brontë's *Jane Eyre*, who extols the benefits of austerity for his schoolgirls while providing every luxury for himself and his family. But so does real life, from self-professed Christians who say they believe Jesus is divine yet blithely reject his teachings on riches and possessions, to philosophy professors who honor the frugal sages while teaching overloads to pay for exotic summer vacations.

As explanations of why the wisdom of the sages falls on such stony ground, however, the ignorance and hypocrisy hypotheses have a common weakness: they both implicitly assume that the arguments in favor of frugal simplicity are decisive, and they ignore the possibility that there could be serious objections to the philosophy of frugality and sound reasons for upholding antifrugal values. We now need to consider this possibility.

THE DANGERS OF FRUGALITY

A danger with adopting any particular lifestyle centered on some principle is that the habit of following the rule becomes too deeply entrenched. It can then easily become an exaggerated trait, even erring toward a vice; and it can make one inflexible when faced with changed circumstances. This is as true of a commitment to frugality as of any other commitment. Four dangers of frugal zealotry are especially worth mentioning.

Mercenariness: Paying constant attention to the cost of everything, comparing prices, calculating unit prices, checking discounts, sniffing out bargains, spotting rip-offs, and so on can, somewhat paradoxically, lead to one becoming excessively concerned with money. Aristippus, a contemporary of Plato's who is one of the few philosophers to champion antifrugal values, was fond of making this point. A dinner guest of his once criticized him for spending so much on expensive food. "Would you not have bought these things yourself if they cost three obols?" Aristippus asked. His friend admitted that he would have done so. In that case, said Aristippus, neatly turning the tables on his critic, "it is not that I am fond of pleasure, but that you are fond of money."[7] The point here is simple enough: thrifty souls may disapprove of the materialistic values associated with wealth, but it is openhandedness and a willingness to spend that really express an indifference to money. The habit of thrift, on the other hand, can become a straitjacket that keeps one from enjoying the good things in life and, in the worse cases, gives rise to miserliness, which can be as serious a failing as profligacy. In Dante's *Inferno*, misers are placed alongside spendthrifts in the fourth circle of hell.

Plato memorably describes the way that thriftiness can give rise to avarice. In the *Republic*, where he matches different personality types to different forms of government, he imagines how the son of a ruined rich man might respond to his situation, basing his account on his tripartite division of the soul into the appetitive, the spirited, and the rational parts:

> Humbled by poverty he turns greedily to making money, and, little by little, saving and working, he amasses property. Don't you think that this person would establish his appetitive and money-making part on the throne, setting it up as a great king within himself, adorning it with golden tiaras and collars and girding it with Persian swords? . . . He makes the rational

and the spirited parts sit on the ground beneath appe-
tite, one on either side, reducing them to slaves. He
won't allow the first to reason about or examine anything except how a little money can be made into great
wealth. And he won't allow the second to value or
admire anything but wealth and wealthy people or to
have any ambition other than the acquisition of wealth
or whatever might contribute to getting it.[8]

The "sunk cost" fallacy: Research by psychologists Daniel
Kahneman and Amos Tversky in the 1970s led them to
conclude that for most human beings a concern to avoid
losses is a more powerful motivator than the desire to realize gains. Many other psychologists have followed in their
footsteps and investigated the phenomenon of loss aversion. A study by Hal Arkes and Catherine Blumer is representative and revealing. Participants in their study were
asked to imagine that they had bought two nonrefundable
tickets, a $100 ticket for a skiing trip to Michigan, and a
$50 ticket for a skiing trip to Wisconsin. They were then
told that the dates of these trips conflicted, so they could
go on only one of them. Even though they were informed
that the Wisconsin trip would be the more enjoyable, most
participants opted for the trip to Michigan. Instead of simply asking which choice would produce most future pleasure, they apparently took into account the "sunk cost" of
the ticket, which from a rational, utilitarian point of view
seems to be irrelevant.[9] Arkes and Blumer suggest that
underlying this preference is an aversion to waste, which
is, of course, a characteristic trait of the frugal zealot.

Conceivably, then, a constant concern for living frugally renders one more susceptible to the sunk cost fallacy, at least in situations involving money.

Ungenerosity: We saw in earlier chapters how often frugality has been associated with other moral virtues and with good character in general. Yet we should remember that our list of terms related to the notion of frugality included several with decidedly negative connotations, such as "parsimonious," "illiberal," "stingy," "closefisted" and "ungenerous." This points to a genuine danger with frugality: cultivating the habit of eschewing wasteful and unnecessary expenditures can easily lead to one becoming habitually ungenerous.[10] This is widely regarded as a moral failing, and understandably so. Aristotle condemns it as the opposite extreme to wastefulness, seeing a wise generosity as the happy mean between these.[11] Moreover, there is plenty of evidence that generous natures are more likely to be happy than tightfists, provided they do not fall into prodigality. One reason for this, presumably, is that they will enjoy better relationships with others. But another reason is that giving itself, like expressing gratitude, tends to improve one's overall mood.[12]

Stagnation: A commitment to frugality will naturally tend to encourage a simple lifestyle, and simplicity is lauded both as a path to serenity and for the way it encourages an appreciation of the little things and the present moment. Clearly, though, it could also, in some cases, signify lethargy, escapism, a drawing in of one's horns, and a rejection of novelty, adventure, or anything that threatens to take a person out of his or her comfort zone. A standard criticism of the Epicurean outlook is that it encourages quietism and escapism. Ivan Goncharov's classic novel *Oblomov* portrays an individual who represents such tendencies taken to an extreme: in the opening chapters the only action Oblomov manages to complete is to shift from his bed to his sofa. Oblomov does have some endearing qualities, including his capacity to enjoy simple pleasures, but his condition is a warning: there are many ways of living simply, as we saw earlier, and some can become a path to, or an excuse for, intellectual, social, moral, and even physical stagnation.

A somewhat analogous argument might be made with respect to society. If human beings had contented themselves with the bare necessities, we would never have made any sort of social, material, or artistic progress. Providing ourselves with superfluities is one of the activities that drives and accompanies progress of various kinds. This connection is made by Voltaire, one of the few philosophers to really enthuse about luxury:

> When scissors, which surely do not date from late antiquity, were invented, what wasn't said against the first people who clipped their nails, and who cut some of the hair that fell down over their nose? They were doubtless called dandies and squanderers, who bought an expensive instrument of vanity to mar the work of the Creator. What an enormous sin to shorten the horny matter which God created at the end of our fingers! It was an insult to Divinity! It was

much worse when shorts and socks were invented. It is well known how furiously the old councilors, who had never worn them, clamored against the young magistrates who showed themselves in this wicked luxury.[13]

In Voltaire's view, wanting, producing, and enjoying luxuries—that is, things that are not strictly necessary—is simply a natural accompaniment, both cause and effect, of progress.[14] Those like Rousseau, who see every step taken away from our natural state as a step away from true happiness, might as well wish that human beings could revert to the condition of apes.

THE APPEAL OF WEALTH

One could fill a book—perhaps several books—with wise admonitions from philosophers, moralists, and purveyors of proverbs warning us about the folly of valuing wealth over the more important things in life, such as duty, virtue, justice, friendship, love, beauty, wisdom, or truth. Nevertheless, throughout history displays of wealth have inspired admiration. Homer delights in describing magnificent palaces shimmering with gold and silver artifacts.[15] The Bible underscores the greatness of Solomon, who "surpassed all the kings of the earth in riches and wisdom," with a detailed account of how he filled his treasurehouses and spent his wealth.[16] Marco Polo is unstinting in his admiration of Kublai Khan's palace, which he describes as "so vast, so rich, and so beautiful, that no man on earth could design anything superior to it."[17] He is equally impressed by the style in which the great khan holds his courts, the splendor of his table settings, and the great quantity of food served at festivals. In such cases, some of the admiration may be directed at the beauty or the sheer magnificence of the spectacle and some at the power symbolized. But the admiration is also inspired in part by the cost in money and labor that such magnificence requires, and even by the extravagance it represents. We shall return to this last point later.

There is, of course, no contradiction between advocating frugal living and viewing wealth as generally a good thing: the steady accumulation of wealth can be one of the goals that motivate frugality. Even when the book of Proverbs tells us to not toil to acquire wealth shortly after saying that "a rich man's wealth is his strong city, and like a high wall protecting him," there is no strict inconsistency. Wealth is viewed positively for the security it provides, so we are not told to avoid it, only to avoid toiling after it, that is, making its acquisition our primary purpose. Stoics like Marcus Aurelius and Seneca offer similar advice.

The chief reasons for regarding wealth as good are fairly obvious: it removes or reduces the burdens of work; it protects one against at least some sorts of adversity; it means you do not need to waste time and mental or emotional energy worrying about money matters; it increases personal freedom; it opens up a wider range of pleasurable experiences; and it increases one's ability to help others. All these benefits—leisure, security, freedom, pleasure, and generosity—are generally associated with happiness.

Two other reasons for valuing wealth, perhaps less often mentioned by moralists but still fairly obvious, are that it increases one's power and raises one's social status. In most societies wealth brings respect and influence: politicians, businessmen, and CEOs jump when the fat cats call. But since this reality rubs against our official egalitarian and democratic ideals, we feel a little less comfortable citing power and prestige as motives for wanting to be wealthy. We have no difficulty, though, understanding Tevye in *Fiddler on the Roof*, when he fantasizes about how, if he were a rich man, he would impress the town with his big, many-roomed, multistaircased house, where the most important men in town would come to fawn on him and ask his advice (which would always be judged wise, since "when you're rich they think you really know").

One other reason for valuing wealth was mentioned earlier in passing: the argument given by Cephalus in Plato's *Republic* that the best thing about being rich is that it removes any temptation to do wrong. A version of this argument is still sometimes heard today in support of paying important public officials handsomely: if they are well paid, it is claimed, they will be less susceptible to corruption. A variation on the argument points to the moral dangers of poverty. Martha Nussbaum observes that one profound problem illuminated by Katherine Boo's *Behind the Beautiful Forevers*, an account of life in a Mumbai slum, is the way severe poverty can force ordinary people who want to be honest into dishonest practices.[18]

Plato, it should be said, does not seem to set much store by Cephalus's thinking. In the idealized city-state described in the *Republic*, wealth itself is viewed negatively as a likely source of moral corruption, which is why the city's guardians are required to live austerely. Too often, he says, people come to desire wealth not as a means to an end but as end in itself. This sort of craving is both irrational and likely to lead to deeper forms of moral corruption, a concern that seems as justified now as in Plato's own time. While some sorts of crime are no doubt more common in impoverished neighborhoods than in prosperous suburbs, no one thinks of Wall Street or other sites of concentrated wealth as the place to go if you seek moral improvement. And while possessing a fortune certainly awakens philanthropic springs in some, it also undeniably encourages arrogance, conceit, and callousness in others. A 2012 study headed by psychologist Paul Piff concluded that individuals of high socioeconomic status were more likely than people in lower socioeconomic groups to act unethically in a number of ways, including lying, cheating, and stealing.[19]

Most people will accept at least a few of the reasons just given for valuing wealth. We may not be willing to sacrifice too much in the way of leisure, pleasure, energy, comfort, security, friends, or moral integrity in order to become wealthy; but in many cultures, and certainly in most modernized societies, having more is generally seen as desirable, all things being equal. Even people who do not buy lottery tickets talk about what they would do if they won the lottery.

There are, though, some well-known pitfalls and illusions here that few us avoid completely. For instance, while

gene of
intelligence
+ talent

it is <u>clearly true that having more money</u> gives us more choices, it is <u>not necessarily true that</u> having more choices will <u>make us happier</u>. On the contrary, as Barry Schwartz persuasively argues in *The Paradox of Choice*, being confronted by too many options often makes us miserable: the decision-making process becomes more complex and draining; our awareness of what we are forgoing becomes more painful.[20] This feeling of being oppressed by an expanded array of options is observable throughout our culture: in the quest by high school seniors for the perfect college; in the bewildering range of alternative settings and gratuitous enhancements with which software designers load up their programs; in the absurd number of hours many of us spend shopping online, comparing hundreds of essentially similar items.

Wealth can also be less than the blessing it is expected to be when its distribution is highly unequal. Family ties, collegial relations, and old friendships can be soured by envy on the one side and arrogance on the other, particularly where the inequality becomes very great over a relatively short period. And inequality is also likely to undermine the benefits of wealth to society at large, an idea made familiar recently by works like Richard Wilkinson and Kate Pickett's *The Spirit Level*, and Joseph Stiglitz's *The Price of Inequality*.[21] According to Wilkinson and Pickett, among wealthy societies, those where income inequality is greater suffer more from a variety of social ills, including higher rates of physical illness, mental illness, and violence, along with lower levels of education, social mobility, and trust. Hence countries like Denmark and Costa Rica report higher levels of happiness than countries like the United States or the United Kingdom, because while there is less wealth swishing around in these societies, the economic and social inequalities are less extreme.

These question marks against the general view that wealth is good naturally raise the broader issue of the connection—or lack thereof—between wealth and happiness. This has been the subject of considerable research in recent years, and something like a consensus has emerged, at least among social scientists. People living in poverty tend to be significantly less happy than those living above the poverty line. This is due both to the obvious sorts of material deprivation that poverty brings, like inadequate food and unhealthy living conditions, and also to the fact that poverty makes one's experience of misfortunes such as ill health, job loss, loneliness, or divorce much worse. But once a moderate level of comfort and security is attained, more wealth does not greatly increase one's happiness. And most people have a "satiation level"—the point at which increased income will make no real difference to their happiness. In the United States in 2012, this point was reckoned to be around $75,000 in high-cost areas, according to a study using Gallup Poll data drawn from over 450,000 respondents.[22]

The existence of a satiation point is in some ways surprising. After all, a much higher income than $75,000 would enable one to travel to exotic places, buy expensive concert tickets, try out fancy restaurants, and in general treat oneself to a few more luxuries. And it seems reasonable to suppose that increasing the number and quality of pleasurable experiences would make one happier. So why does this seem not to occur? Daniel Kahneman suggests one partial explanation that harks back to points made earlier about the simple life: as people become richer, their ability to savor small, simple, everyday pleasures is reduced.[23] A study in which subjects seemed to derive less pleasure from eating chocolate after they had been primed with wealth-related ideas possibly lends support to this hypothesis.

The finding that once we have attained a moderate level of affluence additional wealth does not make us much happier seems to be well established. Nevertheless, people in that situation find it hard to shake off the belief that a little more money will in fact produce more happiness. This illusion is not peculiar to money. There are collectors of all sorts of things, from valuable paintings and vintage cars to railway memorabilia and cow creamers, and some presumably never still the urge to add to their collection, always thinking that happiness lies in that next acquisition. But the fact that money is valuable not in itself but in virtue of its purchasing power—we can exchange it for whatever else we want that is for sale—makes it especially, and universally, desirable. Normal people have no desire for stuff they cannot use. We would regard anyone stockpiling lots of additional cars, refrigerators, tables, or teapots for no clear reason as suffering from a psychological condition. But money is different. We consider it normal to always want more. People buy more lottery tickets as the prize increases to many times what they need for a comfortable, leisured life. Multimillionaires who chase after additional millions are not generally viewed as needing treatment. As Robert and Edward Skidelsky say in *How Much Is Enough? Money and the Good Life*, "Money is the one thing of which there is never enough, for the simple reason that the concept 'enough' has no logical application to it."[24] Or as Wallis Simpson put it, more pithily, "One can never be too rich or too thin."

The illusion that being richer will make us happier is not new, of course. The philosophers of ancient times sought to expose it just as do contemporary critics of materialism and consumerism, and with roughly the same degree of success. Even Aristotle—who, compared to many of the classical thinkers cited so far, was less suspicious of wealth and less convinced about the value of austerity—criticizes those who are driven by an insatiable drive to make money. He sees a certain amount of wealth as, like health, a necessary condition for living well. When performing its proper function, it frees people up to exercise the virtues: for instance, it allows them to cultivate the mind, act generously, and participate in civic life. But for Aristotle money is strictly a means to an end, the end being the good life. Once one has enough for that, to want more is as irrational as wanting more can openers or more kettles than one can possibly use. In this he is at one with the Epicureans and the Stoics.

But while the illusion may not be new, it probably has a stronger hold today than in the past because we can hardly help imbibing certain values, beliefs, attitudes, and desires from the society we are born into. Capitalism, by its very nature, requires constantly expanding markets, which it creates by generating new desires, which consumers can satisfy only by spending money. After more than two centuries on this treadmill we take for granted the desirability of more money no matter how much we already have, just as politicians and economists tend to take for granted the desirability of economic growth regardless of whether it will make people happier. Capitalism also holds out the lure of wealth as a possibility for anyone, whatever his or her current socioeconomic status, and this enhances its appeal. Of course, people have always dreamed of enjoying a dramatic transformation in their circumstances; this is the hope expressed in a fairy tale like "Cinderella," whose protagonist makes the move from household drudge to princess in just a few days. But fairy tales are fantasies; the need for an assist from a fairy godmother is a dead giveaway. Capitalism, however, can point to real-life exemplars from Andrew Carnegie to the latest college dropouts who have sold their start-up tech company for so many billions. The likelihood that you will follow in their footsteps may be small. But it's not impossible!

THE POSITIVE SIDE OF ACQUISITIVENESS

To be wealthy is to possess valuable property; material acquisitiveness is the desire for property of some sort, usually the valuable kind. Most people are acquisitive to some degree. Their desires can be directed toward specific objects—land, cars, books, clothes, cow creamers—or can be for wealth in general; and some desire for money, since this is the most convertible sort of property, is normal in most societies. Given the benefits of moderate wealth mentioned above, this desire is reasonable.

As we have seen, some thinkers distrust even modest acquisitiveness. Diogenes represents the extreme end
of the spectrum, but Plato, too, invariably views it with
suspicion; he traces it to the appetitive part of the soul—
which he compares to the moneymaking part of a city's
population—and warns that the desire to make money,
once aroused, easily becomes insatiable.[25] Most moralists,
though, are troubled only by excessive acquisitiveness,
a.k.a. greed. And some will argue that acquisitiveness in
general, and avarice in particular, might be viewed less
scornfully if we recognize how it may be the expression of
underlying yearnings to which we are more sympathetically disposed. Nietzsche, for instance, offers the fascinating suggestion that avarice and love have a common root
in the desire to possess.[26] And psychologist Kathleen Vohs
reports research demonstrating a link between thinking
about money and being more self-sufficient (although in
the same studies Vohs also finds a link between thinking about money and being less helpful and more self-
centered).[27]

One could also argue that all those sages who go on
about the irrationality of pursuing more wealth than one
needs, the tendency toward insatiability of this particular
desire, or its corrupting effects on a person's moral character should lighten up a little. What they fail to realize
is that for many of those immersed in acquisitive activities, the pursuit of wealth is really a kind of game. We
don't think it is irrational of Serena Williams to keep trying to win more tennis titles, even though she has already
won dozens of tournaments and made millions of dollars.

Competing for titles is what she does. She enjoys the challenge, the quest, and whatever successes she achieves. So why describe entrepreneurs or fund managers in pursuit of further millions that they don't need as irrational? Aren't they basically engaged in the same kind of activity: working out strategy, relishing the cut and thrust of competition, and enjoying a shot of dopamine when they gamble successfully, exploit an opportunity, or close a deal? The psychologists may be right that once you've reached a certain plateau, more money is not going to make you any happier. But the same might be said of Serena Williams and tennis titles. It does not follow that the pursuit of more is pointless, since it is the pursuit itself that gives satisfaction. Perhaps the insatiable moneymakers should be compared to the conqueror who desires more territory or the Don Juan who ceaselessly chases women, both figures used by Albert Camus in *The Myth of Sisyphus* as examples of what he calls the "absurd hero," someone who fully understands the ultimate futility of his project but who, like Sisyphus pushing his rock up the mountain, immerses himself in it all the same, and in doing so finds a kind of happiness.

According to most moralists, however, an insatiable desire for material wealth far in excess of what one really needs is both foolish and reprehensible. Yet determining whether one's desires are excessive is obviously not a straightforward matter. It is all very well to say that our wants should be limited to our natural or rational needs— what we need to live the good life—but these are conceived differently in different societies, and even within a society

the standards may change over time and vary according
to class or social group. Today, for instance, Americans
are frequently told that they should try to sock away at
least a million dollars in their pension funds in order to
ensure a comfortable retirement. Given the general standard of living, the cost of living, longer life spans, and the
cost of medical care in the United States, this can seem a
reasonable aspiration. But to much of the world's population a million dollars in savings is a fantastic amount of
money; people who feel they need that much must seem
somewhat deranged. From the perspective of the middle-
class American, however, it is the seriously rich individuals, the ones who feel they need a fourth home or a fifth
boat, who epitomize greed. If there is a general rule, it
seems to be that a greedy person is someone who desires
more than you do.

Although greed has long been condemned as a moral
failing, there is one familiar argument for viewing it favorably: it drives economic activity, which raises the general
level of prosperity. So what is generally regarded as a private
vice can produce public benefits, an argument famously
and forcefully put forward in Bernard Mandeville's *The
Fable of the Bees*:

> The Root of evil, Avarice,
> That damn'd ill-natur'd baneful Vice,
> Was Slave to Prodigality,
> That Noble Sin; whilst Luxury
> Employ'd a Million of the Poor,
> And odious Pride a Million more . . .

... Thus Vice nursed Ingenuity,
Which join'd with time; and Industry
Had carry'd Life's Conveniencies,
It's real Pleasures, Comforts, Ease,
To such a Height, the very Poor
Lived better than the Rich before.[28]

Adam Smith more or less endorsed this idea in arguing that when individuals single-mindedly pursue "the gratification of their own vain and insatiable desires," they unintentionally, as if "led by an invisible hand," benefit society as a whole.[29] In making this argument, he was reflecting and assisting a broad shift in moral perspective, shared by his friend David Hume, according to which traits should be classified as virtues and vices not by reference to some idealized personality type or lifestyle, but according to their social utility.[30] Thus Hume, in a similar fashion, criticizes "the men of severe morals [who] blame even the most innocent luxury," and offers an early defense of consumerism:

The increase and consumption of all the commodities, which serve to the ornament and pleasure of life, are advantageous to society; because, at the same time that they multiply those innocent gratifications to individuals, they are a kind of storehouse of labour, which, in the exigencies of state, may be turned into a public service. In a nation, where there is no demand for such superfluities, men sink into indolence, lose all enjoyment in life, and are useless to the public.[31]

The acquisitiveness that, by common consent, fuels capitalism has never sat easily with the critique of avarice and greed to be found in most religions. Yet according to Max Weber in *The Protestant Ethic and the Spirit of Capitalism*, it was the somewhat paradoxical coming together of a work ethic that encouraged moneymaking with an ascetic moral code that condemned luxury that made the Protestant countries of northern Europe the primary breeding ground of capitalism, for this combination led to the sort of capital accumulation and large-scale investment that capitalism requires. Nowadays, though, frank expressions of the desire to be rich are less held in check by any religiously informed moral scruples. Business studies is today by far the most popular undergraduate major in the United States, and business students are not usually shy about their motives for choosing this field.

The argument that individual avarice drives economic growth and hence many other social benefits was not unknown before the advent of capitalism, but it has become a staple defense of acquisitiveness in modern times. Moreover, it seems to be a given among economists, corporate boards, and upper management that money is The Great Motivator, that the chief way to get people to work harder and better is to pay them more. To what extent this is true is too big a question to tackle here, but it is worth noting that there are grounds for skepticism. According to psychologist Edward Deci, extrinsic motivations such as money can undermine a person's intrinsic motivation to perform a task. Deci found, for instance, that among students who were given puzzles to solve, those who had initially been rewarded with cash were less likely to persist in trying to solve the puzzles once they had been paid than were the students who received nothing at all.[32] Money can also be a distraction that undermines performance. Dan Ariely conducted research in India that seems to support this idea. Ariely had rural villagers play games that tested memory, creativity, and motor skills. He found that those who were offered the most in prize money (equivalent to five months' income in that part of the world) performed poorly compared to those who were offered less. Similar experiments undertaken using American business students produced similar results.[33] Ariely notes, wryly, that when he presented his findings to some highly paid executives, they remained perfectly convinced that in their own cases monetary rewards improved performance. But then they would, wouldn't they?

In 1964 the Beatles sang, "Money can't buy me love." Travie McCoy's 2010 hit "Billionaire" begins with a frank admission: "I wanna be a billionaire / So freaking bad / Buy all the things I never had." Even though Paul McCartney's conventional platitude carried a whiff of irony, especially given his experience of sudden fame and fortune, while McCoy's song goes on to imagine ways in which he will use his wealth to benefit others, the contrast here does seem to suggest a shift in cultural attitudes. Even so, when in the 1987 film *Wall Street* the real estate speculator and corporate raider Gordon Gecko declares that "greed is good," we the audience understand by convention that the man who says this is bad; and we are duly satisfied when, at the end of the film, we see the bad man who says that greed is good carted off to prison. It seems that our culture is still torn between accepting acquisitiveness as a necessary condition of economic growth and denouncing it as an undesirable character trait that bespeaks false values and encourages unethical conduct.

The Pros and Cons of Extravagance

> When [Aristippus] was reproached for living extrava-
> gantly, he replied, "If extravagance had been a fault, it
> would not have had a place at the festivals of the Gods."[1]

Here are a few synonyms for "extravagant":

liberal	ostentatious	imprudent	wasteful
magnificent	flashy	improvident	unnecessary
lavish	showy	immoderate	reckless
costly	extortionate	excessive	foolish
	unrestrained	profligate	dissipated
		prodigal	superfluous

As with the synonyms for "simple" and "frugal," some of
these are value neutral, others carry normative force. In a few
cases ("liberal," "magnificent") this is positive, but in many
it is negative, suggesting foolishness, wastefulness, or an
unhealthy concern for appearances. Used to describe ways
of living, the concept of extravagance has three main senses:

a. to live beyond one's means

b. to be wasteful, or careless of costs

c. to live expensively, paying out large sums to satisfy one's desires and/or to impress others

One might add another sense, that of being extremely liberal or generous in ways that benefit others. But we generally use other terms to describe this, such as munificent, bounteous, or openhanded; "extravagant" almost always carries the connotation of going *beyond* what is wise or appropriate. Obviously, the three senses identified here are not exclusive. It is only too easy to check all three boxes. Of the three, it is the second and third that are the most interesting, especially when the extravagance is affordable.

EXTRAVAGANCE AS IMPRUDENCE

Living beyond one's means has few defenders. Where this is unavoidable owing to straitened circumstances, it is not usually called extravagance at all; it is just the lesser of two evils, the other evil being something like eviction, sickness, hunger, or some other dire consequences of not going into debt. Where it is avoidable, it is at best foolish, and when it causes others to suffer, it may reasonably be judged a moral failing.

Interestingly, even the sort of fiscal imprudence that causes only the overspender to suffer tends to arouse moralistic criticism. Americans, for instance, are regularly chastised as a group by economists and cultural commentators for their excessive credit-fueled spending and their poor savings habits, especially when they are compared to their thrifty German or Chinese counterparts. The suggestion is that living beyond their means in this manner is irresponsible and, moreover, indicates an inability to resist the temptations that easy credit dangles before them.

Yet this moralistically tinged criticism is confusingly at odds with other messages that capitalism continually broadcasts to us through TV, radio, newspapers, magazines, junk mail, pop-up ads, billboard—every form of media available to it. We are not just constantly and aggressively encouraged to buy stuff on credit—ads for many commodities are often coupled with offers of low-interest loans—but we are even told at times that to be an enthusiastic consumer is to be a good citizen: that consumerism is a form of patriotism. This message was conveyed explicitly after World War II, when consumer demand was needed to rebuild the economy, but it has been promoted more recently also. After the disruption to the New York economy caused by the 9/11 terrorist attacks, New York mayor Rudolph Giuliani made a similar pitch in a radio interview:

> There is a way that everybody can help us, New Yorkers and everybody all over the country. Come here and spend money, just spend a little money. Like go to a store, do your Christmas or holiday shopping now, this weekend.[2]

And with the onset of a recession triggered by the 2008 financial crisis, *Newsweek* issued the same sort of call in 2009 under the headline "Stop Saving Now!"

In our economy, in which 70 percent of activity is derived from consumers, we do need our neighbors to spend. Otherwise we fall into what economist John Maynard Keynes called the "paradox of thrift." . . . It's tempting in the period of contraction to mimic Thoreau, to live simply and deliberately. But if we lose our penchant for gain and risk, we'll lose some of the essence of what makes us American.[3]

In addition to debt-financed consumption, capitalism also encourages and requires debt-financed enterprise. This kind of risk taking has always been integral to the system, and it is certainly part of what Barack Obama was referring to in his 2012 presidential campaign when he called for a "new economic patriotism." Here, too, though, our moral attitude is ambivalent and is largely shaped by hindsight. We applaud budding entrepreneurs—those who stake everything on their visionary idea—when the gamble pays off. These are the inspiring morality tales that the media likes to tell and that stick in our memory. Yet from a statistical perspective, the individuals who empty their own and their spouse's pension plans, take out a second mortgage, and borrow from their parents as they seek to realize their Big Idea are in most cases quite irresponsible. After all, the majority of start-up companies fail. Although the exact numbers depend on how one defines failure, in the United States the typical new business ceases to operate within five years of starting up.[4] And when failure occurs, we are quite ready to criticize the person's imprudence.

Our ambivalence toward taking on debt, and the importance of hindsight in coloring our perception of it as either admirable or foolish, is nowhere more apparent than in attitudes toward spending on higher education. People have long argued that a good education is priceless, not to be measured simply in dollars and cents. On that score, there is something noble about people being willing to take out substantial loans to ensure that they or their children receive a good education; for as a Jewish proverb has it, "an educated man can never be poor." Even those who do think in terms of dollars and cents can cite numerous studies to show that people with degrees will earn far more over the course of their working life than those who never attend or complete college. Yet for many college graduates in the United States, the burden of the debt incurred—which in 2014 averaged $33,000— has become decidedly onerous. And someone who borrows huge sums to get a degree in a subject without a well-defined vocational value, such as dance history or religious studies, is nowadays quite likely to encounter the sort of unsympathetic attitude traditionally reserved for the imprudent. This may reflect an increasingly pervasive materialistic pragmatism. But uncertainty over whether to praise or criticize someone who runs up huge debts for the sake of education also stems from living in changing times. The fact is, for many years now the gap between what students borrow and what they earn after graduation has been growing, and that makes the wisdom of racking up huge debt while in college more questionable.[5]

AFFORDABLE EXTRAVAGANCE

But common or garden imprudence is not especially inter-esting from an ethical standpoint. Much more interesting is the kind of extravagance practiced by those who can afford it.

For example:

- Liza Minnelli's wedding in 2002 cost an estimated $3.5 million.
- The pop star Bono, attending a fund-raiser in Italy, had an urge to wear a particular hat that he'd left behind in Ireland, so he had it flown out to him at a cost of $1,700.
- According to newspaper reports, in 2011 the singer Rihanna spent $23,000 each week on her hair (at which rate she would spend over a million dollars on hair care in the course of a year).
- Paris Hilton had a house that was modeled on her own mansion built for her dog at a cost of $325,000.
- Dennis Kozlowski, the former CEO of Tyco, threw a party for his wife's fortieth birthday on the island of Sardinia at which the guests were handed lux-ury togas, Jimmy Buffet was hired to provide the music, and the centerpiece was an ice sculpture of Michelangelo's *David* that peed vodka.

Something in many of us (and certainly in me) immedi-ately disapproves of—is even disgusted by—this sort of excess. (If you are inclined to say that you have no such reaction, ask yourself if you would be perfectly content to see your suddenly rich parents, spouse, children, or best friend start spending money in this way.) We cannot deny that we experience a little shot of schadenfreude when we read in the newspaper that Liza Minnelli's marriage lasted a mere eighteen months and that Dennis Kozlowski ended up being sent to prison for larceny. But why do we disapprove of their extravagance? And should we?

Some rich people will naturally say that our disapproval is born of envy, and there may be something to that. The editors of celebrity gossip rags clearly believe that we enjoy reading about the misery of the stars. A glance at a recent *National Enquirer* discovers a preponderance of such articles about film stars, including reports of how Alec Baldwin set off an unpleasant family row, how Michael Douglas is going through a divorce while his incarcerated son is being moved to a higher-security prison, and how Zac Efron almost died from a heroin overdose. Our interest in such stories may not be due entirely to mean-spirited envy, though; it could just be that we find it reassuring to learn that the rich are no happier than us.

Why else might we disapprove of extravagance? Some of the distaste people feel is for the sort of character traits that one imagines give rise to spending of the kind mentioned above. In some cases, it just seems fantastically self-indulgent, as when Marie Antoinette had an entire village built purely in order for her to play at being a milkmaid, or when Michael Jackson had a private amusement park constructed on his estate. In others the extravagance seems to be motivated by a desire to flaunt one's wealth: that, presumably, is the point of wearing a Rolex watch with

Sff   character name

diamond inlays and other such items known as "Veblen goods" (named after Thorstein Veblen, the economist who introduced the term "conspicuous consumption"), the main purpose of which is to demonstrate superior status. Sometimes the spending itself can be part of the display, as when some billionaires outbid all comers to secure an artwork they know little about or a star player for the soccer team they own. In such cases we readily infer something negative about the personality behind the purchase. What does it say about such people that they wish to make a show of how rich they are? Are they hoping to make others feel inadequate? Do they have to keep bolstering their own sense of self-worth by these means? Do they judge people primarily by how rich they are?

This line of criticism is similar to the kind that many of the ancient philosophers we have been citing would make. Extravagance is born of ignorance and represents a failure of character. Those who behave in this way have misconceived the nature of the good life for human beings; in the misguided pursuit of status and/or luxurious pleasure, their moral personality becomes warped. This criticism runs close to points made earlier in chapters 2 and 3 and concerns what extravagance says about and does to the individuals who indulge in it. A modern variation on it could be expressed as a critique of what existentialists call "inauthenticity." The forms of inauthenticity are many, but one of the most familiar involves seeking to escape from oneself through acquisitions and indulgence. The eponymous protagonists of Orson Welles's *Citizen Kane* or F. Scott Fitzgerald's *The Great Gatsby* offer paradigmatic examples; the expenditures and displays look like attempts to mask or compensate for an inner emptiness. In such cases our moral-aesthetic distaste may even be mixed with a dash of pity.

Some kinds of extravagance can produce a slightly different and interesting sort of distaste that one might fairly call aesthetic rather than moral. The Bible says that "it is not fitting for a fool to live in luxury,"[6] and that sense of something being not "fit" can be awakened by other sights: the philistine buying up a library, the fifth-rate pianist acquiring a Steinway, the gluttonous boor ordering vintage wine. In some cases this distaste could just be snobbery. We believe that *we* would truly know how to use or appreciate what the rich boor does not really know how to value. But even if we could not justify that sort of claim about ourselves, we might still object to swine wearing pearls on the grounds that others could make better use of them.

All these reasons for disapproving of extravagance concern the character of the indulger, which is viewed as wanting in some respect. From the perspective of virtue ethics (which is the perspective of Plato, Aristotle, and the Stoics) that constitutes a serious moral criticism. For others, though, actions are seriously wrong only if they harm others, and some who think this way will view indulgence with indulgence. If Bono wants to fly his hat to Italy first class, what's the problem? That's the prerogative of the superrich. But can it be argued that when people of ample means are extravagant, they in fact do cause harm to others? Two arguments to support this idea suggest themselves.

One way extravagance may do harm is through its detrimental knock-on effect. The spectacle of some people being extravagant is one of the most important factors encouraging extravagance in others, a process famously described by Thorstein Veblen in *The Theory of the Leisure Class*.[7] People spend money to raise their social status: this is the ulterior motivation behind all sorts of spending, whether on things (houses, cars, clothes, technology, gadgets), experiences (vacations, sports), or events (weddings, parties). And as Juliet Schor argues in *The Overspent American*, keeping up with the Joneses who live down the street has gradually given way to trying to keep up with the usually much richer people seen on television, in commercials, and in other media. These figures provide the new benchmark against which people compare themselves, with the result that they feel still more pressed to earn more in order to buy more.[8] The general consequences of this are bad for most of those concerned as people across the socioeconomic spectrum are led into rounds of competitive conspicuous consumption that leave some broke, few happy, and many dissatisfied, while exacerbating inequalities. The problem is parallel to (and related to) that of inflated incomes. When the people at the top insist on salaries and bonuses in the tens of millions, this affects what people lower down the ladder want, expect, demand, or hope for. So university presidents and CEOs of hospitals also start demanding levels of compensation that are scandalous given the not-for-profit status of their institutions. This has an inflationary effect on other salaries, and the process hurts those much further down the socioeconomic scale who cannot compete, yet who may still have to pay higher rents, tuition fees, medical bills, insurance premiums, and so on that result from (and support) these inflated incomes. In this way the extravagances of the rich fuel a materialistic culture that promises but does not actually deliver happiness. It also indirectly promotes a destructive individualism insofar as it encourages an attitude of seeking the means to enjoy commodities, experiences, and opportunities viewed as things one pays for out of one's own pocket. This reinforces the desire for personal wealth, which makes paying taxes seem less in one's interest, which reduces people's commitment to public expenditure on community goods, which—insofar as it leads to less investment in community goods—encourages the idea that the good in question must be sought and bought privately, and so on. Education and housing offer excellent examples of how this sort of thing plays out.

A second reason for holding that extravagance is harmful is simply that it is so wasteful: the huge sums of money could clearly be put to much better use. This is probably the most common moral objection to it, and the main point seems indisputable. It strikes us with particular force when excess is juxtaposed to serious need. For instance, when one person owns several mansions while thousands go homeless, or where rich diners feast on imported delicacies while the poor all around go hungry. This is the sort of criticism advanced by utilitarians like Peter Singer.

According to Singer's form of utilitarianism, we all have an obligation to promote happiness and alleviate misery where we can. Singer takes it to be obvious that there is something morally wrong with a person gorging himself on expensive food while his next-door neighbor starves, or spending large sums on trivial indulgences while his neighbor dies from want of medicine. And by a simple analogy, there is something wrong with well-off people anywhere indulging themselves in extravagances when the money spent could be used to save or massively improve the quality of many lives; the physical distance between the haves and the have-nots is morally irrelevant. Singer takes this line of reasoning all the way to its logical conclusion, arguing that those of us who can afford it should use our disposable income to help the needy up to the point where the pleasures we forgo are no longer outweighed by improvements in the lives of those helped.[9] Few are prepared to follow him this far, yet many would agree that there is something morally distasteful about at least some forms of extravagance when people are suffering and dying for want of basic necessities. One problem, though, is that perceptions of extravagance are relative to one's cultural benchmark. We might be happy to jump onto Singer's moral high horse in order to criticize the conspicuous consumption and excessive indulgences of celebrities and fat cat bankers. Yet from another point of view, spending habits that middle-class Americans consider perfectly reasonable might equally be viewed by many people in the world as fantastically self-indulgent— even callous. A family of four eating out at a good restaurant in San Francisco and then taking in a movie can easily drop three hundred dollars. That is more than the per capita annual income of countries like Congo and Somalia. It is also more than some families in California spend on food in a month.[10] According to Singer, we have the same obligation to help those in dire need regardless of whether they are close by or far away; so if by forgoing luxuries that add only slightly to our own happiness we could greatly improve the lives of people who lack such basics as food, clean water, housing, and health care, we should do so.

Singer's argument against even what we might call modest extravagance seems powerful, yet it fails to convince most people, or at least it fails to significantly alter their behavior. This could, of course, be attributed to their putting self-interest before duty. But that is too simple. For critics of the strict utilitarian calculation, the discrepancy between our alleged duty and our normal sense of what is acceptable is too great. One problem with Singer's reasoning is that it assumes we have the same obligations to people whether they are friends or strangers, live nearby or on the other side of the world. But in most moral codes and in our ordinary moral thinking, closeness and distance, both literal and metaphorical, do make a difference. Our obligations to those close to us are greater. Another problem is that Singer's argument treats omission as morally equivalent to commission: to spend money on some luxury when it could be used to save lives or alleviate suffering is seen as almost tantamount to causing people to die or to suffer. Here too, though, most moral codes don't treat these as equivalent: we imprison people for murder, not for failing to give enough to charity.

The standard utilitarian response to such objections is to argue that our customary moral beliefs and practices are wrong and should be changed. The fact that most people think a certain way, or that our society has done things a certain way for a long time, or that our "moral intuitions" tell us that this way of carrying on is acceptable, proves nothing. The utilitarian principle that we should strive to maximize happiness and minimize suffering provides grounds for criticizing our conventional (and complacent) morality. To this the other side responds that a practicable ethics cannot just ignore what are virtually universal characteristics of human behavior and human culture. This is well-trodden philosophical ground, and we will not be able to resolve the debate here. It is one of those instances where both sides seem to have very cogent positions.

A different sort of response to the utilitarian critique of extravagance, however, is to defend extravagance on positive grounds, arguing that instead of viewing it as wasteful we should recognize its value for both the individual and society at large. This line of thinking also offers a response to the other criticisms of extravagance coming from the frugal sages and simple livers we have been citing. Remarkably few philosophers in the Western canon seem to have anything good to say about extravagance; but that is all the more reason to consider what might be said in its defense.

ARGUMENTS IN FAVOR OF AFFORDABLE EXTRAVAGANCE

In nearly all the examples of extravagance mentioned so far, the inclination to criticize is triggered by a sense that the spending is excessive or wasteful. As already noted, though, terms like "excessive" and "wasteful" are inherently pejorative: to use them is ipso facto to criticize. But we should beware of feeding on a diet of one-sided examples. Extravagance, even if affordable, is easy to condemn for all the reasons given. We've mentioned Bono's hat, Rihanna's hair, and Liza Minelli's wedding. But we should consider other sorts of examples too, and be willing to acknowledge any good that comes out of even absurd instances of extravagance. When we do this, we find there are in fact good reasons for viewing at least some kinds of extravagance positively.

Extravagance Fuels Economic Growth

In the previous chapter we noted that the advent of capitalism prompted a shift in the moral assessment of traits like avarice and acquisitiveness. What had always been condemned as private vices came to be reassessed by Adam Smith, David Hume, and others on the grounds that they confer public benefits. A similar argument can be made on behalf of extravagance: it is economically fruitful, since one person's extravagance is another person's income.

Exactly how much is spent on "luxury goods" each year depends on how one defines the term. For Diogenes, virtually any possession is a luxury. Most people in the United

States today would probably not think of a smartphone as a luxury but would view expensive artwork in this way. The definition favored by many economists classifies something as a luxury if, as people's income increases, demand for it goes up by more than the rise in income. But on any definition the amount spent on luxuries is huge. According to a report by the management consultant firm Bain & Company, the global market for luxury goods in 2014 was well over $900 billion.[11] When people spend money on luxuries, the argument goes, this increases the demand for goods and services, which creates jobs, which enables those employed to earn more and spend more, which further stimulates economic activity to produce a rising tide that raises all boats. Since those who work pay taxes rather than receive welfare benefits, the good effects of extravagance also include enabling governments to make the sort of public investment in things like education, health care, transportation, and public amenities that improve the quality of life for all.

This is a powerful argument. Its force becomes even greater if one defines extravagance the way some frugal sages would as meaning expenditure on luxuries, where "luxuries" are defined as anything beyond what is necessary for the good life as they conceive it. In that case, we have to acknowledge that the majority of people have employment only because a huge number of people are willing to be extravagant. In the short term, the economy benefits even when people are imprudently extravagant, using credit to buy things they do not really need in a way that leaves them chronically in debt. Those who make and sell things do just as well regardless of how what they provide is paid for. In the longer term, though, the wider economic benefits of this sort of extravagance may fade; for once people are hemorrhaging a good chunk of their monthly income servicing credit card debt, they have less disposable income, and money that they might otherwise spend on goods and services is siphoned into the coffers of the credit card companies. Imprudence can even damage an economy, as was demonstrated in the recession that began in 2008. A major factor in the complex of causes leading to this recession was the amount of debt being carried by American households, including mortgages that could no longer be refinanced and which left people carrying negative equity once the housing bubble burst.

These particular chickens coming home to roost do not, however, disprove the economic benefits of affordable (as opposed to imprudent) extravagance. Common sense and moral philosophy may distinguish between reasonable consumer spending on the one hand and foolish, wasteful, and sickeningly self-indulgent outlays on the other, but economists interested in the effects of these on employment, per capita income, or gross domestic product do not.

Extravagance Fuels Culture

Picture in your mind the Taj Mahal, the palace and gardens at Versailles, the Sistine Chapel, the Library of Congress, the stately homes of England, the terracotta army at Xian, the Hagia Sophia, the Parthenon of Athens, or the crown jewels of the English monarchs. Consider the extravagances of those eighteenth-century aristocrats who employed entire orchestras and commissioned original compositions from the likes of Haydn and Mozart to enliven a dinner party or a dance. Think about where we go and what we do as tourists. Much of the time we queue up and pay good money to admire the results of some long-dead fat cat's extravagance: palaces, castles, tombs, temples, cathedrals, gardens, frescoes, tapestries, sculptures, paintings, jewelry, and other artifacts, nearly all produced at vast expense. Who, when visiting Florence, shakes her head disapprovingly at the spending habits of the Medicis and wishes they had been more frugal? Or goes to see ballet at the Bolshoi in Moscow only to find his enjoyment spoiled by the sight of the theater's lavish fittings? Or considers the house and gardens of Blenheim Palace distasteful rather than beautiful on account of their magnificence? One could argue, in fact, that if everyone had taken the advice of Socrates and the frugal sages, there would hardly be a tourist industry—and not just because we would all be too cheap to travel. Except for a few famous natural wonders, there would be nothing worthwhile for us to stand smilingly in front of when we want our holiday snaps taken.

Here is another rather weighty reason to put a question mark against the recommendation that we should all cut out waste and excess in order to live simply. Extravagance fuels culture. Much of what we think of as the notable achievements of civilization, from the Taj Mahal to the Cadillac, from the Hubble Space Telescope to the Olympic Games, from the art and architecture of the Renaissance to James Bond movies, is the result of individual and collective extravagance. Yet this is the stuff of culture, and we think the world is a lot more interesting and enjoyable because of it. We might note, also, that the precise motives and intentions of those whose extravagance is responsible for some great building, artwork, or other project make little difference to our interest in or appreciation of the result. The pyramids were built to glorify the kings interred within; medieval cathedrals were designed to glorify God; Carnegie libraries were built to provide a valuable public service. We may admire Andrew Carnegie's philanthropic intentions more than we do the egoism of kings who commissioned vast tombs, or the vain self-indulgence of the rich who constructed stately homes. But the tombs and palaces may still be more interesting to visit.

This argument in praise of some sorts of extravagance can be extended to cover the spending of public money also. If the task of government is to promote happiness, and the key to happiness is simple living, then all government needs to do is ensure that everyone has the basic necessities: safety, food, clothing, shelter, and perhaps health care. But of course governments do far more than this. In part this is because, as noted earlier, in a complex modern society far more things are deemed "necessities." These now include things like education, electricity, roads, and many other elements of the infrastructure that makes modern living possible. But governments also spend huge sums to support or subsidize parks, museums, libraries, galleries, opera houses, space telescopes, particle colliders, and all sorts of projects and activities in the natural and social sciences, the arts, the humanities, sport, and popular culture. They do this even though there are millions living in poverty and in spite of the fact that most governments already owe huge sums. (At the end of 2014, the national debt of the United States—the total amount the government owes—was roughly $18 trillion and rising.)[12] Such expenditures could be viewed as excessive and wasteful, analogous to an individual with impoverished relatives and maxed-out credit cards indulging himself with a day at the zoo and a night at the opera. Yet apart from devoted followers of Ayn Rand and others who are ideologically committed to the idea of minimal government, few condemn it all as irresponsible profligacy. Most of us value living in a culturally rich environment and for that reason do not see public spending on "cultural luxuries" as culpably extravagant.

Extravagance Adds Interest and Excitement to Life

The last observations point to a third reason for challenging the philosophers' traditional distrust of extravagance. A wonderful *New Yorker* cartoon, one of those supremely witty cartoons that manage to say a lot with a little, depicts two gravestones side by side. The one on the right bears the inscription "I led a prosperous, but frugal life." The other one is inscribed with an arrow pointing over to the "prosperous, but frugal" grave, and beneath the arrow are written the words "I'm with stupid." This is one of those cases where it is impossible to avoid thinking in reprehensible stereotypes. We all know immediately that the grave on the right contains a man. How? Well, from his epitaph we can safely infer that he was boring, pompous, and smug. Ergo male. Case closed. And the person buried next to him is obviously his wife: critical, frustrated, regretful, but for better or worse attached, probably through some mixture of loyalty and dependence. What is interesting for our purposes is the suggestion that the frugal life is stupid. Why would anyone think that? Why the evident note of regret? There is an obvious answer. The "prosperous but frugal" life is *boring*. This couple's lives were full of opportunities forgone. They failed to drink the milk from the coconut. To quote Ogden Nash:

> One never gets any fun
> Out of things you haven't done.

If the wife could go round again she would do it all differently: she'd go trekking in the Andes, bungee jumping in New Zealand; she'd stand on the Great Wall of China, see the wildlife of the Serengeti, play the tables at Monte Carlo, get high and go skinny-dipping in a thermal spring by moonlight.

This antifrugal attitude toward life is Faustian in the sense embodied by the hero of Goethe's early nineteenth-century drama *Faust*. In Goethe's play, Faust sells his soul to the devil in exchange for the most experientially rich life imaginable. He is indifferent to any time or place except the here and now. His desire is to know firsthand the entire gamut of human experience:

> And what is portioned out to all mankind
> I shall enjoy deep in myself, contain

Within my spirit summit and abyss,
Pile on my breast their agony and bliss,
And thus let my own self grow into theirs, unfettered,
'Til as they are, at last I, too, am shattered.[13]

This attitude is greedily acquisitive, but for experiences rather than possessions. And it embraces a very different conception of the good life from that proposed by the frugal sages. Whereas they are interested in finding the path to serenity and contentment, Faust shuns that ideal in exchange for something less comfortable but more exciting:

Let every wonder be at hand!
Plunge into time's whirl that dazes my sense,
Into the torrent of events!
And let enjoyment, distress,
Annoyance and success
Succeed each other as best they can;
For restless activity proves a man.[14]

He even goes so far as to say that the devil can have his soul the moment he stops restlessly striving after novel experiences and expresses contentment with what he has—in other words, when he achieves precisely that state that the frugal sages call happiness:

If to the moment I should say:
Abide, you are so fair—
Put me in fetters on that day,
I *wish* to perish then, I swear.[15]

Now the regretful wife may not have been positively longing to suffer distress and frustration. But one imagines she
would have been willing to take her chances for the sake
of a more interesting life that included a few high peaks
of real bliss. Some part of her nods in agreement with
Callicles, when he complains that Socrates's conception of
happiness as a contented state in which one feels nothing
to be lacking is the condition of a stone—or a corpse![16]

The sages teach the pleasure of staying put, of tending
one's garden, of chatting with friends over a jug of wine
and a bowl of cheese. They turn their backs on novelty,
adventure, and excitement, all of which might disturb
their cherished peace of mind. But for many a different
ideal has more appeal. The roller coaster may be scary
and uncomfortable, but it is also exhilarating. Faust is the
mythical hero representing this alternative ideal, but there
are many real-life icons who embody it as well: Romantics like Byron and Shelley, adventurers like Slocum and
Shackleton, and all the larger-than-life characters who
make such excellent biographical subjects. This approach
to life is, on the face of it, a legitimate option, one we are
familiar with, at least from observing others, and which
most of us do not despise. On the contrary, it's hard not
to admire it. In fact older people typically like to boast of
Faustian moments in their youth when they threw caution
to the winds and through their imprudence enriched their
experience. So it is really quite remarkable that so few philosophers in the Western canon defend this outlook. One
of the few who come readily to mind is Nietzsche, who
gives this advice in *The Gay Science*:

> The secret for harvesting from existence the great-
> est fruitfulness and the greatest enjoyment is—to
> *live dangerously*! Build your cities on the slopes of
> Vesuvius! Send your ships into uncharted seas! Live
> at war with your peers and yourselves!

Inspiring words. Yet even in Nietzsche's case, this is (as so often with him) all metaphor. Read in context, he is talking here primarily about living dangerously and displaying heroism in the realm of the spirit—that is, in philosophy, science, literature, music, and art. So far as lifestyle goes, Nietzsche lived like a monk without a monastery.

As the example of Callicles in Plato's *Gorgias* shows, advocates of frugal simplicity and the quiet life had their critics even in ancient times. But Faust, with his delight in novelty, his desire for extreme experiences, and his praise of restless activity, represents modernity in general, and the spirit of capitalism in particular. This explains the power of the legend for modern readers, for whom Faust represents something with which we are all famil-iar since it is part of the cultural atmosphere we breathe. Indeed, today there is a certain amount of cultural pres-sure to pursue exotic experiences (which are usually also quite expensive), since doing interesting things is taken as evidence that one is an interesting person. The value of wealth is thus nowadays often perceived to lie less in what it enables one to possess and more in what it enables one to do. Most people today can buy far more stuff than their forebears, owing both to higher incomes and to the lower prices of most commodities. Moreover, the food, clothes, cars, televisions, sound systems, computers, smartphones, cameras, kitchen equipment, and other household gadgets owned by people on quite ordinary incomes are not hopelessly inferior to those found in the houses of the rich. The difference between driving a Lexus and driving a Kia is insignificant compared to the difference between riding in a coach and having to walk everywhere in broken-down boots. Consequently, today, if you are rich and are looking to impress others with a bit of conspicuous consumption, you have to either go big—for instance, a Lamborghini, a yacht, a waterfront property—or go for exotic experiences. No one will be much impressed by the fact that you have the newest iPad. So do millions of others. But being able to announce that you've just come back from sailing to the Bahamas and will soon be off to see the Ring cycle performed in Bayreuth—that sets you apart. Certainly, in my admittedly limited experience of being in the company of very rich people, I have found that one fail-safe conversation starter is to ask them about their recent travels or recreational activities, since this allows them to hold forth on matters that distinguish them from ordinary people.

Psychologists tell us that spending our money on experiences such as vacations, excursions, social gatherings, concerts, or sporting events will generally make us happier than spending it on material things.[17] We quickly adapt to having the new stuff, whereas good memories remain a continuing source of pleasure. This makes sense, but we still need to be aware of how buying experiences can be a form of conspicuous consumption. Acquisitiveness with respect to experiences rather than possessions is nowadays almost a mark of sophistication. The appeal of climbing Everest, or Alpine paragliding, or heading into space with Virgin Galactic does not lie purely in the expected rush or sense of accomplishment. Our almost irrepressible need to document our travels and adventures suggests that we usually keep somewhere in mind the idea of impressing others with our doings. Another *New Yorker* cartoon beautifully captures this aspect of our desire for experiences. A man in an office is shown leaning back in his chair daydreaming, hands clasped behind his head, feet up on his desk, a slight smile on his face. You might expect he's thinking of getting away from work, perhaps to a nice vacation spot. But no. A thought bubble tells us the content of his fantasy. He is daydreaming of himself, sitting in the same office, leaning back in his chair, hands clasped behind his head, but with this difference: on the wall behind him is a framed photograph of the exotic beach where he evidently took a vacation. What he most looks forward to is not being on the beach but *being able to display to others* the evidence of his having been on the beach. Since not working is in itself no longer a badge of honor, what Veblen called "conspicuous leisure" has been replaced by conspicuous recreation.

What might be called "the argument from excitement and adventure" is a powerful reason for questioning the wisdom of any blanket condemnation of extravagance. Seneca may claim that "in any sort of life you will find amusements and recreations and diversions if you choose to count your evils insignificant rather than make them hateful."[18] But this is hardly an argument for turning your back on real enjoyments that are available. The adequacy of British cuisine is no reason to not sample Moroccan or Indonesian. If you have the means to indulge in novel, interesting, and enjoyable experiences, why not go ahead and indulge? The point applies even to small pleasures. A stock character we are all familiar with is the rough, gruff, self-made millionaire who still, even though he no longer needs to economize, refuses to pay a penny more for anything than what he thinks it is worth. He even prides himself on his continuing parsimony, despite it being no longer necessary. But his attitude is arguably quite irrational. If he wants to eat some scallops, see a show, or take the train, why deny himself these pleasures just because they are "overpriced" in the abstract sense of costing more than he was expecting or more than he thinks they are worth? The frugal habit that made sense when money was tight now seems to be a straitjacket from which he cannot free himself, even though it no longer serves any valuable practical purpose. Here we see another possible danger of practicing frugality: it can become a habit that remains rigid in spite of changed circumstances and ends up looking like a foolish addiction to pointless sacrifice.

Extravagance Enhances Our Understanding and Appreciation of Things

A fourth reason for questioning the traditional condemnation of extravagance is that a willingness to spend and indulge can expand our capacities for understanding, appreciation, and expression. We touched on this idea earlier when discussing *Babette's Feast*. Take food and drink as an example. Simple fare can be a fine thing, provided it is not so simple as to be nutritionally deficient, and over-indulging in haute cuisine may perhaps diminish one's ability to enjoy more ordinary dishes. But it is also true that sampling different cuisines and occasionally trying out novel foods—which can be expensive—helps to refine one's palette. Not only is the variety itself enjoyable—even Epicurus recognizes that—but experiencing a wider range of foods, with respect to both quality and variety, yields a certain kind of knowledge. You learn how to appreciate flavors, textures, and combinations that at first might seem strange or even repellent (as I did when I moved from Britain to Canada and for the first time had bacon and eggs drenched in maple syrup, or as visitors to Scotland do when they sample their first deep-fried Mars bar). You also learn to discriminate between high and low quality—between, say, Bud Ice Light and a genuine beer. Since food is often an important element in national and regional cultures, one's understanding of a culture is enhanced through becoming familiar with its culinary arts, whether it be curries in India, kebabs in Turkey, or beans on toast in Britain. And having extensive experience of diverse cuisines may also improve your own abilities in the kitchen.

Similar arguments obviously apply to things other than food. Consider music. Is it foolishly extravagant for a violinist to pay $50,000 for a violin? Yes, if she is a mediocre player. But if she is good enough, a poorer instrument may limit her musical expression as well as the pleasure that both she and her audience derive from her playing. Is it a waste of money to pay $200 for a concert ticket? Not if you are able to discriminate between superlative and merely excellent playing, or if you wish to cultivate the sort of ear that can appreciate this difference. It is easy to see how the same sort of reasoning could justify extravagance in many areas of life and culture. In an earlier chapter we noted how a concentrated high-quality diet of anything might have the negative effect of making it harder to enjoy what is commonplace. This may be true. But it must also be admitted that exposing ourselves to variety and quality—which is often expensive—can help enlarge our appreciative capacities and thereby enrich our lives.

CAN EXTRAVAGANCE BE A DUTY?

In addition to the arguments considered above, there is another, more radical reason to question the idea that frugal simplicity is always preferable to lavish spending and luxurious indulgence. In some circumstances extravagance may be obligatory.

As was noted earlier, lavish displays of all kinds have long been enjoyed, from victory parades and seasonal festivals in ancient times to the opening ceremonies of the modern Olympic Games. But the justification for the expenditures involved does not simply lie in the pleasure provided: quite often the display has great symbolic importance. On December 31, 1999, countries around the world put on spectacular celebrations to mark the turn of the millennium. Imagine a sizable country deciding to go dirt cheap on its celebrations—say, just having the head of state let off a small box of discounted fireworks. The country would be an object of ridicule from abroad, and its own citizens would likely feel not just disappointment but some degree of shame. A head of state visiting a foreign capital does not expect to be taken out for dinner at a local greasy spoon, and the citizens of the receiving country expect their government to put on a decent reception for their visitors. Failure to do so is thought to reflect badly on the country as a whole. Something similar but on a smaller scale informs the treatment of visitors to various institutions and organizations. Going too cheap would be felt as a lack of respect; putting on a show is understood to indicate respect and friendship. People take pride in the collectives they belong to, from their family and hometown to their college, their workplace, and their country. They typically feel that they are in some sense represented by the collective and naturally wish to appear in a good light, generous rather than parsimonious, grand rather than grubby.

There are other situations, too, where extravagance can be viewed as fulfilling a duty. The aristocrat of old (think *Downton Abbey*) who oversaw a large estate including a huge house, a large household, agricultural lands, extensive stables, and a pack of hounds may well have felt an obligation to provide employment to house servants, laborers, grooms, and gamekeepers. No one really needs a valet, any more than one needs a pack of hounds. But if a whole local economy depends on a few members of the upper class living in the style to which they have become accustomed, one can easily imagine those few feeling duty bound to keep playing their roles. And others may be disappointed or even critical if they do anything less, just as celebrities from the slums who have made it big might disappoint their old comrades if they failed to make a display of bling. We like to see these people fulfilling their designated social roles, and society imposes a subtle pressure on them to behave accordingly: princesses are supposed to wear diamonds; pop stars are supposed to drive Porsches.

We might note here that Aristotle, who as we observed earlier is less inclined to praise poverty, and is less suspicious of wealth than most of the philosophers cited in previous chapters, allows a place in his ethics for these kinds of extravagance—the kind that involve practicing the virtue of magnificence.[19] Magnificence, in this sense, involves lavish spending either on public goods, such as a temple, or on private matters, such as one's house or a wedding. Like any other virtue, it has to be accompanied by wisdom. Individuals who spend excessively purely to show off their wealth are guilty of vulgarity. Those who through unnecessary penny-pinching fall short of producing something fine that is within their reach display niggardliness. People who attempt a display of magnificence that they can't really afford are foolish. But for those few who have the means, lavish spending done with taste and a sense of responsibility on worthwhile projects can legitimately be considered virtuous. It is important to recognize, though, that Aristotle does not *advocate* magnificence as a necessary component of the good life. After all, most people are not in a position to exercise it. In this respect it is unlike temperance, or generosity, or most other virtues. He includes it in his catalog of the virtues not because he thinks it is something we should all aspire to, but because he wishes to acknowledge and explicate the common sentiment on this matter. Those who are fortunate enough to be capable of magnificence should behave accordingly if they are to live as well as they might. But to be incapable of magnificence is not a misfortune, like sickness or friendlessness, for happiness does not require it.

Obligatory extravagance is also characteristic of gift-giving ceremonies such as the potlatches practiced by some Native American tribes of the Pacific Northwest. A potlatch could be part of an economic system within which those who have accumulated property redistribute it to those in need. But it could also be a competitive event where individuals, families, and tribes seek to raise their status by giving away more than their rivals do. In some cases, property would even be destroyed as a way of demonstrating superiority. Here, too, going against the values of the system by embracing an ethic of frugality would be seen as a dereliction of duty.

The fact that there are deep-rooted social conventions and expectations that cause people to feel under an obligation to be extravagant does not, however, prove that the extravagance in question is justified. As we noted earlier when discussing the utilitarian critique of extravagance, even deep-rooted traditions and conventions can be criticized, the most obvious grounds for doing so being that they are contrary to the common good. When heads of state or top officials of government or publicly funded agencies gather together, why should taxpayers foot the bill for elaborate displays, luxurious accommodations, first-class travel, expensive banquets, and so on? Plato's *Republic* offers a very different model, according to which public officials are required to live simply—a condition imposed on them both to discourage the wrong sort of people from going into politics for the wrong reasons, and to ensure that those in power can focus on what matters, free from distractions and corrupting influences.[20] Nothing in the last two thousand years of political history has proved Plato's anxieties to be misplaced. The symbolic significance of state events and all the trappings of power should perhaps be harnessed to express different values, including sympathy for and a commitment to help the less fortunate. The aristocratic estate could still provide employment for many if it were converted to a worker's cooperative. Displays of bling could be routinely scorned as symptomatic of shallow personalities. The philosophy of frugality encourages us to entertain these critical perspectives.

Nevertheless, most of us, at one time or another, will feel some sort of moral pressure to eschew frugality. One obvious instance of this concerns gift giving. Giving gifts can be a complex social interaction, and we may feel obliged to be extravagant relative to our own beliefs or preferred practices for various reasons: perhaps because we are expected to give something equal in value to what we have ourselves received, or expect to receive, or have previously given to someone else; perhaps because the occasion for giving is governed by conventions that dictate the sort of gift that is appropriate; perhaps because we feel we ought to conform to what we know other gift-givers will be doing; or perhaps just because we are anxious not to disappoint the recipient.

An interesting phenomenon related to this point is the aversion some people have to giving (or receiving) secondhand gifts. Obviously, for your typical tightwad, giving used items is not a problem. In fact it is perfectly rational: you save money and maybe give a better present than you could otherwise afford. So why would anyone have any objection to doing this? There may be a hint here of a preference for the pure, the unsullied—dare one say it, for the virginal. Some people may also feel that a whiff of shame attaches to used gifts, since secondhand items might be viewed as indicating an inability to buy new. But today the more common anxiety that steers people away from secondhand gifts probably concerns what the gift is supposed to symbolize. Gifts are intended to express affection; that is their widely accepted official meaning. And although it is crass to simply equate the monetary value of a present with the depth of feeling it conveys, we still do connect its symbolic value to the sort of sacrifice it represents. All things being equal, a costlier gift involves a greater sacrifice, and this is recognized by the recipient. Buying used, on the other hand, makes it look as if you are trying to cut costs while expressing affection, and that strikes some as tacky.

Another situation in which many people feel obliged to be extravagant is when they are called on to celebrate a special occasion such as a wedding, a bar mitzvah, or a birthday. Weddings, especially, seem to prompt a "no expense spared" attitude. Ordinary folk obviously do not indulge in the sort of multimillion-dollar extravagance that accompanied the nuptials of the daughter of steel magnate Lakshmi Mittal at a cost of $78 million (he booked the Palace of Versailles for the reception). But given that the average cost of weddings in the United States in 2012 was over $28,000 (in Manhattan it was over $76,000) and the average annual household income that year was around $45,000, it is clear that many people do dig deep for elaborate weddings;[21] and those who do are in a sense more extravagant than the celebrities, since they have a harder time covering the costs. They may be less extravagant in the sense of lavish indulgence, but they are more extravagant in the sense of being imprudent. There is no way that Ben Franklin would approve of spending thousands on some overpriced clothes, a little jewelry, and an all-night party, when the money could be used to pay off credit card debt or make a down payment on a house.

Why do people do this? In part, perhaps, because there is a bravado tradition of reckless folly where romance is concerned. The financial sacrifice may be foolish, but folly signifies passion, certainty, and commitment. This is an idea imbibed through countless romances in books, in the movies, and on TV. Love is a blind raging passion that cares not a hang for the future, that counts not the cost and will always find a way. Wisdom in the form of a prudent frugality, by contrast, could be interpreted as a sign of caution, doubt, and a low-burning flame. There is no reason to suppose there is any truth in this. (Nor, for that matter, is there any solid evidence for the idea often advanced by critics of extravagance that the cost of a marriage is inversely proportional to its duration.) But the bravado tradition combined with other cultural conventions and expectations is undoubtedly capable of creating a sense of obligation. According to Rebecca Mead, author of *One Perfect Day: The Selling of the American Wedding*, "you're made to feel guilty if you try to cut corners, as if to do so is to cheapen your love."[22] To go cheap on a wedding and eschew all the expensive trimmings could easily disappoint and even offend many people. This is especially the case in cultures where a person's identity, status, and honor are closely tied to those of his or her family. And in many societies the obligation to unfetter one's wallet often extends beyond the ceremony itself to such matters as dowries. In China, for instance, large dowries are often expected by and from both sets of parents; and to not offer an adequate dowry would involve a serious loss of face.[23]

To understand, however, is not necessarily to accept or endorse. As with extravagance on the part of public officials, so with private extravagance over gifts, weddings, and the like, there are reasonable grounds for being critical. People who go into serious long-term debt for the sake of a lavish wedding celebration would probably be better off bucking the convention that leads them down this road. Those who do have the means to be extravagant in the gifts they give their children should probably think harder about the likely subtle effects of their actions on the character of the recipients and the quality of their relationship with them. They might also consider how what they do affects others through peer pressure, raising materialistic expectations or aspirations in some, creating dissatisfaction in others. Here, too, the outlook promoted by the champions of frugal simplicity can provide a critical lens through which to view both people's behavior (including our own) and the conventions that influence it.

CHAPTER 6

The Philosophy of Frugality in a Modern Economy

We have seen that in a rich tradition of philosophical reflection on the nature of the good life, the consensus of the sages, from Socrates to Thoreau, is that a life of frugal simplicity is preferable to one of luxury and extravagance. Within that tradition, luxury and extravagance have few champions. Frugality and simple living are held to promote virtue and secure happiness. Wealth, acquisitiveness, and indulgence are distrusted both for their deleterious effects on a person's character and because they typically fail to deliver the happiness they promise. Philosophers have tended to ignore many of the arguments on the other side of the ledger, yet some of these are fairly obvious and have evidently been found persuasive by millions of people. Frugality risks breeding parsimoniousness; it restricts the pursuit of excitement, adventure, and varied or interesting experiences, while simple living can easily induce stagnation. Wealth provides security and leisure; it also expands one's freedom and range of available pleasures. Novelty and luxury are enjoyable in themselves and enable one to cultivate a refined sensibility. Ambition underlies individual achievement, greed fuels economic growth, and extravagance not only drives much economic activity but is also responsible for many of the most impressive cultural productions and achievements of civilization. In some circumstances, extravagance can even be considered a moral obligation.

From all of this emerges a suspicion that the wisdom of the frugal sages, or at least a good part of it, may be seriously outdated. It is pleasant to read and easy to cite approvingly the wise sayings of the Buddha, Jesus, Epicurus, Epictetus, Seneca, Boethius, and the rest. But perhaps much of their advice made more sense in premodern times when most people's circumstances were very different from what they are now.

One obvious difference is that in modernized societies at peace, life is far more secure for everyone than it ever used to be. From prehistorical times to at least the nineteenth century, life expectancy was much lower. The death of infants and children was commonplace, as was the death of women in childbirth; without antibiotics, minor infections and injuries at any age could easily become fatal; science, technology, and government programs offered less protection against natural disasters, accidents, sickness, and other misfortunes; hunger was a common experience; political power was exercised more oppressively; violent crime was more prevalent; and for most people judicial protection was limited and unreliable. In these circumstances, when most people feel themselves to be highly vulnerable to what Hamlet memorably lamented as "the heartache, and the thousand natural shocks that flesh is heir to," the goals and values posited by the champions of frugal simplicity make a lot of sense. A typical peasant in medieval Europe, or an antebellum North American homesteader, or people anywhere trying to subsist in challenging conditions would probably settle quite readily for a longish life in which their basic needs were met and they managed to avoid calamities brought on by nature, sickness, poverty, injustice, or war. Their chief hope, for which they prayed every day, was to be delivered from evil and given their daily bread. But the much greater material security that most people in affluent societies now enjoy makes such an outlook seem almost culpably unambitious. Personal tragedy can still strike, of course, but it does so much less often than in times past, thanks primarily to massive advances in medical science. We no longer have to worry that every small injury might lead to a mortal infection, or that every fever might prove fatal. In these circumstances, it is not surprising that when I ask my students if they could be content with the Epicurean ideal of frugal simplicity and peace of mind, most consider it insufficient. It seems unexciting, even uninteresting. They expect and desire more from life than a cup of wine, some bread and cheese, and a few friends to share them with.

A second major difference between today and times past that prompts these much higher hopes and aspirations is that the vocational opportunities open to most people are considerably greater today than in any previous century. "What do you want to be when you grow up?" would have been a pointless question so far as the majority of people were concerned through most of the preceding centuries. Most careers were off-limits to women. Illiterate farmhands could have little real expectation of embarking on some other profession. Today the situation is quite different. This is not to deny that in the United States today there is a pervasive mythology that exaggerates the degree of social mobility. But myths can influence a person's attitudes as surely as any other kind of belief. If I believe I can go from log cabin to president, I'm less likely to be content with a log cabin. Nor is it to deny that in recent decades, and especially since the recession of 2008, many people have experienced diminished employment prospects, even in relatively wealthy countries. But if we view things over a longer time span, we have to recognize the radical difference between today and the way things were at any time prior to the Second World War, when far fewer working-class people could consider going to college or pursuing professional careers.

The shift toward a more egalitarian society, the closing of the social distance between classes, and the partial erosion of entrenched castes (again, the time span to consider here covers many centuries, not just the past few decades) all encourage individual ambition, and this ambition is continually spurred by parents, teachers, graduation speakers, employers, and commercial interests of every kind. We are taught from our earliest years to aim high, pursue our dreams, be all we can be, shoot for the moon, reach for the stars, and all the rest of it. The cultural icons we are encouraged to admire, in sport, politics, business, entertainment, and science, are the individuals who strive and succeed, not those who content themselves with a static, humble existence. Knowing one's place is no longer taught and admired the way it once was.

Another huge and relevant difference between the world today and the world of just a century ago, let alone the world of Epicurus, is the vastly greater range of recreational opportunities that we now enjoy. These have been transformed and multiplied beyond anyone's expectations over the past century or so, even for people with relatively few resources. This is surely one of the most important cultural revolutions that has taken place in modern times. Epicurus may have been content with a jug of wine, a bowl of cheese, and a friend to converse with, but he lived before television, movies, mystery novels, classical orchestras, jazz, rock concerts, the World Cup, the Super Bowl, Disneyland, video games, package tours, downhill skiing, bowling alleys, white-water tubing, art galleries, science museums, and French restaurants. Some of these, like foreign travel or attending major sporting events, may be beyond our means. But many cost little or nothing and are available at all times to almost everyone. If pleasure is good, as Epicurus teaches, why wouldn't someone want to sample the many and diverse pleasures that the world now offers?

All these developments, particularly the increased security, the growth in opportunities, and the expansion of recreational options, are generally hailed as a good thing, and rightly so. Yet they also open up new avenues for dissatisfaction, the sort of problems that Stoic philosophers warn us about. As the likelihood of tragic loss or utter destitution diminishes, so does our tolerance for painful reversals of fortune. As the possibilities for bettering ourselves educationally, professionally, socially, and financially expand, we are more likely to become dissatisfied with modest circumstances. And as the smorgasbord of available amusement and entertainment grows, it is easy to become jaded, to take too much for granted, to find simple pleasures less appealing, and to experience even uncommon pleasures less intensely. Children who grow up accustomed to Hollywood movies, television dramas, video games, and the Internet are unlikely to feel the same kind of excitement when the circus comes to town as did their nineteenth-century forebears for whom this would be the outstanding event of the year.

On top of all this, there is the obvious fact that while many of our new forms of recreation are readily available to all, many are forms of consumption that require money. Indeed, the very activity of consuming is now itself a major recreation. Consequently, the lure of all these purchasable pleasures is now a powerful force pulling us toward busier lives centered on earning and spending. As Joanne Ciulla notes in *The Working Life*, "consumption creates a *need* to work even when the desire to work is weak. . . . The market tempts people with more leisure options than they can afford or have time to enjoy."[1] As a result, people can easily find themselves alternating between various treadmills: the hedonic treadmill of pursuing happiness, the status treadmill requiring conspicuous consumption, and the treadmill of work undertaken to finance one's activity on the other two treadmills.

Paradoxically, then, some of the same factors that have diminished the appeal of frugality and simplicity are also responsible for regenerating interest in the ideals of simple living. While many find the dynamism of modern times exciting, many others find it threatening, confusing, or exhausting. And the majority probably have both reactions! Modernity is characterized by constant change, which brings with it instability, unpredictability, complexity, and confusion. Rapid transformation of technology is the most obvious sphere where this is happening, but constant change also affects social relations between employers and employees, parents and children, teachers and students, as well as the way we interact with service providers, neighbors, friends, and strangers. It relates to the way we shop, study, communicate, and travel, to the way children play, and to the way old people approach the end of life. It is hardly surprising, therefore, that one often runs into nostalgia for a time when life was simpler. But nostalgia for simplicity is nothing new; in fact, it seems to be almost the default attitude among champions of simplicity. This connection is worth considering more closely.

THE NOSTALGIC APPEAL OF SIMPLICITY

Nostalgia is a fascinating phenomenon in its own right, and it seems to be extraordinarily common both as an individual experience and across cultures as a persistent motif in both oral and written literary traditions. We have all heard older people comparing the present unfavorably with the past in spite of—or even because of—the obvious material improvements in the standard of living. Most of us over the age of twenty-five have probably done this ourselves, and very often the fond remembrance involves describing how life was simpler in some of the senses identified in chapter 1. People recollect, for instance, how they lived cheaply, were closer to nature, were more self-sufficient, enjoyed uncomplicated daily routines, and contented themselves with humble pleasures. The underlying idea is that things were better because they were simpler.

But nostalgia for simplicity is not confined to individuals reminiscing. Across cultures it is also a persistent motif in oral and literary traditions. In religion, philosophy, and literature, nostalgia for simplicity has often taken the form of harking back to an unsullied past or a golden age of happiness and virtue. The biblical account of Adam and Eve in paradise is paradigmatic, but there are many others. The Greek poet Hesiod, writing over two and a half thousand years ago, laments the sorry condition of the world he lives in compared to that inhabited by the first humans, a "golden race of men," who lived "free from toil and grief . . . for the fruitful earth unforced bare them fruit abundantly."[2] The Roman poet Ovid (43 BCE–17 CE) similarly describes a golden age when

> of her own accord the earth produced
> A store of every fruit. The harrow touched her not,
> nor did the ploughshare wound her fields.
> And man content with given food,

And none compelling, gathered arbute fruits
And wild strawberries on the mountain sides.[3]

The lines underscore not just the absence of toil or tools, but also the idea of not wanting more than what suffices, and the notion of living harmoniously with nature. In these idyllic circumstances there was no need for laws, since "rectitude spontaneous in the heart prevailed."

Several of the frugal sages we have cited have made their own contributions to this genre. Seneca, for instance, looks back to a happier era and diagnoses the reason it passed away:

> the age before architects and builders was the happy one. It was burgeoning luxury that gave birth to the practice of hewing timbers square [and various other needless excesses]. Thatch protected free men; under marble and gold dwells slavery.[4]

Boethius offers a quintessential example of nostalgia that reaches back far beyond anyone's actual experience:

> O happy was that long lost age
> Content with nature's faithful fruits
> Which knew not slothful luxury.
> They would not eat before due time
> Their meal of acorns quickly found,
> And did not know the subtlety
> Of making honey sweeten wine,
> Or how the power of Tyrian dyes
> Could colour shining flocks of silk.

A grassy couch gave healthy sleep,
A gliding river healthy drink;
Men did not plunder all the world
And cut a path across the seas
With merchandise for foreign shores.
War horns were silent in those days . . .
Would that our age could now return
To those pure ways of leading life.
But now the passion to possess
Burns fiercer than Mount Etna's fire.[5]

Here, too, we encounter familiar themes: closeness to nature, contentment in simple pleasures, absence of luxury, lack of acquisitiveness, and moral purity. The desire to possess more than is necessary shifts people away from a life in harmony with nature to one where they seek to "plunder all the world." In *Utopia*, Thomas More describes a society that in many ways is like that recalled by Seneca and Boethius, one without property, luxury, and their attendant evils. But perhaps the most eloquent representative of this sort of nostalgia for a lost world of idyllic simplicity is Rousseau. In his *Discourse on the Origins of Inequality* he imagines man in the state of nature:

> I see him satisfying his hunger under an oak, quenching his thirst at the first stream, finding his bed at the foot of the same tree that furnished his meal; and therewith his needs are satisfied.[6]

This is the fancy that underpins Rousseau's moral and political philosophy. He places great store on the harmony with nature enjoyed by "savage man." What we think of as civilized humanity exists in a fallen state, for which humanity itself is to blame:

> most of our ills are our own work, and . . . we would have avoided almost all of them by preserving the simple, uniform, and solitary way of life prescribed to us by nature.[7]

Rousseau's fanciful vision is rather peculiar in imagining human beings to be happy with a "solitary way of life," but like many others he takes the key to this happiness to be the limited character and scope of the individual's wants: "His desires do not exceed his physical needs, the only goods he knows in the universe are nourishment, a female, and repose"[8] (in other words, dinner, a hump in the sack, and next day a late breakfast). Whereas Seneca and Boethius see the seeds of dissatisfaction being sown when people start desiring luxuries, Rousseau blames the introduction of private property. This led to the division of labor, which reduced self-sufficiency, and increased specialization led to greater reliance on laborsaving devices. Rousseau describes these as "a source of evil" for future generations since they led to the production of yet more commodities that people sought to acquire, grew accustomed to possessing, and hated to be without. It is probably safe to say that he would not have approved of the smartphone.

Interestingly, nostalgia for simplicity is not confined to oldsters; it can kick in surprisingly early in life. One of Bob Dylan's earliest songs, "Bob Dylan's Dream," written when he was twenty-two, is a classic expression of the sentiment. The singer tells how he dreamed of a happy time in the past when he and his friends hung out together around an old woodstove, chatting, laughing, telling stories, and singing songs, desiring nothing beyond present pleasures and company. The key to this happiness is the lack of complexity in their lives, moral, material, and aspirational, which makes possible a cherished social unity. Like the feeling of nostalgia itself, the song is ambivalent: it both celebrates and laments what has been lost. But the dominant mood, which comes through especially at the end, is sadness and regret. The singer would gladly give up any amount of material wealth to recover the simple life that was, but the expression of this wish is bound up with his recognition that his wishing is in vain. We should not forget, though, that what has been described is a dream, a framing that leaves open the possibility that the memory is an illusion.

Bucolic scenes have long been a favorite subject for visual artists also, presumably for the same reasons that they appealed to poets. Nor is this sort of nostalgia unique to Western art. It is noticeable that today in China for instance, amid urbanization and industrialization on an unprecedented scale, the most widely reproduced sort of art, hung on restaurant walls and sold to tourists, depicts unsullied natural landscapes in which if there is any human presence, it is likely to be an old man in peasant garb sitting tranquilly with a fishing pole by a river.

Nostalgia for a simpler and more stable existence is certainly not confined to philosophy and the arts; it is a pervasive phenomenon that manifests itself in many and varied ways: politicians harking back to a time before the country went to the dogs; teachers remembering how students used to be more diligent and respectful; parents recalling how as children they played all summer long outside rather than hunched over electronic devices. Yet like Bob Dylan's dream, such recollections are likely to be rose-tinted, so a dose of skepticism is usually in order. Corruption and incivility are hardly new in politics. If children were more respectful and obedient, it was perhaps because their elders punished transgressions so brutally; and one reason they played outside so much was because small houses inhabited by large families were overcrowded. It may be true that when an old Ford broke down, you could fix it on the spot with a nylon stocking and a ballpoint pen, whereas today's cars are more like computers on wheels that require high-tech servicing; but then today's cars are far less likely to break down in the first place.

People readily trace dissatisfaction with their own lives or with the world to ways in which they have moved away from simplicity—in their routines, relationships, circumstances, and lifestyle. The sense of loss that accompanies this dissatisfaction is presumably likely to be more common, and more pronounced, when the complicating changes are radical and come quickly. Since, as Marx pointed out, constant change is a defining feature of modernity, we can expect it to trigger a longing for simpler times, and we see this longing expressed not only in a large body of literature but also in the deliberate lifestyle choices that some people make: downsizing, downshifting, going back to the land, growing one's own food, choosing greater self-sufficiency over consumerism, and seeking to preserve or revive traditional crafts like basket weaving and quilt making. A similar motive has given rise to the Slow Movement, a general term for the various ways in which people seek to combat the frenetic pace of modern life. Examples of this trend, described in detail by Carl Honoré in *In Praise of Slowness*, include Slow Food, Slow Cities, Slow Sex (all originating in Italy), the Sloth Club (Japan), the Society for the Deceleration of Time (Austria), and the Long Now Foundation.[9]

The nostalgic component that generally seems to be present in any "back to basics" movement invites the criticism that the philosophical outlook associated with it (a) rests on a rose-tinted view of the past, and (b) is unsuited to the modern world. This distrust of the nostalgic sensibility is understandable. While it is undoubtedly true that modern lifestyles produce various forms of alienation— for instance, from nature, work, tradition, and community—another kind of alienation is to be estranged from one's own time and the culture one lives in. We recognize this readily in some spheres. To be an engaged scientist is to be *au fait* with the most recent theories, discoveries, and technologies. The most important artists and writers of today participate in some sort of dialogue with their contemporaries, and their work speaks to contemporary issues. Few people would think it particularly admirable for a person to read books while refusing to watch films, or to listen to classical music while remaining ignorant of more recently evolved musical genres. But analogous arguments can be made with respect to lifestyle. To live "off the grid," metaphorically speaking, may limit our understanding of and ability to participate in the world we happen to have been thrust into.

On the other hand, champions of simple living can respond to this criticism with the well-taken point that it is no bad thing to be alienated from the worst aspects of contemporary culture—materialism, consumerism, individualism, technology fetishism, shallow hedonism, or the cult of celebrities. The fact that the Internet this afternoon is humming with the latest gossip about Kim Kardashian's cosmetic surgery is and should be of supreme indifference to anyone who has a life worth living. The fact that millions eat junk food, watch junk TV, buy lots of unnecessary stuff, and waste inordinate amounts of time messing about with their smartphones to no great purpose is not a reason to do the same. From the perspective of the simplifiers, what they are embracing is not an outmoded philosophy sunk in nostalgia but a reorientation of values that, if adopted, will help people live happier and more meaningful lives.

There is also an important positive aspect to nostalgia for the way things used to be done that should not be overlooked. It sometimes arises from a desire that people feel to be connected to their forebears, to the daily activities and patterns of life practiced by previous generations. Establishing this connection is satisfying, perhaps especially when one is also passing along certain sorts of knowledge and experience to the next generation; it expresses a kind of respect, a kind of loyalty; it maintains the chain; and it places individuals within something greater than themselves, rather as saying prayers or participating in traditional rituals does. This is one reason why people will sing traditional songs and tell old folktales to their children, pass on the simple games they used to play when young, make their own maple syrup rather than buying it in the supermarket, or go to the same place each year for their vacation rather than somewhere more exotic.

As we have seen throughout the preceding chapters, the debate between advocates of frugal simplicity and Faustian seekers of adventure, pleasure, power, or profit is not new. The clash between Socrates and Callicles in Plato's *Gorgias*, written almost two and a half millennia ago, lays down some of the main arguments and points of disagreement. Subsequent discussions have built on these, and for the most part have focused on the question of what kind of lifestyle and mind-set is most likely to make a person happy, with some auxiliary discussion of moral virtue and the well-being of society. The philosophical fraternity have invariably sided with Socrates, holding that both individuals and societies are happier and more virtuous when they embrace frugal values. There are some arguments, however, that have figured hardly at all until quite recently; they simply didn't occur to many people prior to the advent of capitalism and industrialization. Two are especially important, although they pull in opposite directions: the argument that frugality, if practiced widely, would have dire economic consequences for society as a whole; and the argument that a widespread shift toward simpler living is urgently required in order to prevent further irreversible harm to earth's natural environment and to head off potentially catastrophic climate change. We will consider the first of these arguments here and the second in the next chapter.

ECONOMIC GROWTH AND WELL-BEING

The economic argument against frugality is fairly simple. Economic prosperity makes people happier. Prosperity is created by economic growth, which is fueled by people *not* being especially frugal. Thus the philosophy of frugal simplicity, if adopted by enough people, would be disastrous for the economy and result in many people being less happy.

In chapter 4 we noted the origins of this argument in the work of eighteenth-century thinkers like Bernard Mandeville and Adam Smith. The advent of capitalism precipitated a shift in values. What had traditionally been regarded as flaws in an individual's character—traits such as greed, avarice, acquisitiveness, extravagance, or a taste for luxury—came to be viewed more positively insofar as they promoted the public good by fueling economic activity from which everyone benefited. There had, of course, always been plenty of rampant hypocrisy on the part of those who preached a Christian ethic of self-denial while pursuing and relishing wealth and luxury. But it was with the emergence of dynamic market economies (growing rapidly on the basis of an increased population), global trade, modern banking, and industrialization that the tension between the professed moral values of Christianity and the economic needs of society became seriously stretched.

Today, the belief that economic growth is a good thing is a basic assumption shared by the great majority of economists, political theorists, and politicians. As economist Diane Coyle remarks, "virtually every society in the modern world has come to be focused on the achievement of economic growth."[10] This is what most people everywhere seem to want, and no mainstream politician, whether democratically elected or not, would dream of opposing this goal.

Since the end of the Second World War, the single most important statistic used for measuring economic growth has been a country's gross domestic product (GDP), which is the monetary value of all the finished goods and services produced within the country over a specified period of time. From its first introduction into economic discourse, many people, including many economists, have had misgivings about how this figure might be misleading or even misused. For one thing, it can give an inaccurate idea of what is actually going on, since a lot of economic activity isn't taken into account: for instance, unpaid work such as child rearing, undeclared work like babysitting, people doing things for themselves, from growing their own vegetables to building their own houses, bartering, black market transactions, and so on. The more of these sorts of unrecorded economic activities there are, the more likely it is that a country's GDP will be seriously underestimated. In recent times this problem of accurately measuring GDP has become still more difficult in economies where there has been a shift from manufacturing to service industries and information processing. How does one determine productivity and the monetary value of work in fields like teaching, nursing, journalism, data analysis, or social work?

The more fundamental objection to centering economic policy on GDP, however, is that this figure does not necessarily correlate with the well-being of either individuals or society as a whole. Many things that help raise a country's GDP—for instance, natural disasters that boost construction, diseases that require medical treatment, or high crime rates that fuel prison building and sell burglar alarms—are highly undesirable in themselves. Moreover, the increased wealth indicated by a higher GDP can be very unevenly distributed, in which case it may make little difference to most people's lives. For instance, between 1999 and 2013, per capita GDP in the United States rose by about 25 percent, yet during that same period the median household income declined by 8.7 percent.[11] And even where rising GDP does reflect a general increase in material prosperity, social scientists remain divided over the extent to which it brings about an increase in the general level of happiness.[12] Those who oppose using GDP to guide government policy have likened what they see as a misguided obsession with it, on the part of many economists and politicians, to a driver paying attention to only one gauge on a car's dashboard, the speedometer, while ignoring those that measure such important things as fuel level, engine temperature, or oil pressure.[13] Some even argue that the excessive focus on GDP has been a major obstacle to progress in many areas, including material prosperity.[14]

For these reasons numerous alternatives to GDP as measures of a society's well-being have been proposed. One that has attracted quite a lot of attention is the Gross National Happiness Index pioneered by the government of Bhutan. Others include the Human Development Index, which emphasizes life expectancy, education, and standard of living, and the Social Progress Index, which uses fifty-two indicators, including such things as health, safety, sustainability, and individual freedom. Yet in spite of all these criticisms, reservations, and alternative indexes, GDP remains important for economists and policy makers because it is a single number that, even if it oversimplifies matters, provides some sort of basic unit with which to make comparisons between countries and over time. And the assumption that there is *some* correlation between GDP and general well-being isn't fanciful; countries with the highest GDP per capita typically rank high on other positive indexes, while those with relatively low GDP per capita typically don't. This is Diane Coyle's view:

> Economic growth contributes to happiness, and GDP growth should remain a policy target. . . . There's no doubt that in a number of ways GDP is a flawed statistic as a measure of welfare. But any replacement would be flawed too, not to mention much harder for many countries to collect and measure; at least with the familiar GDP statistics we know what we're getting.[15]

The argument about the usefulness of GDP, or per capita GDP, as an indicator of individual or social well-being is really a technical debate within a larger philosophical discussion about values and goals. On one side are those who believe that economic growth should be a primary, overarching goal of social policy on the grounds that material prosperity is the key to happiness. On the other side are the many critics of this view who, as the earlier chapters made clear, belong to a venerable tradition. Some, like Amartya Sen and Joseph Stiglitz, stress the importance of other goods, such as justice, freedom, equality, autonomy, security, health, and education. Others, like Richard Easterlin and Gregg Easterbrook, question the assumed link between wealth and well-being. Easterlin's research identified what has become known as the "happiness-income paradox" (a.k.a. the "Easterlin paradox"). The paradox is that although within a given society at a given time the rich tend to be happier than the poor, this connection between income and happiness is not apparent when geographical or historical comparisons are made. People in wealthy countries (those with a relatively high per capita income) are not on the whole happier than people in less wealthy (but not impoverished) countries. And although per capita income in the United States rose steadily over three decades following World War II, individuals in the 1970s did not report being any happier than individuals in the 1940s.[16]

Naturally, these claims have been disputed. Diane Coyle, for instance, writes: "The new conventional wisdom about happiness and growth is mistaken. Growth *does* make us happier, easily seen perhaps as the mirror of the unhappiness caused by economic recession."[17] But Easterlin and others reject this argument. They agree that in the short term, economic upturns or downturns produce corresponding swings in the levels of reported happiness. But in the long term the paradox still holds, and data drawn from the last forty years continues to support the main idea. For instance, between 1990 and 2005, China, South Korea, and Chile all experienced high rates of economic growth and increases in per capita income but no increase in reported life satisfaction.[18]

A great deal of interesting research has been done by social scientists over the past few decades into the conditions and distribution of happiness. "Happiness economics" is now a field within economics; "positive psychology" is a flourishing movement within psychology. However, definitions, findings, interpretations, explanations, and conclusions are still somewhat unsettled and disputed. There is particular unease about the usual method of measuring how happy people are, which, in one way or another, basically consists in asking them how happy they feel. This approach is open to the objection that what people say about their subjective states may not be reliable or easily compared with what others say. Individuals may wish to project a happy state, or feel under an obligation to do so, or be deceiving themselves about their condition— as an old joke has it, many couples are unhappily married, but they just don't realize it. And there may be significant variation in the terms people use to describe how they feel; asked how they are doing, it's possible that one person's "Can't complain" reflects the same state of mind as another person's "Doing great!"

Nevertheless, certain conclusions seem now to be increasingly well-established and generally accepted. Daniel Kahneman and Angus Deaton, two of the leading researchers in the field, drew the following conclusions from data collected by Gallup surveys that involved over 450,000 US residents.[19] They found that the connection between income and subjective well-being is different depending on what sort of subjective state is being measured. A distinction can be drawn between "emotional well-being" and "life evaluation." Emotional well-being, or experienced happiness, refers to a person's day-to-day experiences of feelings such as joy, anger, boredom, pleasure, anxiety, or engagement. The people who count as happier on this scale are those who experience such feelings more frequently, more intensely, and for longer periods. Life evaluation, on the other hand, concerns what sort of answer people give to the question "How satisfied are you with your life as a whole these days?"

In line with many other studies, the Gallup data revealed that people's emotional well-being rises with household income, but only up to a certain point. Getting out of poverty, achieving a fairly secure level of material comfort, makes a big difference to the subjective quality of their everyday lives. But this positive effect of higher income tails off at around $75,000 per annum (in 2010 dollars); beyond that point, extra money does not seem to make much difference. This is not the case with respect to people's life evaluations, however. It is true that if one considers raw dollar increases in household income, the positive effect of such increases seems to dwindle as one gets richer. So an extra $10,000 per annum will not do much for the life satisfaction of someone already enjoying an annual income of $200,000, whereas it is likely to raise significantly the life satisfaction of someone making $50,000. But if, instead, one considers and compares percentage increases in income, then it seems that these raise the life satisfaction of everyone to a similar extent. So a 50 percent increase in income has roughly the same effect on the life evaluation of someone making $100,000 as on someone making $50,000.

There also seems to be fairly wide acceptance of the idea that people in most societies place great store on their relative social standing; so even if everyone is better off in objective or absolute terms, this won't necessarily lead them to feel more satisfied with their lives if their position in the social hierarchy has not changed.[20] When hardly anyone could afford a car, being without one would make few people unhappy. But once most of one's peer have cars, owning one is no big deal, and being unable to afford one becomes a source of dissatisfaction. Similarly, people will generally be happier living in a 1,500-square-foot house surrounded by houses of a similar size than in a 2,000-square-foot house surrounded by mansions. This concern with relative social standing can be seen in other primates, which suggests to some that it may be the result of evolutionary conditioning. And it offers a plausible partial explanation of the happiness-income paradox: increasing our income and being able to buy more stuff does not make us much happier if those around us are experiencing the same thing, since our relative social standing remains the same. Another explanation, endorsed by many of the sages discussed in earlier chapters, is that the things that matter most to us do not require significant wealth. So once we are freed from the stresses of poverty, our happiness is determined primarily by such things as the quality of our relationships and whether we are engaged in satisfying work. These explanations are not exclusive, of course.

There is thus on the one hand a fair amount of evidence of some correlation between material prosperity and happiness, but on the other hand several important qualifications to be taken into account regarding what kind of subjective well-being is in question, the diminishing marginal returns beyond a certain level of income, and the importance of relative rather than absolute social standing. One other problem worth noting is the fact that the correlations that have been observed may hold only for particular times and places. In societies that place a high value on wealth, it stands to reason that the wealthy are likely to feel pretty good about themselves. But we should be careful about forming generalizations or shaping policies on the basis of such correlations. In a society where blonde hair is considered especially beautiful, people with blonde hair will probably tend to be happier; but so what? The correlation may be real, but it does not reveal some deep truth connecting happiness with being blonde, nor does it provide a reason for the government to subsidize hair dye.

WHAT IF FRUGALITY WENT VIRAL?

With these observations regarding economic growth and happiness as background, let us return to this question: What if everyone embraced frugal simplicity? Imagine the various movements advocating simplification, slowness, downsizing, and downshifting really taking off, with people everywhere rushing to embrace the frugal lifestyle. The rich eschew extravagance; the well-off sell off their luxury items; used clothing and furniture stores are packed; everywhere people embrace self-sufficiency and stop paying others to mow their lawns, fix their toilets, paint their houses, or cook their meals. And all this happens right before Christmas!

The immediate consequences by any reckoning would be dire. Manufacturers of large- and small-ticket items, from cars to cookie trays, would soon be laying off workers, as would thousands of retailers, restaurants, boutiques, salons, and other providers of nonessential services. Whole spheres of the economy devoted to recreation and entertainment would virtually collapse as people cut back on expensive tickets for musical, theatrical, and sporting events. Colleges would see their enrollment plummet as young people decided to avoid taking out hefty student loans. It would probably be easier to say which businesses would survive than which would perish. Thrift stores, eBay, and Craigslist would presumably do well. Mechanics who mend and service stuff, thereby helping us to make do with what we have rather than buy replacements, might also thrive. But most businesses would struggle.

Even undertakers, usually immune from market fluctuations, would suffer since everyone would be opting for cardboard coffins rather than lined oak with brass handles.

The basic problem is that the sort of economy we have requires a fairly high level of continuous economic activity just to keep functioning. In particular, it requires lots of people to keep buying lots of stuff. As economist Paul Krugman tirelessly reminds *New York Times* readers, this is the key to understanding the recession that began in 2008:

> It's always important to remember that what ails the U.S. economy right now isn't lack of productive capacity, but lack of demand. The housing bust, the overhang of household debt and ill-timed cuts in public spending have created a situation in which nobody wants to spend; and because your spending is my income and my spending is your income, this leads to a depressed economy over all.[21]

If getting and spending were to fall below a certain level, the economy would stall, like a plane that allowed its speed to drop below a critical point. Were this to happen, millions would be thrown out of work, with disastrous consequences. Those without capital would sink into poverty. Those already hard up might benefit somewhat from falling prices, but they would have even fewer opportunities to get out of poverty. Government revenues from taxes would fall, while expenditures to help the needy would go up, eroding the government's ability to finance or subsidize important public goods such as education or environmental protection. And it is not just everyone's material well-being that is at stake. Involuntary unemployment often leads to depression. According to a 2013 Gallup Poll, 12.4 percent of Americans who were unemployed reported having been treated for depression, which is more than twice the rate for people who have full-time jobs. Among the long-term unemployed—those who had been out of work for more than twenty-seven weeks—the depression rate was 18 percent.[22] A further, less obvious consequence of a failing economy, which makes the road to recovery that much harder to find, is that it leads people to be less adventurous, since in hard times they are less willing to risk losing what they have; prosperity, opportunity, and confidence, by contrast, tend to encourage innovation.[23]

Enough said. A modern capitalist economy is certainly a clunky machine, subject to periodic booms and busts, wreaking havoc on communities centered on industries that have died or moved elsewhere, forcing millions to work harder than they wish to, denying millions the opportunity for adequately paid work, and condemning tens of millions to life below the poverty line. Nevertheless, life as we know it, and as many more or less like it, would grind to a halt if enough people embraced the frugal ideal. The buoyancy of a modern economy depends heavily on people's willingness to spend more than they need to on essentials, and to spend plenty more on inessentials. This is not simply because there needs to be in general a sufficiently high level of getting and spending. Innovation, too, requires at least some people to have an antifrugal mind-set. Often, the first versions of a new technology that enter the market are expensive and not always very efficient. The vanguard customers who bought the first laptops or digital cameras paid far more for quite a bit less than those who shrewdly waited for the price to come down, for the imperfections to be ironed out, and for the benefits of standardization and compatibility that eventually arrived once enough people embraced the new technology. The frugal approach is here parasitic on the activity of spendthrifts. Yet without the spendthrifts, the innovative technology, from which we all benefit and which eventually drives a significant amount of economic activity, might never be considered commercially viable.

Of course, the likelihood of frugal zealotry going viral overnight is remote. The majority of people enjoy consuming. One can imagine such an event occurring in response to a collapsing economy, but a radical overnight change of mind-set is unlikely to be the cause of that collapse. A slightly more plausible scenario, however, is one in which frugal or anticonsumerist values gradually gain ground, perhaps owing to mounting concerns about the environment, or perhaps just because people become surfeited with consuming. Possibly we will start to look back on the past half century or so as a slightly embarrassing, though understandable, temporary phase when people in wealthy societies reacted to the novelty of having a level of purchasing power unprecedented in human history by buying loads of stuff just because they could, rather as people who have been underfed for years might gorge on a feast spread before them beyond the point where eating is either healthy or pleasurable. If frugality were slowly to become fashionable, the economy would not go over a cliff, but it could well slide slowly into a depression that would continue so long as demand remained low. That possibility will be enough for some to conclude that the champions of frugal simplicity are hopelessly naive, and that their ideals are not viable.

WHY INCREASED FRUGALITY NEED NOT HAVE DIRE CONSEQUENCES

These arguments were hardly considered by the frugal sages discussed in earlier chapters. Their economies, and their economic theories, were so much simpler than ours. Socrates may describe his Republic as "luxurious" and "fevered" compared to his first ideal, the bucolic community decried by Glaucon as a "city of pigs," but it is nevertheless utterly simple compared to the sort of society most people live in today. That does not mean, though, that the critique of frugality just presented is decisive. The basic idea—that our current economic system is fueled by consumer demand and that a severe reduction in this demand would have huge repercussions—is clearly correct. But it does not follow that the philosophy of frugal simplicity is hopelessly outmoded or misguided. A number of responses to this charge are available.

First, while it is important to recognize that there are real costs to a society embracing frugal values and becoming less consumerist, there are also some clear benefits. This is obvious with respect to certain kinds of spending. Take smoking, for example. If people stopped smoking cigarettes (a no-brainer for anyone with frugal tendencies), cigarette manufacturers would go out of business, thousands of jobs would be lost, cigarette retailers would see their profits shrink, and tax revenues from cigarette sales would dry up. But these costs would all be worth paying since millions of people would be in better health and therefore, one assumes, happier. This in itself would be reason enough to cheer, but the knock-on benefits to society at large would also be considerable: fewer people suffering from lung cancer, cardiovascular diseases, emphysema, diabetes, and numerous other illnesses would free up medical resources to service other needs; health-care costs (including insurance premiums) would be reduced for everyone, particularly the government; and fewer workdays would be lost owing to smoking-related causes. (A 2013 study by Gallup estimated that smoking cost the US economy around \$278 billion per year.)[24] A similar point could be made for sugary drinks and snack foods heavy in sugar, fat, and salt, few of which would appear on the frugal zealot's shopping list, and which many public health experts believe are partly responsible for the obesity epidemic that has appeared in many countries over the past few decades. Hundreds of thousands of people earn their living by making, marketing, or selling these products. But given that obesity is now one of the leading health problems globally, being strongly linked to heart disease and diabetes, it would obviously be a good thing overall if the market for sodas and junk food shrank dramatically. It would be even better if this trend went hand in hand with an increased interest in people growing their own food, since this would bring improved mental and physical health for many people through increased consumption of healthy fruits and vegetables, a more active lifestyle, more time spent outside, and closer contact with nature.

This is hardly a complete response, of course. Most things we buy are not especially harmful to us, nor do they carry such obvious social costs as cigarettes do. But the general point being made is certainly worth keeping in mind: even though our economy may require a fairly high level of demand to keep running, not all demand is to be encouraged or cheered. Some kinds of consumption carry decidedly negative consequences for both individuals and society as a whole. But a more radical and comprehensive response is needed if the advocates of frugal simplicity are to meet the objection that their philosophy is misguided given modern economic conditions.

Such a response is available and it is cogent. The argument that our economic well-being depends on our maintaining or even increasing current levels of production and consumption suffers from a failure of imagination. It imagines changing one term—demand—while holding everything else constant. Our economy and society are assumed to be set up pretty much as they are today, but with people spending much less, doing more things for themselves, and generally seeking fulfillment in the ways that ancient philosophers and contemporary psychologists recommend. If that happened, it is quite likely that the consequences for many people would be dismal, since a significant reduction in demand for goods and services would lead to high levels of unemployment. And that is the crux of the problem: *people losing their jobs* and consequently sinking into poverty with all that that entails—anxiety, depression, poorer health, increasing government deficits, and so on.

It is important to keep this in mind. The problem is not that there wouldn't be enough food produced for people to eat well. It is estimated that 30 to 50 percent of all food produced in the world—between 1.2 and 2 billion metric tons—is currently wasted owing to inefficient methods of harvesting, storing, and transporting it, along with wastage at the point of sale or consumption.[25] Approximately 40 percent of the food in the United States is not eaten, and most of this wastage occurs at the point of retail or in the household. For various reasons, particularly the relatively low cost of food as a proportion of household income, American households now throw out roughly a quarter of all the food they buy, about ten times the amount discarded by consumers in Southeast Asia.[26]

Nor is the problem that there wouldn't be enough adequate housing. Homelessness is, of course, a current problem. Even before the 2008 recession the National Law Center on Homelessness and Poverty estimated that in a given year between 2.3 and 3.5 million people experienced homelessness in the United States.[27] But against that we should also set the figure of 18.5 million—the number of vacant homes in the United States according to a report by Amnesty International.[28] We might also throw in the fact that the average house size in the United States in 2013 was just under 2,600 square feet compared to 1,660 square feet in 1973.[29] So while some people may lack adequate housing, this isn't because there is a real shortage of accommodation, or of materials, or of skilled labor; it is because we allow market forces to determine housing outcomes, including what houses cost to buy or rent, and how the available housing is distributed—a system that results in some people living in broken-down trailers or even sleeping in doorways while nearby mansions sit unoccupied.

Similar points could be made with respect to other basic necessities. In general, technologically advanced and prosperous societies like the United States possess easily enough wealth, resources, and talent for every member of the society to live comfortably. The problem is not a shortage of stuff to go around. The problem that a fall in consumer demand would create has to do entirely with how things are organized, specifically, with the economic arrangements we currently have regarding working hours, conditions, compensation, benefits, and so on.

There are two fairly obvious ways to try to forestall the problem of widespread unemployment following a drop in consumer demand: find alternative worthwhile employment for those who have been laid off, and promote a general reduction in the number of hours people work.

Easier said than done, of course. And to be sure, these proposals will strike many readers, especially in the United States, as hopelessly utopian. The notion that unemployed workers should be "found" new jobs or provided with the retraining they need to reenter the workforce raises obvious questions: Who is supposed to find or create these jobs? And who is supposed to pay for the retraining? The idea of shorter hours and longer holidays no doubt appeals to most people; but how is it possible to ensure that employers go along with this, especially if they are convinced that doing so is against their interests?

We should distinguish, though, between different kinds of utopianism. The questions just posed do have answers: the government could help create jobs, fund retraining, and promote a reduction in working hours. Such suggestions may reasonably be called utopian insofar as they are unlikely to be implemented by the people who currently hold political power in countries like the United States— the politicians, and the rich business leaders who exert tremendous influence over the politicians, lobbying them around the clock, bankrolling electoral campaigns, offering lucrative sinecures, and threatening to withdraw support if their interests are not promoted. Most of these people—for the sake of brevity we might call them "the ruling class"—are committed, from either conviction or self-interest, or both, to the capitalist system in something like its present form. There is, of course, a spectrum of opinion within this group, from libertarians like Grover Norquist, founder and president of Americans for Tax Reform—who famously said he would like to shrink the government "down to the size where we can drown it in the bathtub"—to mainstream liberals who believe an important function of government is to ameliorate capitalism's more unpleasant side effects. But in the current political climate in the United States and most other large, advanced capitalist countries, few of those roaming the corridors of power seem willing to advocate the level of government intervention in the economy that would be required to create an environment in which living simply but not in poverty is a viable option for all. An ideological commitment to the "wisdom" of market forces over government intervention is deeply entrenched; the perceived self-interest of the better-off, who do not see themselves as beneficiaries of such intervention, is very strong.

But it is important to recognize that the obstacles just described are purely political. There is no knockdown *theoretical* objection either to the idea that the government could fund alternative employment and retraining for unemployed workers, or to the idea of a general reduction in working hours. Regarding the first of these, most governments already do this to some extent. For instance, part of the US government's response to the 2008 recession was to give money to the states for them to use on improving infrastructure and education. An even more striking example is what governments did at the outbreak of the Second World War. Throughout the 1930s in the United States and the United Kingdom there was high unemployment, and those without jobs experienced serious material deprivation. When war came, the governments immediately orchestrated things to ensure that full use was made of the labor power available: factories were retooled, workers were retrained, and in a very short time there were jobs for everyone. One reason government could do this, of course, is that there was widespread agreement about the national goal toward which all this new activity was directed—namely, victory over Germany and Japan. At the present time it is admittedly hard to imagine anything approaching that sort of consensus for another great national project. But the point here is not that the solution to economic problems like unemployment is easy to put into effect; the point is that the problem does not lie in some intrinsic feature of modern economies or in some mathematical formula discovered by clever economists that blocks the path to full employment the way the law of gravity prevents us from jumping over our houses.

There is no shortage of worthwhile work that needs doing. Infrastructure needs repairing; schools and hospitals need upgrading; public parks, large and small, need to be improved and adequately staffed; public transport in many places is woefully inadequate; there is a virtually unlimited amount of research to be undertaken in medicine, alternative energy, and other scientific fields. And there are plenty of people who want to work. The example of what happened at the beginning of the Second World War proves that the present ongoing inefficiency is not necessary, as does the work undertaken in the United States by the Civilian Conservation Corps in the 1930s, one of the most popular and successful elements of the New Deal. Enlightened public policy could establish worthwhile goals that benefit everyone and ensure that anyone who wished to work could be employed in projects aimed at realizing these goals. The fact that economically advanced countries are now much richer than in 1940, and have at their disposal vastly superior technology, only makes this argument stronger.

Having the government fund work and training schemes is one measure that would help offset job losses due to a general reduction in demand should the philosophy of simple living win more adherents. The other measure suggested is to engineer a reduction in the number of hours worked by each person in a full-time job. The basic idea here is not rocket science. Ten people working forty-hour weeks with three weeks' holiday a year each adds up to an annual total of 19,600 hours worked per year. Fifteen people working thirty hours a week with six weeks' holiday a year adds up to an annual total of 20,700 hours worked. The second scenario has many obvious advantages. The five additional people who are employed rather than unemployed will pay taxes rather than be in need of welfare. A shorter working week and longer holidays means the workforce will feel less tired, be more productive while at work, and, one assumes, be generally happier and healthier since their lives will be less stressful. Those with children will be able to spend more time with them, a situation that also has various knock-on benefits both for the families and for society as a whole.

There are two obvious problems with trying to reduce the working week: (a) doing so will raise labor costs for most employers; (b) many workers need, or want, all the money they can get, which is why a lot of people work overtime if it is available. But these objections are hardly decisive. To think they are is, once again, to think of the proposal in isolation from other changes that could and should accompany it. Under the present system in the United States, for instance, employers often prefer to have few employees working relatively long hours since this reduces the amount companies have to pay in health insurance, pension contributions, and other benefits. Some employers prefer to hire part-timers for the same reason, since they don't have to provide benefits for workers whose hours fall below a certain threshold—one reason why so many college courses are now taught by part-time adjuncts. Thus an important obstacle to the happy medium—more people being sufficiently employed and compensated without being overworked or keeping others out of the workforce—is the cost to employers of providing benefits such as health insurance and pension schemes. But the system of linking such benefits to the workplace came about owing to contingent historical circumstances. There is nothing necessary, or efficient, or desirable about it. A national health-care system under which everyone receives free or inexpensive heath care as they need it, paid for out of taxes, is perfectly viable. So too is a social security system that guarantees all people an adequate pension when they reach retirement age. The feasibility of such systems is proved by the fact that something like them already works in several prosperous countries such as Australia, Denmark, the Netherlands, and Canada. And as Juliet Schor points out in her discussion of the possible economic consequences of people consuming less, the United States has much greater resources at its disposal for publicly beneficial investment than any other country.[30]

Universal health care and decent state pensions for all, paid for out of taxes, make it possible for employers to employ more people working shorter hours. It could also be part of a broad package that makes it much easier for people to live comfortably on less, thereby reducing the pressure they feel to work longer hours. Other measures that would have a similar effect include improved public education (so parents don't feel pressurized to send their kids to private schools or move to affluent school districts), good public transport, and decent affordable public housing that, along with cost controls on private rentals, could help lower housing costs in general.

Even if all these things were available, some people would no doubt still be driven to make lots of money and enjoy a more extravagant lifestyle. But the goal of the policies mentioned is not to eliminate voluntary extravagance; it is to make reduced working hours viable—even desirable—for many more people. This would help us move away from the current situation, where millions are unemployed or underemployed while many others feel overworked, to a more rational and efficient distribution of work. And this, in turn, would mean that large numbers of people could choose to reduce their level of consumption without this throwing millions out of work and into poverty.

These suggestions obviously involve a greater degree of government intervention into the economy than many people, particularly those on the political right, consider desirable. Their repeated mantra is that the free market is the most efficient mechanism for motivating the provision and governing the distribution of just about anything, whether it be wealth, jobs, goods, services, housing, health care, energy, or education. Yet the way things operate in the United States and other capitalist countries is clearly not terribly efficient. To say it again, there is plenty of work that needs doing; there are millions who would like to do this work rather than be unemployed; there is unprecedented wealth swilling around the system; yet much of the wealth ends up in the pockets of a small minority. The richest 0.01 percent of Americans own over 10 percent of the wealth in the United States, the top 0.1 percent own over 20 percent, and the wealthiest 1 percent account for over 60 percent.[31]

Economists skeptical about the potential benefits of government playing a more active role in the economy along the lines suggested here like to point to places where they say such socialistic experiments have been tried and have failed. For instance, they will point to problems said to be caused by the institution of a thirty-five-hour working week in France. But what is strikingly obvious about these objections is their ideological motivation. You would think that when France tried putting this idea into practice in 2000, the most reasonable response would be something like this: "Here's an interesting experiment; let's hope it works, because if it does, that would be good news for all of us! Less work, more play, less stress, more time spent with family and friends." Instead, it's a foregone conclusion that free-market advocates like the *Economist* will condemn the idea from the outset and pronounce it a failure on a regular basis.[32] The truth, though, is that the "experts" disagree over how successful this experiment has been. Some argue that the thirty-five-hour week is a bit of a myth. Many French workers, especially white-collar workers, routinely work well over thirty-five hours; it is just that beyond that threshold additional hours count as overtime.[33] The World Bank issued a report stating that limiting the workweek had little measurable effect on the efficiency of an economy.[34] And the French labor force certainly remains one of the most productive in Europe, ranking seventh among OECD members in 2011.[35] Yet as Jean Baker, codirector of the Center for Economic and Policy Research, observed, "economists look at France as a country with a 35-hour work week, a government that accounts for more than half of GDP, and provides its citizens with top-notch healthcare and childcare—and want to say that this can't work. They almost get angry that it does."[36]

WHY DO WE WORK SO HARD?

Back in 1930, the economist John Maynard Keynes predicted that the continuous increase in productivity characteristic of industrial capitalism would lead within a century to much more leisure for everyone, with the typical working week being reduced to about fifteen hours. This has obviously not come about. To be sure, in virtually all relatively prosperous countries the average number of hours worked annually has fallen over the last few decades. Between 1950 and 2010, in the United States, for instance, this number dropped from 1,908 to 1,695, in Canada from 2,079 to 1,711, in Denmark from 2,144 to 1,523, and even in Japan, famed for its workaholism, the average number of hours worked per year went from a high of 2,224 in 1961 to 1,706 in 2011.[37] But even the lackadaisical Danes are still working twice as hard as Keynes predicted. Given the increases in productivity and prosperity in the industrialized world, one could have reasonably hoped for more. People in the United Kingdom are now four times better off than they were in 1930, but they work only 20 percent less, and that is fairly typical of other advanced economies. The rich, who used to relish their idleness, now boast about how hard they work, while for many of the poor, unemployment is a persistent curse. Moreover, according to economist Staffan Linder, economic growth is typically accompanied by a sense that we have less time available for the things we wish to do. This feeling is not mistaken, but the lack of time is in large part due to the fact that members of affluent societies will opt for more money over more leisure if given the choice. They then start to carry the mentality and values of workplace productivity into every part of their lives, resulting in what Linder calls the "harried leisure class."[38] Advocates of simple living naturally see this trend toward increasing busyness, whether objectively real or subjectively felt, as something to be combated since the expansion and enjoyment of leisure have always been considered to be among the main benefits of choosing to live simply.

So why was Keynes wrong? According to Robert and Edward Skidelsky in *How Much Is Enough?* his mistake was to underestimate the difficulty of reining in the forces unleashed by capitalism, particularly people's desire for ever-increasing wealth and the things it can buy. Our natural concern for improved relative status, hardwired into us by evolution, is inflamed by the capitalist system, complete with incessant advertising and free-market ideology, so that we always want more than we have and more than we really need. [39]

This explanation for why we still work much harder than we need to has some plausibility. But I would suggest that the problem is not solely, or even mainly, that most people are driven by an insatiable desire for more. Rather, as Juliet Schor argues in *The Overworked American*, the main problem is that individuals are at the mercy of the system.[40] Many would prefer to work less than they do, but for various reasons they don't feel that they have much choice. One obvious obstacle to working less is that one's employer may not offer this option. As noted above, it is usually in the employer's interest to have a smaller number of employees working long hours rather than spreading the work over a larger workforce. And even if working fewer hours is technically an option, many employees will be reluctant to work less for fear that doing so will send the signal that they are insufficiently motivated or committed to the work. Another obvious problem is the fact that many jobs pay poorly, so people work overtime or take on more than one job. No doubt some people who take on all this extra work are driven by avarice; but far more are motivated simply by the need to make enough to pay the bills. Here it is not the workers who insatiably crave more money, but the bosses (which includes the top executives and the big shareholders). They are the ones who, although often fabulously wealthy themselves, insist on paying their lower-grade employees subsistence wages.

The system also includes the way that market forces determine the cost of living. Ideally this is supposed to benefit the consumer as suppliers compete for custom by lowering their prices. But although things work this way with respect to items like computers or cameras, in some crucial spheres the market drives prices up. The most obvious of these is housing. Normally everyone cheers when prices of a commodity drop, for who doesn't want to see cheaper plane tickets or lower gas prices? But economists treat house prices differently. A fall in house prices is a "slump," and it is typically reported as bad news. But why? One reason is that if you own a house, an increase in its value means an increase in your net worth. People are pleased by this, even if the corresponding rise in other house prices means that they are not necessarily any better off. True, they can sell their house for more, but they then have to spend more to buy something similar. A second reason for cheering a rise in house prices is that one can borrow using one's house as collateral, so the higher its value, the more one can borrow. Yet most people don't need to borrow sums so large that a hefty increase in the value of their house is necessary to secure the loan. A third reason is that a rise in house prices means high demand for houses, which means work for those who provide the goods and services involved in building and equipping new houses, improving old ones, and helping people move.

This last reason for viewing an increase in house prices positively makes some sense, although even here rising prices are not so much good in themselves as a sign of something else that is good—namely, the prospect of increased economic activity. But on the other side of the ledger high property values have some significant drawbacks. Most obviously, they make it impossible for many people to buy a house. And in population centers like London or San Francisco, where property values are especially high, rents will also be exorbitant. So those on modest incomes must either devote a good chunk of what they earn to paying the rent, or settle for a long unenjoyable commute.

Market forces are also responsible for escalating costs in health care and higher education. The problem for people without much money is that these things, like housing, cannot reasonably be considered optional luxuries. Diseases and injuries can threaten one's life; disabilities and pain can seriously reduce one's quality of life. That is why people are willing to bankrupt themselves in order to get treatment for themselves or their family members. The need for a college education is obviously not quite of the same order: failing to get into the college of your choice may be disappointing, but it is rarely fatal. All the same, for anyone hoping to pursue any sort of professional career today, a college degree is indispensable. And even though in some countries (e.g., France, Germany, Sweden, Brazil) it is still possible to get a decent education and a respectable qualification quite cheaply, there are far more where this is not true.

The minimum wage, working hours and conditions, public transport, and the cost of essentials like housing, health care, and education are all aspects of the system we live in that government could do something about to make simple living easier to achieve for those who want it. But we are also pressured to make more money by features of our economic and cultural environment that government policies cannot easily influence. The Skidelskys emphasize people's uncontrolled desire for wealth, status, and stuff; and frugal purists might criticize any kind of consumption that is "relational" in the sense that it is fueled by one's concern for how one stands in relation to others rather than by an authentic need for the thing in question. But this criticism is too simple. As Judith Lichtenberg points out, our needs form a spectrum from absolute necessities to sheer luxuries. And while some relational desires are morally problematic—for instance, the desire for superiority over others—some can be understood more sympathetically. Our desire to be on a more or less equal footing with our peers is tied to our deep-seated need for self-respect. And some relational consumption is forced on us by the surrounding infrastructure. Think of cars, telephones, cell phones, computers, or Internet access. At first they are luxuries; but once a critical mass of people acquire them, they become requirements of a normal integrated lifestyle. As Judith Lichtenberg puts it, "invention is the mother of necessity."[41]

So if many people in the modern world are spending more time at work than they would like to, this is not primarily because their desire for more money, stuff, and status is out of control. To a great extent they are pressed into this behavior by the system they find themselves participating in. The Skidelskys and others are surely right, though, in questioning the assumption that unlimited economic growth is a good thing, and in criticizing the blind drive for growth that motivates the policies favored by mainstream economists and politicians. Yes, economic growth has clearly improved the lives of millions and brought into being many wonderful things from airplanes to iPhones. But as Jürgen Habermas has tirelessly argued, our technical cleverness has outpaced our moral wisdom. And this is the case not just in areas like weaponry or medicine. Many societies, most obviously the United States, are awash with wealth and talent yet plagued by unemployment, poverty, crime, and environmental problems. The top universities are engines of brilliant research, yet the majority of students in the lower socioeconomic tiers leave high school woefully uneducated. Medical science provides a stream of astonishing breakthroughs, but millions continue to suffer from preventable diseases.

Why these paradoxes? One obvious reason is that large complex societies are very difficult things to organize and control. Policies made with the best intentions will often have unforeseen and undesirable consequences, as all economists recognize. But ideology and interests also play a huge role, as is well illustrated by the political opposition in the United States to reforming an absurdly inefficient health-care system or to introducing a carbon tax (a measure supported by an overwhelming majority of economists).

The philosophy that advocates frugal simplicity does not necessarily entail a particular political line or specific economic policy, but its general outlook naturally tilts toward a position that is critical of consumerism and rejects the values of Wall Street. Consumerism misguidedly seeks happiness and meaning in the acquisition of things; corporate capitalism is driven by the desire for ever more wealth and measures everything by its contribution to this end. Frugal zealots and radical simplifiers at the fundamentalist end of the spectrum will denounce these capitalistic values wholesale, perhaps following in the footsteps of Diogenes or Thoreau in opting for a lifestyle removed from the mainstream. Those of a more moderate persuasion will acknowledge the many benefits brought by economic growth, but will see these as insufficiently realized so long as they are distributed so inequitably and require so many to keep slogging away on the working-getting-spending treadmill. They will thus naturally favor government policies that, by making the basic elements of the good life easy to obtain, free all people to live more simply if they choose.

CHAPTER 7

The Environmentalist Case for Simple Living

The basic environmentalist argument in favor of frugal simplicity is pretty straightforward and will be familiar to most readers. Over the past two centuries, industrialization and the rapid growth in population have massively increased the impact of human beings on the natural environment. Much of this impact is negative: smog; acid rain; polluted rivers, lakes, and seas; contaminated groundwater; litter; garbage dumps; toxic waste; soil erosion; deforestation; extinction or threatened extinction of plant and animal species; habitat destruction; reduced biodiversity; and, perhaps most significant of all in the long term, global warming. Consumerism, extravagance, and wastefulness increase the damage being done; living frugally and simply, by contrast, reduces one's ecological footprint. The philosophy of frugality thus expresses the outlook and advocates the lifestyle that will best help preserve nature's beauties and sustain earth's fragile ecosystems.

HISTORICAL BACKGROUND

From ancient times up to the nineteenth century, the philosophical champions of frugal simplicity did not give much thought to environmentalist arguments. Like their contemporaries, they paid little attention to the impact of humans on the natural environment. There were two main reasons for this. First, the low population and preindustrial modes of production meant that the impact was light. The dramatic difference between our current situation and that which obtained prior to the Industrial Revolution is captured in two graphs, one charting population growth, the other indicating the increase in greenhouse gases in the atmosphere.

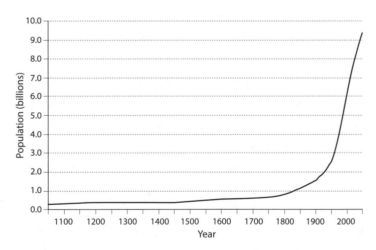

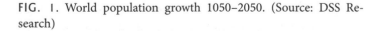

FIG. 1. World population growth 1050–2050. (Source: DSS Research)

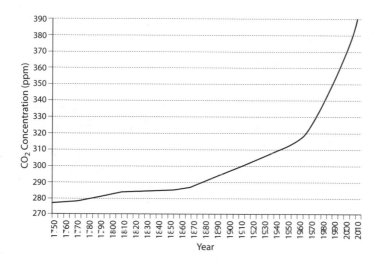

FIG. 2. Changes in atmospheric CO_2 concentrations 1750–2010. (Source: Carbon Dioxide Information Analysis Center, NOAA ESRL)

The other main reason for the absence until recently of environmentalist arguments in favor of simple living was that life for most people was hard and insecure. With hunger, sickness, natural disasters, and other serious misfortunes as ever-present possibilities, nature was typically viewed as a resource to be exploited rather than a value to be protected. Moreover, this attitude accorded with the way Christian theologians understood the "dominion mandate" given to Adam and Eve in Genesis:

> And God blessed them, and said unto them, Be fruitful, and multiply, and replenish the earth, and subdue it: and have dominion over the fish of the sea, and over the fowl of the air, and over every living thing that moveth upon the earth.[1]

God goes on to explain that every herb-bearing seed and every fruit-bearing tree was also created for humanity's benefit. This anthropocentric outlook meshed easily with the Aristotelian view that, since "nature makes nothing in vain," animals, and therefore also the plants that animals eat, ultimately "exist for the sake of man."[2] Such a view would have seemed natural to all Europeans through the Middle Ages and beyond. Sentimental attitudes toward nature were a luxury that, if they had thought about the matter at all, they would have felt they could not afford.

The assumption that everything in nature was made for our benefit and should be viewed as subordinate to our purposes remained dominant through the early modern period, although during this time dissenting voices began to chip away at this way of thinking. The discovery of both new and extinct species fueled the rise of a new kind of biology that studied plants and animals for their intrinsic interest quite apart from any useful function they might serve.[3] With the passing of the medieval worldview, the distinction between human beings and animals came to seem less absolute, even before Darwin; after the seventeenth century keeping pets (animals viewed as companions rather than as sources of meat or as workers) became much more common. And the expansion of cities to house a growing population prompted nostalgia among the new urban dwellers for natural landscapes and fresh air.

The view of nature as something that is more than just raw material for human purposes really began to gain ground with the advent of Romanticism, which not coincidentally arose as the Industrial Revolution gathered steam. The greater security that industrialization ushered in also underlay the Romantic celebration of wild and untamed landscapes—craggy mountains, bleak moorland, tempestuous seas. Nature came to seem less threatening, and as fear of famine receded, people no longer wished to see every bit of land cultivated or producing food.[4]

Romanticism embraced values that went hand in hand with a philosophy of simple living: a distrust of the artificial or excessively ornate, a new respect for the lives of ordinary folk, a desire to live and feel at home in nature, and a celebration of nature as a source of joy and inspiration. It is thus no surprise to find so many advocates of simplicity among Romantics and those influenced by them. Wordsworth, for instance, writing lyrical poems in "the language of common men," does not just express his profound enjoyment of and sense of gratitude toward nature; he makes a point of singing the praises of its humbler beauties rather than its famed spectacles: daffodils, a cuckoo, a skylark, the lesser celandine, the sun in the morning, the quiet of an evening. Thoreau shares this delight in the commonplace—*Walden* is a catalog of pleasures of this kind—but he is more alert to the growing alienation from nature that industrial society brings about, and to the damage it can inflict. For this reason he has more of a claim to being recognized as a pioneer of environmentalism.

Other late nineteenth- and early twentieth-century critics of the environmental ravages of industrial capitalism include artists, writers, and reformers like John Ruskin, William Morris, and Edward Carpenter. To varying degrees they extol simplicity, and do so primarily because it brings one close to nature, although it has to be admitted that Ruskin and Morris, being aficionados of fine art and architecture, preferred a fairly luxurious form of simple living. In America John Muir, often identified as the "patron saint" and the first great moving spirit of modern environmentalism, described himself as a disciple of Thoreau and for a time emulated his hero by living for several years in a small cabin in Yosemite.

Today environmentalism is a worldwide intellectual, moral, and political movement, and every thinking person is aware of the need to limit the damage being done to earth's ecosystems by human activity. There has been a growing awareness that behind all the goods and services we consume is a vast amount of industrial activity much of which depletes resources, pollutes soil, water, and air, destroys habitats, and contributes to global warming. Most of the food we eat is produced by industrial-scale agriculture that uses huge quantities of chemical fertilizers and pesticides, as well as water and energy. Acres of woodland and farmland are destroyed each day to make land available for more McMansions. Technology in many areas may have become cleaner, but this in itself cannot fix the problem. We think of the digital revolution as environmentally friendly, yet by the end of the twentieth century the manufacturing of each computer was generating 140 pounds of solid waste a year, some of it hazardous, and 12 million computers (300,000 tons) were being junked each year, mainly into landfills.[5] Motor vehicles are undoubtedly becoming cleaner with respect to the amount of energy they consume and in the sort of exhaust they put out; but these improvements are more than offset by the rapid increase in the number of cars on the road in places like China and India.

THE ENVIRONMENTALIST ARGUMENT

Nearly all contemporary advocates of frugal simplicity will contend that the more people who embrace their outlook, the better it will be for the natural environment. How strong an argument is this?

The grounds for making it seem fairly obvious. At the level of individual actions and lifestyle choices, there is often a straightforward connection between being frugal and reducing one's ecological footprint. Reduce, reuse, recycle. This is the familiar slogan shared by both frugal zealots and environmentalists. Books, articles, and blogs abound advocating "ecofrugality" and advising us how to simultaneously save money and the environment by following practices such as these:

- walking or cycling instead of driving
- installing energy-efficient appliances
- turning off unnecessary lights
- drying clothes on the line
- raking leaves instead of using a leafblower
- eating leftovers
- sharing tools
- buying only what you need and using until it is worn out
- buying used items when possible

- drinking tap water instead of bottled water
- turning down the thermostat
- washing only full loads of laundry
- reusing wrapping paper (or, better, making reusable gift bags)

Each of these measures, in addition to saving money, reduces the consumption of energy either directly, as when you turn off unnecessary lights, or indirectly by reducing demand for the production of new commodities. And as ecofrugalist Keith Heidorn says: "Reduction of waste in any form is a win for the environment. Reduction of material and energy use is a win for the planet and all life forms."[6]

Essentially the same argument is made in favor of other aspects of simple living. Increasing self-sufficiency by growing some of your own food is cleaner and greener than buying the products of industrial agriculture that are produced with chemical fertilizers and pesticides, involve a high level of wastage, and consume additional energy through being packaged and transported. Contenting oneself with simple pleasures close to home as opposed to buying expensive toys or exotic experiences reduces both energy consumption and the production of waste. Moreover, the connection between simplicity and environmental protection runs both ways: by preserving natural beauty we ensure that the important simple (and usually free) pleasure of enjoying nature will continue to be available—and those who enjoy it will perhaps be more likely to adopt green practices.

Communities can also create institutions and pursue policies that simultaneously help people live more cheaply and protect the environment. Good public transport reduces energy consumption, pollution, and congestion. Public parks and gardens improve air quality in cities and allow people to enjoy greenery, beauty, and open spaces to play in without having their own large private gardens. Allotments or community gardens encourage local food production. Libraries limit the need for individual acquisitions.

These are the sort of arguments that advocates of frugal simplicity can and do make. On the whole they are reasonable. Nevertheless, we have to recognize that legitimate questions can be raised concerning the supposed environmental benefits of frugality and simplicity. Consideration of some of these possible objections will help us form a more judicious assessment of the environmentalist argument.

OBJECTIONS TO THE ENVIRONMENTALIST ARGUMENT

Ecological Impacts Are Difficult to Calculate

Determining the precise environmental impact of any particular activity or purchasing decision is often extraordinarily difficult given the number of variables and the complexity of their interaction. For instance, there are scientifically respectable studies suggesting that the production of biofuels, like ethanol made from corn, releases more greenhouse gases, at least in the short term, than are released by the production and use of conventional gasoline.[7] Solar panels produce electricity with zero emissions, but manufacturing the photovoltaic panels (and in some setups the batteries they charge) requires the mining of rare metals and produces toxic waste.[8] Plug-in hybrid cars emit less exhaust than regular cars, but this reduction in their eco footprint may be partially offset by the additional energy used in manufacturing their batteries, by their consumption of electricity from the grid (much of which is still produced by burning coal), and by their owners' propensity to drive more miles since the cost per mile is lower (an example of what energy economists call the "rebound effect"). A study comparing the environmental impact of disposable and reusable diapers concluded that whether the latter are better for the environment depends on how they are laundered (i.e., on such factors as size of laundry load, water temperature, and drying technique).[9] Apples imported to the United Kingdom from New Zealand may have a smaller total environmental impact, in terms of energy consumed in production and transportation, than locally grown apples because they are grown in more favorable conditions—but only in spring and summer when the comparison is with English apples that have had to be stored in refrigerators for several months.[10]

The basic point being made here is undoubtedly correct. Ecosystems are complex, and comparisons between the long-term effects of different practices or technologies are difficult. So there are times when the truth is counterintuitive. But this hardly justifies a general skepticism regarding the environmental benefits of frugal practices and simple living. Walking or cycling clearly does pollute less than driving a car; a clothesline uses less energy than a dryer; drinking tap water creates less waste than buying bottled water. The skeptical argument performs a useful service in reminding us of complexities and indeterminacies we might be inclined to overlook, but it simply has no purchase on most straightforward frugal measures of the sort listed above.

Simplicity Is Not Always Green

Some aspects of simple living are actually worse for the environment than the less rustic alternatives. For instance, we have seen that for many people living close to nature and being self-sufficient are important components of an ideally simple lifestyle. But as David Owen argues in *Green Metropolis*, if this means rural living, it is unlikely to be better for the environment than living in a city.[11] Living in the countryside usually means a detached house, which takes a lot more energy to heat than a city apartment that is typically more compact and surrounded on all sides but one by other apartments. It also usually involves a lot more driving compared to life in big cities where there is extensive public transport and where walking is often preferable to driving. If part of being self-sufficient and harking back to simpler times is heating the house with wood you've cut, this is probably worse for the environment than heating with gas. Even when the wood is properly dried and burned in an efficient modern stove of the type approved by the US Environmental Protection Agency, burning wood still gives off far more fine-particle pollution than does heating with oil or gas furnaces.[12]

If simple living has to be inexpensive, there is the additional problem that the frugal option is often not very green, while the green option can be quite pricey. The cheapest fruit and vegetables are produced on an industrial scale with massive amounts of pesticide and fertilizer; organic alternatives can be two or three times as expensive. The policy of repairing and reusing rather than replacing is a frugal strategy familiar to all card-carrying tightwads, but new appliances such as water heaters, refrigerators, and washing machines often meet higher EPA standards of efficiency. Signing up for electricity from renewable sources may help support the shift toward green energy, but it will usually mean higher monthly electricity bills.

Once again, the argument makes a fair point. Simple living, as we have already observed, encompasses many ideas and practices, and there are times when some of these conflict. As with the previous objection, the appropriate response is not to deny this but to acknowledge where it is true. Here too, though, the point being made hardly constitutes a wholesale objection to the environmentalist case for frugal simplicity. Most frugal practices clearly do reduce one's ecological footprint. The more people choose to live in smaller houses, walk or cycle rather than drive, compost their waste, turn off unnecessary lights, put on a sweater rather than turn up the thermostat, and so on, the better. Except in the case of inefficient or polluting machines, getting by with what you have rather than throwing stuff away and buying unnecessary replacements reduces both waste and the demand for industrially produced stuff, as does buying used items where possible.

A specific example of how criticism of a supposedly green practice associated with simple living may make a legitimate point without amounting to a devastating objection is provided by the debate over locavorism. Locavores are people who prefer food that is produced locally, say within a hundred miles of where they live. So given a choice, they will buy local apples rather than apples shipped from thousands of miles away, and they will look to eat what is in season where they live insofar as this is possible. Obviously, locavores differ in how seriously and rigorously they apply these principles, but the thinking behind the philosophy is common to all. Locally produced food, they argue, is usually better quality since it is fresh. Because it is often produced on a small scale by Community Supported Agriculture (CSAs), organic farms, community gardens, or backyards, it is healthier and more trustworthy than what comes from industrial agriculture, where fruit and vegetables are drenched in pesticides and animals are pumped full of steroids and antibiotics. It typically requires less energy to produce and transport. In towns and cities a desire for local produce encourages small farming enterprises and community gardens on vacant lots, which improves the urban landscape with pleasing areas of greenery. Buying local is also a way of engaging with and supporting one's local community, keeping money circulating around where one lives, helping to sustain local economic activity rather than sending the dollars off to some distant agribusiness. Last but not least, locavorism encourages home gardening, which in addition to these other benefits gets people outside, exercising, and in touch with nature. (It would also, as best-selling locavore Michael Pollan argues, make suburbia a lot more interesting if some of the lawns were converted to vegetable gardens.)[13]

To each of these points skeptics and critics can offer counterarguments. Fresh local food is the best available only when it is the sort of thing that grows well locally: Florida oranges, even after refrigeration and shipping, are always going to be better than anything grown in cooler climes. It isn't necessarily true that what you buy at the farmers' market is more trustworthy than supermarket produce shipped from large farms; the latter, unlike the former, is subject to inspection and has to satisfy government regulations. The amount of energy that goes into producing and delivering any food item can be devilishly difficult to calculate, but it is a mistake to assume that local always means less. As Michael Specter observes in a *New Yorker* article on the concept of carbon footprints:

> Many factors influence the carbon footprint of a product: water use, cultivation and harvesting methods, quantity and type of fertilizer, even the type of fuel used to make the package. Sea-freight emissions are less than a sixtieth of those associated with airplanes, and you don't have to build highways to berth a ship.[14]

Although it seems counterintuitive, the berries you col-
lect at a pick-your-own farm a few miles from where you
live, to which you've made a special journey in your car,
may have a bigger carbon footprint per berry than the
ones in the supermarket that have been shipped in bulk
from another continent.[15] Community gardens within
a city may be pleasing to the eye, but if the idea is to
reduce energy consumption and carbon emissions, the
land they occupy would be better used to site high-rise
apartments—by far the most efficient sort of residence.
As for supporting the local economy, skeptics will argue
that small-scale farming and gardening is generally quite
inefficient; that is why, compared to agribusiness, which
has all the advantages of scale, CSAs and small organic
farms often struggle to be commercially viable, and their
prices tend to be high. The skeptics will also point out
that any little good we do by eating locally produced food
is swamped by the fact that most of the things we spend
money on are nonedible commodities, usually made in
and shipped from faraway places.

In this debate both sides have reasonable arguments.
What the critics of locavorism fail to appreciate, though,
is that the preference for homegrown or local produce is
typically one element in a package, a general outlook and
set of commitments to a certain form of life. It may har-
bor some inefficiencies and inconsistencies—whose way
of living does not?—but it is nonetheless part of a worthwhile attempt to realize certain values; and if more people
shared those values and sought to put them into effect,
the environment really would benefit and the world really

would be a better place. Small organic farms do treat animals more humanely than do factory farms, pollute less, and cause less soil erosion. Homegrown vegetables generally are more nutritious and satisfying than those produced on a large scale. Farmers' markets, CSAs, and small local shops provide occasions for interaction that are lost when megastores take over. Gardening is a way for people to be less alienated from nature. The "victory gardens" that people dug in backyards and on waste ground during the Second World War made good sense then since they increased self-sufficiency at both the domestic and the national level. And although we no longer have a Great National Cause to which everyone is devoted, it would surely still be a good thing for households and communities to be more rather less productive, and more rather than less self-sufficient, especially where this would be environmentally beneficial rather than harmful.

The Choices of Individuals Make No Real Difference

The small things people do to reduce their ecological footprint by living more simply or frugally make a minuscule difference. They may give these people a warm fuzzy feeling inside for doing their bit to save the planet, but what really decides whether we can reduce the rate of global warming, make our air cleaner and our water purer, save species from going extinct, and so on, are the actions of governments and corporations, along with technological innovations. In the case of global warming, for instance, what will really make a difference are measures such as the introduction of a carbon tax, the replacing of coal-fired power stations by cleaner forms of energy production, and the enforcement of stricter regulations governing industrial pollution and vehicular emissions. Individuals' remembering to turn the lights off, or choosing to walk to work, barely moves the needle. The value of such actions is subjective rather than objective.

This is a commonly heard argument, but I think it is a poor one. It is true, of course, that the fate of our environment will be determined most of all by the big decisions made by the big players—the politicians who make the laws, the experts who advise them, the agencies that enforce the laws, and the corporations that enjoy outsized political influence and whose large-scale industrial enterprises have a significant environmental impact. But this hardly proves that there is no point in any of us trying to reduce the negative impact that as individuals we have on the environment. One could just as well argue that there is not much point in voting in an election where it is a foregone conclusion that a single vote will not affect the outcome; or that a family shouldn't worry about wasting water during a drought since the amount involved is trivial, especially compared to the quantities being used or misused by large factories and farms; or that we shouldn't feel any compunction about failing to declare little bits of additional income to the tax office since the tax we thereby avoid paying is a drop in the ocean compared to the billions that big business and the superrich manage to avoid paying.

The objection is misguided in two ways. First, and most obviously, although the impact on the environment of each individual action may be minute, when millions of people do the same thing, the impact can be huge. State and municipal authorities that prohibit the watering of lawns during a drought are not being stupid: the actions of individuals, multiplied many times, make a difference. And the larger the population, the bigger the difference made. If everyone who could do so conserved energy in all the ways that frugal zealots recommend—turning off unnecessary lights, drying clothes on the line, choosing fuel-efficient vehicles, driving less, consuming less, and so on—our overall consumption of fossil fuels would dramatically decrease, which all of us, except oil company executives, agree would be a good thing. If everyone were to completely ignore the EPA guidelines on disposing of household waste, pouring used motor oil and other toxic materials into the ground while flushing old medicines down the toilet, the consequences for the water supply would be serious.

Second, encouraging individuals to participate in the general project of reducing the harm we are doing to the environment is worthwhile not just because they then, as individuals, do less harm, but also because it helps to foster concern for the environment as the default attitude in a society, an attitude that gradually gains ground until it becomes widespread. And as it becomes more widespread, its practical value increases. The growth of recycling offers a good example of this.

Recycling of certain materials, like iron, bronze, or timber, has been practiced from time immemorial, but it was only in the 1970s that municipalities began recycling programs. The environmental benefits of recycling seem obvious: it conserves resources, saves energy (since recycling a material usually takes less energy than producing it from scratch), reduces greenhouse gas emissions and other forms of air pollution, and reduces the amount of waste going into landfills. Naturally, recycling has its critics. Economist Michael Munger, for instance, argues that quite a lot of recycling is inefficient, even absurd. He describes how in Raleigh, North Carolina, the municipal authority wished to discontinue recycling green glass. Making fresh glass from virgin materials is usually cheaper and takes less total energy than manufacturing it from cullet, the ground-up glass produced from recycled bottles and jars. But people in Raleigh, because they were committed to the idea of recycling, voted to require that glass be included in the recycling program. Consequently, it would be collected, sorted, and then taken to the landfill, an exercise in pointless inefficiency. Munger also describes a ridiculous scene he witnessed in Chile of people spending their Saturday morning driving out to a recycling center where they queued for a long time, engines running, just to deposit a few bottles and cans in the recycling bins.[16]

Practices like these certainly seem silly on the face of it, and no doubt there are plenty of other specific examples of well-intentioned policies that aim to reduce waste, pollution, or energy consumption but which fail on all these counts. Nevertheless, skepticism toward recycling on the basis of such cases rests on a somewhat blinkered perspective that focuses on details and fails to pay enough attention to the broader and longer-term context. As noted earlier, many environmental questions are extremely complex. To what extent a particular act of recycling, or a particular recycling program, is environmentally beneficial depends on many things: what is being recycled (recycling aluminum cans saves a lot more energy than recycling glass); where the recycling takes place (recycled green glass is less useful in Britain than in France since Britain does not produce much wine); the methods used (slum dwellers sifting through trash burn less fuel than do high-tech processing plants, but the latter are safer places to work); the quality of the technology employed; how many people participate in the program; and what happens to the waste if it is not recycled. In the same way, whether or not recycling is cost-effective depends on a whole host of variables.

But what seems undeniable is that, in general, the more people become committed to recycling—and also to buying recycled goods, a preference driven by the same values—the more efficient recycling becomes, both in terms of cost and in terms of its beneficial environmental impact. As more people do it, the benefits of scale kick in. A truck driving around a neighborhood covers the same number of miles but collects far more stuff. Less waste goes to the landfill. Recycling plants become bigger in order to handle increased volume. Collection methods and sorting processes improve. All of this has in fact happened, and the various kinds of improvement are mutually reinforcing. Better sorting technology at the recycling plant means that households don't need to sort, which makes recycling easier and boosts participation. This makes further investment in recycling technology viable, which leads to better-quality recylate, which makes products made from the recyclate more competitive. And as recycling becomes standard practice, things start to be manufactured with recycling in view, leading to further efficiencies and even eventually to "upcycling," where waste is used to produce something of greater value, as opposed to "downcycling," where what is made from the waste is lower in quality.[17]

The growth of recycling programs, and their increasing efficiency and value, illustrate the general point that the small actions of individuals can have an impact beyond themselves, so to speak. Encouraging all people to make their small contributions to protecting the environment helps make environmental concern the normal and natural way of thinking throughout an entire community. And as this happens, so the practical effectiveness of individual actions increases. Narrowly focused skepticism about the value of individual measures fails to recognize this.

Our Best Hope Lies in Technological Innovation

The best hope for reversing environmental damage already done and for protecting the environment from further harm is better science and technology. But the development and application of science and technology are expensive. It is possible only on the basis of economic growth, and economic growth is driven by consumer demand. So those who embrace and advocate frugal simplicity, by slowing economic growth, also slow down the sort of technological innovation that represents the most likely and most effective long-term solution to the environmental problems we face. There are many examples of this process (consumption promoting environmentally beneficial technology) already at work. Rising demand for energy means that producing it should be profitable, which encourages research into cleaner, renewable energy. Increasing demand for fresh water drives continuing research into desalination. The computer revolution, which has been fueled to a considerable extent by demand for consumer products like laptops and smartphones, makes possible a reduction in the need for material products such as cassette tapes, vinyl records, paper memos, newspapers, books, and so on. In general, selling stuff is what provides businesses with the funds to undertake research and development, and the prospect of selling more stuff gives them a motive to do this. The increased amount paid in income tax, business tax, and sales tax during a period of economic growth allows governments to pay for environmental protection programs, the vital gathering of information, and research into possible solutions to our current problems.

Prima facie this is quite a plausible argument, although as with some of the other arguments considered above, it is hard to assess definitively because the interaction of the various factors involved is so complex. Yet the reasoning is suspiciously convoluted. One obvious point that will occur to many people immediately is that our present environmental problems have arisen largely *because* of technology. Factories pollute rivers, soil, and the atmosphere; the burning of fossil fuels is the main cause of global warming; bigger vessels and advanced fishing technology have brought about a precipitous decline in fishing stocks; industrial-scale agriculture exhausts soil and uses

pesticides that contaminate groundwater and harm wildlife. So the idea that salvation lies in more and better technology will strike many as naive, ironic, even paradoxical.

Of course, that does not show it to be false. But there
is something undeniably odd about the proposition that
the best way to protect the environment is to burn lots of
energy and consume lots of stuff so that we can afford to
research ways to solve the problems created by our burning lots of energy and consuming lots of stuff. One might
argue along analogous lines that the best response to the
epidemic of obesity in the United States is for people to
keep eating too much and exercising too little, since the
more people are afflicted, the more likely it is that medical science and pharmacology will come up with effective
treatments. Technological fixes can certainly be wondrous;
but it defies common sense to step up the very activities
that have helped bring about the problems that need fix-
ing. It is surely more reasonable to begin addressing any
problem by first trying to reduce the ongoing damage
being done. If you suspect you have emphysema, the first
thing to do is to stop smoking, even if you've read that a
remarkable new treatment may be available some time in
the future. Failing to take this obvious first step when the
problem is pressing, as it is in the case of global warming,
is downright irresponsible.

As for the claim that we need a consumption-fueled
economic boom to provide governments with the tax revenues needed to support research that will help protect
the environment, the argument would be stronger if the
governments of prosperous countries really were strapped

for cash and at a loss as to how to bring in more. But this is not their situation. The extreme wealth, measured these days in hundreds of millions or even billions of dollars, that is enjoyed by individuals in the upper social tiers indicates that there is plenty of money within the system. More progressive tax policies, perhaps including the sort of consumption tax advocated by Robert Frank,[18] along with a carbon tax as recommended by legions of economists, could provide the means for much greater public investment in environmental protection. So, too, could a realignment of spending priorities. The Obama administration's proposed budget for 2015 allocated 55 percent of discretionary spending ($640 billion) to the military, compared to just 3 percent ($38 billion) to the Environmental Protection Agency and the Department of Energy combined.[19] In Canada, the United Kingdom, China, Russia, India, Brazil, and most other large economies, a similar, if less extreme, imbalance can be seen: the amount spent by most governments on defense dwarfs the amount devoted to environmental protection.

The environmentalist argument for living simply goes beyond most of the traditional reasons given for choosing this lifestyle. Whereas Cynics, Epicureans, Stoics, Franciscans, Buddhists, Jains, and other schools that advocate simple living have usually concerned themselves primarily with the well-being of the individual making the choice, the environmentalist argument rests on a commitment to other, less self-interested values such as ensuring clean air and water, conserving existing ecosystems, and preserving natural beauty. Of course, we all have an interest in realizing these goals; but the focus is much less on what is good for us as individuals and much more on what is good for all humanity and, ultimately, for the planet, which includes at least some of its nonhuman life-forms. For this reason, the argument supports a stronger sort of moral imperative. The advice offered by Epicurus or Epictetus constitutes what Kant calls counsels of prudence; these tell us what we should do if we want to be happy. The environmentalist imperatives, by contrast, tell us that we have a serious moral obligation to reduce our detrimental impact on the natural environment by shifting toward a simpler lifestyle, at least in some respects.

The objections to this argument that we have considered should not be dismissed out of hand. They make legitimate points. Calculating environmental impacts is complicated; some truths are counterintuitive; there are times when simplicity, frugality, and greenness don't coincide; the impact of any individual actions is minute compared to the impact of corporate practices and government policies; technological innovation has a major role to play in environmental protection. But none of these points undermines the general thesis that more people shifting their lifestyle in the direction of frugal simplicity would help to reduce our collective ecological footprint. That argument can reasonably be added to the battery of arguments developed by the frugal sages of earlier times in favor of simplicity. The objections are valuable, though, in reminding us that just because something *seems* right or *feels* right does not mean that objectively speaking it *is* right. Effective environmentalism has to be open-minded enough and self-critical enough to acknowledge this. The problems we currently face are too important for us to let ideology obscure truth. But with the same open-mindedness, the skeptics who advance these objections have to recognize that the road the world is currently on—the relentless and apparently endless pursuit of economic growth and consumer satisfaction with little regard for environmental consequences—could well be a road to disaster.

Conclusion

The author of Ecclesiastes famously opined that "there is nothing new under the sun." In his *Meditations*, Marcus Aurelius agrees:

> Look at the past—empire succeeding empire—and from that, extrapolate the future: the same thing. No escape from the rhythm of events. Which is why observing life for forty years is as good as a thousand. Would you really see anything new?[1]

These authors have been celebrated as founts of wisdom for two millennia, and deservedly so. But they are wrong about this. The scientific revolution, the Industrial Revolution, and the advent of capitalism transformed the world, changing everything utterly. As a result some strains in the frugal tradition are less relevant or less appealing today. Asceticism, for instance, has usually been motivated by a concern to produce hardiness, physical and spiritual purity, or some sort of enlightenment. But for people living in a relatively secure, comfortable, and secularized world, these reasons for embracing asceticism have less purchase.

Hardiness is not so likely to be required; the notion of purity, detached from religion, need involve only modest abstemiousness; private, experiential enlightenment compares poorly with publicly accessible knowledge based on evidence and argument.

Other aspects of frugal simplicity, however, remain obviously relevant. Fiscal prudence is as sensible today as at any other time, for both individuals and institutions, as was demonstrated by the collapse of the US housing bubble in 2007, following which millions were left owing far more on their mortgages than they could really afford or than their houses were worth. Being able and willing to live cheaply—the core notion of frugality—are still virtues that the majority of people across the globe must practice of necessity. There may be more people today than in the past who can rationally choose to ditch time-honored thrifty measures and live expensively while staying within their means. But the majority are not in that position, and even those who are can still feel insecure. They may not face the prospect of civil war, exile, famine, or plague; but in a constantly changing world there is a fair chance of losing one's job, or of finding that one's particular expertise is no longer in demand.

Interestingly, almost paradoxically, several of the senses of simplicity identified in chapter 1 refer to ways of living that are out of sync with modern lifestyles yet also enjoy a renewed appeal. Moreover, their appeal is largely due to just those elements in the way we live now that threaten to render these forms of simple living passé.

Take being close to nature, for instance. People have been moving from the countryside to cities ever since the Industrial Revolution, and between 1950 and 2005 the world's urban population is estimated to have quadrupled. More than half the world's population now live in cities, and this urbanizing trend is predicted to continue. By 2005, 74 percent of the population in developed regions lived in urban settlements, and the United Nations predicts that by 2030 the proportion will have increased to 81 percent.[2] Although one regularly hears talk of a reverse trend, perhaps among hipsters seeking authenticity or oldsters returning to their roots, the magnetic pull of cities is formidable, especially on the young. Cities are where one finds work, opportunities, connections, and culture. Yet many city-dwellers still feel, consciously or unconsciously, a need to connect with nature. That is one reason why so many seek to recharge their batteries through taking their vacations in natural surroundings, by the sea, by lakes, in the mountains and the forest. The simplicity of a country cottage or cabin, removed from all the physical and digital bustle of modern urban life, has probably never held greater appeal than it does today, when it contrasts more than ever with people's daily situation and lifestyle.

Or consider self-sufficiency, another of the values traditionally associated with frugal simplicity. The more one is integrated into modern society, the less self-sufficient one becomes, and not just because so much today depends on electricity. Contemporary life at work and at home relies on an increasingly complex material and informational infrastructure. Furthermore, for many people these days

the paid work they do is more specialized, more consuming, and better compensated than work done in the
past. As a result they are more likely, and better able, to
pay other people to do things they might formerly have
done for themselves, such as child minding, house cleaning, snow removal, home maintenance, or car repair, and
they are less likely to bother growing their own food, or
making and mending their own clothes. Small forms of
self-sufficiency, like knitting your own sweaters or drying
your own herbs, are largely just gestures, symbols of an
aspiration rather than serious reductions in dependency.
For all that, they should not be despised. Doing things
for yourself is inherently satisfying; it expresses a desire
for independence that deserves respect; and as Matthew
Crawford argues in *Shop Class as Soulcraft*, it is healthy
in that it helps to keep us from living too abstractly—that
is, too cerebrally, too narrowly, and at too great a distance
from the elements of life.[3] Like the desire to reconnect with
nature, the impulse to be more self-sufficient, even if only
in ways that are virtually symbolic, is an understandable
reaction to the feeling that the tide of contemporary life is
continually pulling us in the other direction.

Something similar could be said regarding the enjoyment of simple pleasures. Thanks to rising affluence,
technological innovation, and globalization, many of us
now have an unprecedented number and variety of pleasurable recreational activities available to us. It would be
churlish to complain about this; and it would be absurd
to turn one's back on all these possible enjoyments like a
stern Calvinist with Luddite tendencies. Why not sample

exotic cuisine, play newly invented games, take in new art forms, and check out the marvelous new technologies? Even some of the pleasures we think of as simple, like taking a bike ride or listening to recorded music, often rest on modern inventions. Nevertheless, the simple pleasures praised by Epicurus, particularly those wrapped up with friendship, remain basic; the more exotic experiences are dispensable. And it is the sometimes exhausting proliferation of enticing experiences on offer that at times helps us to realize this, and to appreciate those foundational pleasures recommended by Epicurus and his fellow sages.

The paradox of the same factors making the philosophy of frugal simplicity both passé and timely can even be seen in connection with our ability and propensity to buy things. Exactly how the cost of living today compares to the cost of living in years gone by is a tricky calculation. In the United States, adjusting for inflation, items such as college tuition, health care, and other services provided by local workers have become much more expensive over the past decade or two; things like clothing and computers, which are largely produced in factories abroad that are either highly mechanized or staffed by low-wage workers, have become considerably cheaper.[4] One also has to consider changes in income, which affects how many hours a person must work to afford any particular item, as well as improvements in the quality of the items bought. One thing is beyond doubt, though: today it is much easier for almost everyone to buy lots of stuff. Clothes, kitchenware, household items, books, toys, and technology, all of decent quality, are remarkably cheap nowadays, and for frugal zealots who buy things secondhand or on sale if possible, the cost of many items has become negligible.

The upside of this is that if you are not poor, you don't need to penny-pinch in order to afford a pair of shoes, a chest of drawers, some golf clubs, or a digital camera. The downside is that many people gradually accumulate far more stuff than they need and end up being positively oppressed by it as it fills closets, attics, basements, and garages. In extreme cases this propensity to acquire and hoard becomes patho-logical; it can dominate a person's life and require treatment as a psychological disorder. In less serious cases, people call in the services of a professional declutterer. The problem is not confined to a few eccentrics. In 2009 the United States had 2.3 billion square feet of space in self-storage units. Ten percent of households were renting one of these units, and half of these units were used simply to store stuff that there was no room for at home (even though the average house size was larger than ever).[5] In the United Kingdom the need for help with decluttering is common enough for there to be an Association of Professional Declutterers & Organisers. Here again, the very forces that seem to make traditional thrift less relevant (since so much is now so cheap) create a new reason for wanting to simplify.

One feature of modern life that perhaps especially fuels a yearning for simplicity is the rapid rate of technologi-cal, social, and cultural change. Some people relish this, of course. Like surfers, they enjoy riding the wave. They are unsympathetic to the simplifiers' tendency to look back-ward, and they find the ideal of a slower, more stable—they might say "static"—world rather boring. This is the mind-set behind Facebook's cheerful mantra, "Move fast and break things." But for many the rate of change creates all sorts of problems and anxieties. Traditional ways have to be abandoned; cherished communities disintegrate; once-valued skills become useless; secure jobs are outsourced or lost to machines. Often those who suffer most are at the bottom of the socioeconomic order, the people who lack the sort of education and information-related skills that are particularly prized in today's economy. Yet even those who are well equipped to keep up can find the rate of change exhausting and a slower, more stable form of life appealing.

Marx was one of the first to identify constant change as the hallmark of capitalism, and hence of modernity. Yet although he fully recognizes its disruptive effects on tra-ditional society, this is not the basis for his critique of the system. He criticizes capitalism for its exploitative char-acter, its proneness to crisis, and its immiseration of the masses, but he virtually celebrates the way it continually revolutionizes the means of production, thereby releas-ing the hitherto unimagined power of human intelligence and labor. Nevertheless, his vision of socialism still carries some traces of the tradition that praises simplicity. The rational harnessing of the technological power unleashed by capitalism is expected to release us from the drudgery of tedious, unwanted work. The end of class struggle will lead to an era of unprecedented stability. And in one of his few references to how life will be in a future communist society, his imagination alights on a bucolic ideal in which, since labor specialization is no longer required, one will be able "to hunt in the morning, fish in the afternoon, rear cattle in the evening, and criticize after dinner."[6]

Marx never thought, though, that voluntary simplicity or back-to-nature movements had any revolutionary potential. For him, the way to overcome the pains of modernity was to push on through in order to reap the full benefits of technological progress. By contrast, contemporary advocates of frugal simplicity often do claim that the changes in outlook and lifestyle they prescribe have the power to transform society. As Cecile Andrews, who founded the organizations Seeds of Simplicity, puts it, voluntary simplicity is "the Trojan horse of social change."[7] The basic belief, or hope, is that a reaction to the glut of consumerism that has characterized Western society since the Second World War will set in, and that this, in conjunction with growing concern over environmental dangers, particularly global warming, will lead increasing numbers of people to embrace frugality, simplicity, slowness, and associated values. According to some accounts, the millennial generation (roughly those born between 1980 and 2000) exhibit some signs of this trend. They are less interested in home ownership, happy to share cars rather than buy them, and savvy at using technology to save money and keep things simple through using companies like Zipcar (transport), Airbnb (accommodation), and thredUP (clothes). The pendulum is changing direction; a cultural sea change is at hand.

Maybe. I for one would be happy to believe that the frugal zealots and voluntary simplifiers are capable of pioneering a general shift in habits and values. They certainly perform a valuable social function, calling attention to the follies of, and trying to apply the brakes to, what they see as a runaway consumer culture, the culture criticized by Juliet Schor, Robert Frank, and others. One problem, though, is that light brakes don't have much effect on a juggernaut. Another problem is that even those who are trying to apply the brakes can hardly avoid simultaneously riding the juggernaut, adding to its weight and momentum. A few people are radically frugal, but most of us who are generally sympathetic to the philosophy of frugality still come to want and expect ever-better consumer goodies— more energy-efficient machines, smarter phones, faster computers, and cooler apps. We may criticize consumerism and worry that everything is changing more quickly than we can handle wisely, yet we have the same interest as everyone else in using the new technologies and adapting to change.

Some who desire more radical social change might even argue that the advocates of frugal simplicity effectively encourage people to accept an unfair economic system. Just as Jesus's precept to "render unto Caesar that which is Caesar's" has been criticized for endorsing exploitation and inequality, so the advice of the frugal sages could be seen as telling people not to ask for a bigger piece of the pie, but to learn instead the joys of living on crumbs. But this criticism is misguided. The teachers of frugal simplicity criticize avarice and consumerism on the grounds that working ever harder to make ever more money to buy ever more stuff is not the road to a satisfying life. This seems basically correct, and there is plenty of evidence to back it up. The alternative is to argue that working, getting, and spending are the essential ingredients of human happiness—and it is fairly clear who stands to benefit most from that message.

Still, behind this radical critique there is perhaps a legitimate suspicion that the philosophy of frugality often has a rather individualistic and quietistic tinge to it. I husband my means, grow my beans, and keep myself spiritually clean, looking down on the poor suckers who are less enlightened, and feeling good about my small ecological footprint. Some frugal sages are certainly open to this criticism, but not all. In fact, one of the differences between the ancient schools of Epicureanism and Stoicism has to do with just this issue. Both schools seek peace of mind; but whereas Epicureans were inclined to withdraw from the world, minimizing political involvements since they are so liable to lead to frustration, the Stoics encouraged a strong sense of civic duty and looked to cultivate a frame of mind that will not be unduly disturbed by the annoyances and disappointments that such involvements inevitably bring. One can obviously advocate frugal simplicity in a nonindividualistic way. Indeed, the Stoics explicitly argued that the less we concern ourselves with private goods, the more we will be able to contribute to the public good. Moreover, in today's world, individualism finds its primary expression in consumerism and the competitive pursuit of wealth and status. So the critique of these tendencies is often also a critique of individualism.

Just as there is no necessary conflict between simple living and a concern for community, so there need be no contradiction between living simply and wanting to enjoy the fruits of civilization. A problem arises here only when our ability to enjoy these fruits depends on our having considerable private means. Public policy informed by the philosophy of frugality would thus try to ensure that this is not the case. In practical terms this involves two general goals. First, making sure that basic needs like food, housing, health care, child care, education, and transportation are available to all at low cost; and second, ensuring that, where feasible, other goods are available as public amenities rather than private privileges. These other goods include such things as access to areas of natural beauty, public beaches, trails, parks, gardens, libraries, sports facilities, art galleries, museums, concerts, lectures, and so on. This is already done to different degrees in various countries, but in many areas policies serving these ends could be extended considerably. In the United States, for instance, there is free universal education from ages six to seventeen, but the high cost of housing, day care, health care, and college makes it difficult for people to live on little without anxiety and a dispiriting sense of being at the bottom of the socioeconomic heap, this latter feeling being reinforced by the many visible indicators of inequality. There are some fabulous public amenities, from the great national parks to the Smithsonian Institution, the largest complex of museums and research centers in the world— all free—but there are also many areas where what J. K. Galbraith observed in the 1950s remains true: "public services have failed to keep abreast of private consumption," producing "an atmosphere of private opulence and public squalor."[8]

There is nothing very new or complicated about this argument for policies that help to realize some of the key values espoused by the frugal sages. The thrust of the argument is obviously egalitarian: the idea is to make the important sources of enjoyment and fulfillment available to everyone, not just to the well-off. A sound reason for doing this, apart from considerations of fairness, is that it makes it easier and more rational for people to opt for simple living. The reasoning here is prudential rather than moral. It does not appeal to the supposedly edifying effects of practicing the "monkish virtues." Rather, the idea is to promote peace of mind by lessening the anxiety many people experience over their ability to meet basic needs, to provide ready access to the most important sources of pleasure, and to make it easier for individuals to choose a more leisured lifestyle.

Giving people this choice is one important way of expanding their freedom, another basic value that more or less everyone claims to champion. If the only way to secure the basic elements of a good life is to work much harder than one would like, or than should be necessary in a rationally ordered society, that is a significant limitation on one's freedom (although it is not a limitation that seems to trouble those who, in the name of freedom, rigorously oppose the expansion of publicly funded goods). Freedom was certainly valued by the philosophers of ancient times as a key ingredient in their conception of the good life. But an interesting and significant difference between them and us is that we tend to be more pluralistic in what we allow to count as a good use of that freedom. Whereas Plato and Aristotle seem to assume that there is a specific kind of life that is ideal (and which by coincidence happens to be the philosophical life), most people today assume that there is no single model of *the* good life. Within certain parameters—that is, provided a person sufficiently enjoys such things as the satisfaction of basic needs, autonomy, political and religious freedom, mental health, and satisfying relationships—we recognize that many kinds of life may be fulfilling, including some far removed from the life of frugal simplicity. But that life still has much to recommend it for the values it expresses and the responsibilities it accepts. It remains one of the surest paths to contentment, and there are good reasons to associate it with wisdom.

Acknowledgments

I had no luck applying for grants to spend a year doing hands-on research into luxurious living and extravagant spending. I am grateful, though, for a summer stipend from the National Endowment for the Humanities that supported some of the early writing. Any views, findings, conclusions, or recommendations expressed in this book do not necessarily reflect those of the National Endowment for the Humanities. I would also like to acknowledge the institutional support provided by Alfred University, its College of Liberal Arts and Sciences, and my colleagues in the Division of Human Studies.

My thinking first turned toward frugality as a philosophical topic when I offered an honors course at Alfred in 2002 with the title Tightwaddery: The Good Life on a Dollar a Day. Although the course included some light-hearted practical components (such as having the students learn to cut each other's hair), it also involved much discussion of classic philosophical writings by thinkers like Epicurus and Thoreau, and contemporary social commentary by scholars such as Sut Jhally and Juliet Schor. I have taught the course several times since, along with a related course on happiness, and am grateful to the students in all these classes for everything that I learned from them. I also received valuable feedback from various people who attended the Bergren Forum at Alfred University in December 2012 where I first presented some of the ideas contained in the book.

Questions about simple or extravagant living readily provoke interesting conversations and entertaining anec-dotes. Consequently, there are many individuals who have contributed (sometimes unwittingly, perhaps) to my thinking on these topics. I would particularly like to thank the following: Mark Alfino, Bob Amico, Gordon Atlas, Cecilia Beach, Robert Bingham, Bonnie Booman, Sylvia Bryant, John Buckwalter, Beka Chase, Sarah Chase, Dan Cherneff, Jean Cherneff, Lila Cherneff, Peter Cherneff, Rose Cherneff, Chris Churchill, Ann Cobb, Jack Cobb, Max Cobb, Priscilla Cobb, Bill Dibrell, Paul Dingman, Beth Ann Dobie, Joe Dosch, Vicki Eaklor, Nancy Evange-lista, Juliana Gray, Allen Grove, Sam Hone-Studer, Chris Horner, Ben Howard, Amy Jacobson, Lou Lichtman, Fenna Mandolang, Randy Mayes, Mary McGee, Drew McInnes, Mary McInnes, Rahul Mehta, Dudley Merchant, Susan Merchant, Susan Morehouse, Otto Muller, Gary Ostrower, Tom Peterson, Rob Price, Becky Prophet, Craig Prophet, Melissa Ryan, Marilyn Saxton, Rosemary Shea, Sandra Singer, Jeff Slutyter-Beltrao, Djuna Thurley, and Hester Velmans.

Two anonymous reviewers chosen by Princeton Univer-sity Press provided useful feedback on the entire manuscript.

Lauren Lepow helped to improve the final text in many ways through her superb copyediting. And Rob Tempio offered invaluable assistance, support, and sound advice throughout. I am grateful to them all.

Finally, special thanks go to my immediate family, Vicky, Sophie, and Emily, for their love, support, and various contributions. As always, my deepest debt is to Vicky, for reading and critiquing the entire manuscript, and for everything else as well.

Notes

INTRODUCTION

1. Widely read books urging frugality and/or simple living, or critiquing consumerism, include the following: Amy Dacyczyn, *The Complete Tightwad Gazette* (New York: Villard, 1998); John de Graaf et al., *Affluenza: The All-Consuming Epidemic*, 2nd ed. (San Francisco: Berrett-Koehler, 2005); Juliet Schor, *The Overspent American: Why We Want What We Don't Need* (New York: Harper, 1999); Charles Long, *How to Survive without a Salary: Learning How to Live the Conserver Lifestyle* (Toronto: Warwick Publishing, 1988); Jeff Yeager, *The Ultimate Cheapskate's Road Map to True Riches: A Practical (and Fun) Guide to Enjoying Life More by Spending Less* (New York: Broadway Books, 2008); Vicki Robin and Joe Dominguez, *Your Money or Your Life: 9 Steps to Transforming Your Relationship with Money and Achieving Financial Independence* (New York: Penguin, 1992); Gregory Karp, *Living Rich by Spending Smart: How to Get More of What You Really Want* (Upper Saddle River, NJ: FT Press, 2008); Lauren Weber, *In Cheap We Trust: The Story of a Misunderstood American Virtue* (New York: Little, Brown and Company, 2009); Solomon Shepherd, *The Lost Art of Frugality: A Frug's Philosophy* (N.p.: HCL, 2002); Ed Romney, *Living Well on Practically Nothing* (Boulder, CO: Paladin Press, 2001).
2. Representative websites devoted to frugality or simple living include the following: Simple Living Network, The Simple Dollar, Value of Simple, The Minimalistas, Center for a New American Dream, Slow Movement, Degrowth, The Dollar Stretcher, Happy Simple Living, and Choosing Voluntary Simplicity.
3. William B. Irvine, *A Guide to the Good Life: The Ancient Art of Stoic Joy* (Oxford: Oxford University Press, 2009).

CHAPTER I: WHAT IS SIMPLICITY?

1. Benjamin Franklin, *Autobiography*, in *Autobiography and Other Writings*, ed. Ormand Seavey (Oxford: Oxford University Press, 1993), p. 85.
2. Ibid., pp. 81–82.
3. Ibid., p. 82.
4. Franklin, "The Way to Wealth," in *Autobiography and Other Writings*, pp. 264–74.
5. Other debt-ridden characters in Victorian fiction include, for instance, Rawdon Crawley in Thackeray's *Vanity Fair*, William Dorrit in Dickens's *Little Dorrit*, and Dr. Lydgate in George Eliot's *Middlemarch*.
6. Diogenes Laërtius, *The Lives and Opinions of Eminent Philosophers*, trans. C. D. Yonge (London: G. Bell and Sons, 1915), p. 230.
7. Epicurus, "Fragments," in *The Stoic and Epicurean Philosophers*, ed. Whitney J. Oates (New York: Modern Library, 1940), p. 44.
8. Daniel Defoe, *Robinson Crusoe* (New York: Norton, 1994), p. 86.
9. See Jean-Jacques Rousseau, *Emile; or, On Education*, trans. Allan Bloom (New York: Basic Books, 1979), pp. 184–86.
10. See M. Billerbeck, "The Ideal Cynic from Epictetus to Julian," in *The Cynics: The Cynic Movement in Antiquity and Its Legacy*, ed. R. Bracht Branham and Marie Odile Goulet-Cazé (Riverside: University of California Press, 2000), p. 226.
11. Marcus Aurelius, *Meditations*, XI, trans. Gregory Hays (New York: Modern Library, 2003), p. 150.
12. William Wordsworth, "The Tables Turned," in *The Prelude, Selected Poems and Sonnets*, ed. Carlos Baker (New York: Holt, Rinehart and Winston, 1954), p. 77.
13. Henry David Thoreau, *Walden and Civil Disobedience*, ed. Owen Thomas (New York: Norton, 1966), p. 61.
14. Ibid., p. 75.
15. Ibid., p. 88.
16. Ibid., p. 213.
17. Epicurus, "Fragments," in *The Stoic and Epicurean Philosophers*, p. 46.
18. Epicurus, "Principal Doctrines," in *The Stoic and Epicurean Philosophers*, p. 37.
19. Epicurus, "Fragments," in *The Stoic and Epicurean Philosophers*, p. 48.
20. For a vivid account of some of the early Christian ascetics, see Jean Kazez, *The Weight of Things: Philosophy and the Good Life* (Oxford: Blackwell, 2007), pp. 18–23.
21. See Friedrich Nietzsche, *On the Genealogy of Morals*, Third Essay, in *Basic Writings of Nietzsche*, trans. Walter Kaufmann (New York: Modern Library, 1968).

22. W. B. Yeats, "The Lake Isle of Innisfree," in *W. B. Yeats: Selected Poetry* (London: Macmillan, 1974), p. 16.
23. See Roy Baumeister and John Tierney, *Willpower: Rediscovering the Greatest Human Strength* (New York: Penguin, 2011).
24. Arthur Schopenhauer, "Aphorisms on the Wisdom of Life," in *Parerga and Paralipomena*, trans. E.F.J. Payne (Oxford: Clarendon Press, 1974), p. 417.
25. See Rudiger Safranski, *Schopenhauer and the Wild Years of Philosophy*, trans. Ewald Osers (Cambridge, MA: Harvard University Press, 1987), pp. 283–85.
26. Franklin, *Autobiography and Other Writings*, p. 229.
27. Ibid., p. 230.
28. Michel de Montaigne, "On Ancient Customs," in *The Complete Essays*, trans. and ed. M. A. Screech (New York: Penguin, 1987), p. 332.

CHAPTER 2: WHY SIMPLE LIVING IS SUPPOSED TO IMPROVE US

1. The distinction between virtues useful to self and virtues useful to others is taken from Hume's *An Enquiry Concerning the Principles of Morals*.
2. In one sense, utilitarians and other consequentialists close the gap between the moral and the prudential: for them, if an action promotes the general happiness, then that is a moral reason for doing it. But the arguments considered in chapter 3 mainly concern the happiness of the agent, not the happiness of everyone. They all have this form: if you practice frugal simplicity, you are more likely to be happy. Calling such reasons "prudential" has a solid philosophical pedigree derived from Kant, who labels them "counsels of prudence," and also accords well with common usage today.
3. See Plato, *Republic*, bk. 4, trans. G.M.A. Grube, revised by C.D.C. Reeve, in *Plato: Complete Works*, ed. John Cooper (Indianapolis: Hackett, 1997).
4. Cited in Julie Kerr, *Life in the Medieval Cloister* (London: Continuum, 2009), p. 43.
5. Frederick Rudolph, *The American College and University* (Athens: University of Georgia Press, 1990), p. 124.
6. Cited in ibid., p. 121.
7. Cited in ibid.
8. See ibid., pp. 122–23.
9. In fact there are other examples. Voltaire, for instance, made a fortune in 1728 when he teamed up with a mathematician to buy all the lottery tickets issued by the French government, realizing the prize being offered was much greater than the amount he would pay for the tickets.

10. Epicurus, Fragment 47, in *The Stoic and Epicurean Philosophers*, p. 47.
11. Marcus Aurelius, *Meditations*, p. 10.
12. Seneca, Letter on Holidays, in *The Stoic Philosophy of Seneca*, trans. Moses Hadas (New York: Norton, 1958), p. 180.
13. Seneca, "On Tranquility of Mind," in *The Stoic Philosophy of Seneca*, p. 120.
14. Proverbs 23:4.
15. Ibid., 5:9.
16. Ibid., 28:4.
17. Ecclesiastes 2:24.
18. 1 Timothy 6:10.
19. Plato, *Republic*, 1.331ab.
20. One of the best-known original examples of laconic speech is the phrase with which Spartan women handed departing warriors their shields: "With it, or on it," they would say, meaning that the man should only return either with honor or dead.
21. Jean-Jacques Rousseau, *First Discourse*, in *The First and Second Discourses*, trans. Roger D. and Judith R. Masters (New York: St. Martin's Press, 1964), p. 43.
22. The Spartans were defeated militarily by Thebes in 372 BC. Xenophon thought this happened because they had become soft and corrupt. Aristotle argued that their methods were well suited to times of war but not to times of peace. Plato suggests that in neglecting culture, their way of life became unbalanced. See H. Mitchell, *Sparta* (Cambridge: Cambridge University Press, 1952), p. 203. According to Mitchell, Spartan opposition to wealth and luxury has often been exaggerated: some men became rich and corrupt; many women were fond of jewelry.
23. Diogenes Laërtius, *Lives and Opinions*, p. 226.
24. Plato, *Republic*, 2.369b–372e.
25. Epicurus, Letter to Menoeceus, in *The Stoic and Epicurean Philosophers*, p. 31.
26. See Friedrich Nietzsche, *The Gay Science*, Aphorisms 110 and 344, in *The Gay Science*, trans. Walter Kaufmann (New York: Vintage, 1974).
27. See Jürgen Habermas, *The Theory of Communicative Action*, vol. 1, *Reason and the Rationalization of Society*, trans. Thomas McCarthy (Boston: Beacon Press, 1981).
28. Plutarch, *Makers of Rome*, trans. Ian Scott-Kilvert (New York: Penguin, 1965), p. 123.
29. Boethius, *The Consolation of Philosophy*, trans. V. E. Watts (New York: Penguin, 1969), p. 67.
30. Seneca, "On Providence," in *The Stoic Philosophy of Seneca*, p. 44.

31. Schopenhauer, "Aphorisms on the Wisdom of Life," in *Parerga and Paralipomena*, pp. 321–22.

32. Ibid., p. 331.

33. Some virtue ethicists might claim that quite apart from the specific arguments considered in this chapter, frugality just *is* one of the virtues and is therefore a good thing. Certainly some virtue ethicists write about virtues in this way at times. For instance, Rosalind Hursthouse in her book *On Virtue Ethics* (Oxford: Oxford University Press, 1999) writes, "According to virtue ethics, what is wrong with lying, when it is wrong, is not that it is unjust . . . but that it is dishonest, and dishonesty is a vice" (p. 6). While I believe the revival of virtue ethics has been an excellent thing in many ways, I have little sympathy with the idea that a character trait is good or bad *in itself*. To my way of thinking, we value those traits we call virtues, just as we value things like justice, freedom, truth, or beauty, because we believe they are associated, either causally or constitutively, with someone's happiness (understood in a rich sense, not merely as a succession of pleasant subjective experiences). To say that we value frugality because it is a virtue seems to me to be an empty statement, since a virtue is precisely a trait that we value.

CHAPTER 3: WHY SIMPLE LIVING IS THOUGHT TO MAKE US HAPPIER

1. Marcus Aurelius, *Meditations*, IV.

2. Seneca, Letters, in *The Stoic Philosophy of Seneca*, p. 244.

3. Proverbs 28:19.

4. Hesiod, *Works and Days*, in Hesiod, *Works and Days and Theogony,* trans. Stanley Lombardo (Indianapolis, IN: Hackett), line 310.

5. *The Rule of Saint Benedict*, trans. Abbot Justin McCann (Westminster: The Newman Press, 1952), chap. 48, "On the Daily Manual Labor."

6. Franklin, "The Way to Wealth," in *Autobiography and Other Writings*, p. 268.

7. W. H. Davies, "Leisure," in *Collected Poems of William H. Davies* (New York: Knopf, 1927), p. 18.

8. William Wordsworth, "Expostulation and Reply," in *The Prelude, Selected Poems and Sonnets*, p. 76.

9. Paul Lafargue, *The Right to Be Lazy and Other Studies*, trans. Charles H. Kerr (Chicago: Charles H. Kerr & Company, 1907), p. 30.

10. Bertrand Russell, "In Praise of Idleness," in *In Praise of Idleness and Other Essays* (New York: Unwin Books, 1962), p. 12.

11. See Bob Black, "The Abolition of Work," in *The Abolition of Work and Other Essays* (Port Townsend, WA: Loompanics Unlimited,

1986), and Alain de Botton, *The Pleasures and Sorrows of Work* (New York: Vintage, 2010). Other works on this theme include Anders Hayden, *Sharing the Work, Saving the Planet* (London: Zed, 2000); Juliet Schor, *The Overworked American: The Unexpected Decline of Leisure* (New York: Basic Books, 1992); and Madeleine Bunting, *Willing Slaves: How the Overwork Culture Is Ruining Our Lives* (New York: Harper, 2005).

12. Schopenhauer, *Parerga and Paralipomena*, p. 351.

13. Seneca, "On Tranquility of Mind," in *The Stoic Philosophy of Seneca*, p. 91.

14. Karl Marx, *Economic and Philosophic Manuscripts of 1844*, in *The Marx-Engels Reader*, 2nd ed., ed. Robert C. Tucker (New York: Norton, 1978), p. 74.

15. Alain de Botton, "Workers of the World, Relax," *New York Times*, September 6, 2004.

16. Sam Volk, "For the Love of Money," *New York Times*, January 18, 2014.

17. Barbara Ehrenreich, *Nickel and Dimed: On (Not) Getting By in America* (New York: Metropolitan Books/Henry Holt & Company, 2001).

18. Epicurus, "Fragments," in *The Stoic and Epicurean Philosophers*, p. 50.

19. Seneca, "Consolation to Helvia," in *The Stoic Philosophy of Seneca*, p. 111.

20. Boethius, *The Consolation of Philosophy*, p. 66.

21. Thoreau, *Walden*, p. 88.

22. See Kazez, *The Weight of Things*, chap. 5.

23. Epicurus, "Fragments," in *The Stoic and Epicurean Philosophers*, p. 51.

24. Robert and Edward Skidelsky, *How Much Is Enough? Money and the Good Life* (New York: Other Press, 2012), p. 40.

25. Cited in ibid., p. 39.

26. Plato, *Republic*, 442a.

27. Epicurus, "Fragments," in *The Stoic and Epicurean Philosophers*, p. 41.

28. "Zadie Smith's Rules for Writers," *Guardian*, February 22, 2010.

29. Dave Bruno, *The 100 Thing Challenge: How I Got Rid of Almost Everything, Remade My Life, and Regained My Soul* (New York: William Morrow, 2010).

30. See Daniel Gilbert, *Stumbling on Happiness* (New York: Vintage, 2007).

31. Jerome M. Segal, *Graceful Simplicity: Toward a Philosophy and Politics of Simple Living* (New York: Henry Holt, 1999), pp. 52–53.

32. John Rawls, *A Theory of Justice* (Cambridge, MA: Harvard University Press, 1970), p. 440.
33. Marcus Aurelius, *Meditations*, XII.
34. See Thomas More, *Utopia*, trans. Clarence Miller (New Haven, CT: Yale University Press, 2014), bk.2, chap. 4.
35. Henry Howard, "The Means to Attain a Happy Life," in *The Poems of Henry Howard, Earl of Surrey* (Seattle: University of Washington Press, 1920), p. 94.
36. Schopenhauer, *Parerga and Paralipomena*, p. 404.
37. Ibid., pp. 405–6.
38. Matthew 6:25–34 (King James Version).
39. Marcus Aurelius, *Meditations*, VII, p. 86.
40. Seneca, "On the Shortness of Life," in *The Stoic Philosophy of Seneca*, p. 57.
41. Seneca, Letters, in *The Stoic Philosophy of Seneca*, p. 179.
42. Ibid., pp. 178–79.
43. Alice Park, "Study: Stress Shrinks the Brain and Lowers Our Ability to Cope with Adversity," *Time*, January 9, 2012.
44. Elizabeth W. Dunn and Michael Norton, "Don't Indulge. Be Happy," *New York Times*, July 7, 2012.
45. Simon Laham, *The Science of Sin* (New York: Three Rivers Press, 2012), p. 53.
46. For research supporting the general idea that becoming accustomed to something as the norm interferes with our ability to derive enjoyment from lesser versions of that sort of thing, see Christopher Hsee, Reid Hastie, and Jinquin Chen, "Hedonomics: Bridging Decision Research with Happiness Research," *Perspectives on Psychological Science* 3, no. 3 (2008): 224–43.
47. Ralph Waldo Emerson, "The American Scholar," in *Selections from Ralph Waldo Emerson*, ed. Stephen E. Whicher (Boston: Houghton Mifflin, 1957), p. 78.
48. Marcus Aurelius, *Meditations*, III, p. 28.
49. Ibid., p. 27.
50. Seneca, "Consolation of Helva," in *The Stoic Philosophy of Seneca*, p. 117.
51. Epicurus, "Fragments," in *The Stoic and Epicurean Philosophers*, p. 51.
52. Upton Sinclair, *I, Candidate for Governor: And How I Got Licked* (Berkeley: University of California Press, 1994).
53. See Mihaly Csikszentmihalyi, *Flow: The Psychology of Optimal Experience* (New York: Harper & Row, 1990).
54. The term "frugal zealot" is taken from Dacyczyn, author of *The Complete Tightwad Gazette*.
55. International Naturist Federation website: http://www.inf-fni.org/.

56. Epicurus, *The Stoic and Epicurean Philosophers*, p. 42.
57. Thoreau, *Walden*, pp. 88–89.
58. See E. O. Wilson, *Biophilia* (Cambridge, MA: Harvard University Press, 1984). See also Erich Fromm, *The Heart of Man: Its Genius for Good and Evil* (New York: Harper & Row, 1964).
59. See Richard Louv, *Last Child in the Woods: Saving Our Children from Nature-Deficit Disorder* (Chapel Hill, NC: Algonquin, 2008).
60. See "A Prescription for Better Health: Go Alfresco." *Harvard Health Publications*, July 2010.
61. Robert and Edward Skidelsky include "harmony with nature" in their list of seven basic elements of the good life. See Skidelsky and Skidelsky, *How Much Is Enough?*, pp. 162–63.
62. "City vs. Country: Who Is Healthier?" *Wall Street Journal*, July 12, 2011.

CHAPTER 4: WHY THE PHILOSOPHY OF FRUGALITY IS A HARD SELL

1. See Plato, *Republic*, 2.369a.
2. Pew Research Center, "Gen Nexters Say Getting Rich Is Their Generation's Top Goal," January 23, 2007.
3. Alicia Hansen, "How Much Implicit Tax Revenue Did Lotteries Raise in FY2010?" Tax Foundation, December 28, 2010.
4. Mark Gillespie, "Lotteries Most Popular Form of Gambling for Americans," *Gallup Poll Monthly*, no. 405 (January 1999).
5. Daniel P. Ray and Yasmin Ghahremani, "Credit Card Statistics, Industry Facts, Debt Statistics," http://www.creditcards.com/credit-card-news/credit-card-industry-facts-personal-debt-statistics-1276.php.
6. BBA Statistics, April 3, 2012.
7. Diogenes Laërtius, *Lives and Opinions*, p. 83.
8. Plato, *Republic*, 8.553cd.
9. Hal R. Arkes and Catherine Blumer, "The Psychology of Sunk Cost," *Organizational Behavior and Decision Processes* 35 (1985): 124–40.
10. I am indebted to Lou Lichtman and Gordon Atlas for pointing out this problem.
11. Aristotle, *Nicomachean Ethics* (1119b–1122a), in *The Basic Works of Aristotle*, ed. Richard McKeon (New York: Random House, 1941).
12. See Sonja Lyubomirsky, *The How of Happiness: A New Approach to Getting the Life You Want* (New York: Penguin Press, 2008), pp. 92–94.
13. Voltaire, "Luxury," in *Philosophical Dictionary*, trans. Peter Gay (New York: Basic Books, 1962), p. 369.
14. Ibid.
15. See, for instance, *Odyssey*, bk. 4.

16. See 1 Kings 10:16–26.

17. See *The Travels of Marco Polo, the Venetian*, trans. and ed. William Marsden, reedited by Thomas Wright (New York: Doubleday, 1948), bk. 2, chaps. 6–13.

18. Martha Nussbaum, "How to Write about Poverty," *Times Literary Supplement*, October 10, 2012.

19. Paul K. Piff et al., "Higher Social Class Predicts Increased Unethical Behavior," *Proceedings of the National Academy of the Sciences of the United States of America* 109, no. 11 (2012): 4086–91.

20. See Barry Schwartz, *The Paradox of Choice* (New York: HarperCollins, 2004).

21. Richard Wilkinson and Kate Pickett, *The Spirit Level: Why More Equal Societies Almost Always Do Better* (London: Bloomsbury, 2009); Joseph Stiglitz, *The Price of Inequality: How Today's Divided Society Endangers Our Future* (New York: Norton, 2013). It should be noted that Wilkinson and Pickett's methodology, evidence, and conclusions have been challenged. See, for instance, Peter Saunders, "Beware False Prophets: Equality, the Good Society and the Spirit Level," *Policy Exchange*, July 8, 2010.

22. Daniel Kahneman and Angus Deaton, "High Income Improves Evaluation of Life but Not Emotional Well-Being, *Proceedings of the National Academy of Sciences of the United States of America*, August 4, 2010.

23. See Daniel Kahneman, *Thinking Fast and Slow* (New York: Farrar, Straus and Giroux, 2011), p. 396.

24. Skidelsky and Skidelsky, *How Much Is Enough?*, p. 75.

25. Plato, *Republic*, 4.442a.

26. Nietzsche, *The Gay Science*, bk. 1, 14.

27. See Kathleen D. Vohs, Nicole L. Mead, and Miranda R. Goode, "The Psychological Consequences of Money," *Science* 314, no. 5802 (November 2006): 1154–56.

28. Bernard Mandeville, "The Grumbling Hive," in *The Fable of the Bees, or Private Vices, Publick Benefits*, ed. Irwin Primer (New York: Capricorn Books, 1962), lines 177–202.

29. Adam Smith, *The Theory of Moral Sentiments* (Oxford: Oxford University Press, 1979), p. 184.

30. See Skidelsky and Skidelsky, *How Much Is Enough?*, pp. 49–53.

31. David Hume, "On Refinement in the Arts," in *Essays: Moral, Political, and Literary* (Indianapolis, IN: Liberty Fund, 1985), p. 272.

32. See Edward Deci, *Why We Do What We Do: Understanding Self-Motivation* (New York: Penguin, 1996).

33. See Dan Ariely, "What's the Value of a Big Bonus?" *New York Times*, November 19, 2008.

CHAPTER 5: THE PROS AND CONS OF EXTRAVAGANCE

1. Diogenes Laërtius, *Lives and Opinions*, p. 83.
2. CNN.com Transcripts, September 21, 2001, http://transcripts.cnn.com/TRANSCRIPTS/0109/21/se.20.html.
3. "Stop Saving Now!" *Newsweek*, March 13, 2009.
4. Scott Shane, "Start Up Failure Rates: The Definitive Numbers," *Small Business Trends*, December 17, 2012.
5. See Phil Izzo, "Congratulations to the Class of 2014, Most Indebted Ever," *Wall Street Journal*, May 16, 2014.
6. Proverbs 19:10.
7. Thorstein Veblen, *The Theory of the Leisure Class: An Economic Study of Institutions* (New York: Dover, 1994), chap. 4.
8. Schor, *The Overspent American*.
9. Peter Singer, "The Singer Solution to World Poverty," *New York Times*, September 5, 1999.
10. According to the US Bureau of Labor Statistics, Report 1042, April 2013, consumer units whose income placed them in the lowest 20 percent spent on average $3,547 in 2011 on food, which averages out to $296 per month. http://www.bls.gov/cex/csxann11.pdf.
11. Claudia D'Arpizio et al., "Luxury Goods Worldwide Market Study Fall–Winter 2014: The Rise of the Borderless Consumer," *Bain Report*, December 31, 2014.
12. Federal Reserve Economic Data, https://research.stlouisfed.org/fred2/series/GFDEBTN.
13. Goethe, *Faust*, trans. Walter Kaufmann (New York: Anchor Books, 1963), lines 1770–75.
14. Ibid., lines 1753–59.
15. Ibid., lines 1699–1702.
16. Plato, *Gorgias*, 492e, in *Plato: Complete Works*.
17. See, for instance, Leaf Van Boven and Thomas Gilovitch, "To Do or to Have? That Is the Question," *Journal of Personality and Social Psychology* 85, no. 6 (2003): 1193–1202.
18. Seneca, "On Tranquility of Mind," in *The Stoic Philosophy of Seneca*, p. 93.
19. See Aristotle, *Nicomachean Ethics*, bk. 4.
20. Plato, *Republic*, 3.416c–417b.
21. Melanie Hicken, "Average Wedding Bill in 2012: $28,400." CNN Money, http://money.cnn.com/2013/03/10/pf/wedding-cost/.
22. Cited in "The Wedding Industrial Complex," *Newsweek*, June 15, 2013.
23. See Malcolm Moore, "Chinese Brides Go for Gold as Their Dowries Get Bigger and Bigger," *Telegraph*, January 4, 2013.

CHAPTER 6: THE PHILOSOPHY OF FRUGALITY IN A MODERN ECONOMY

1. Joanne Ciulla, *The Working Life: The Promise and Betrayal of Modern Work* (New York: Three Rivers Press, 2000), p. 200.
2. Hesiod, *Works and Days*, lines 133–39.
3. Ovid, *Metamorphoses*, bk. 1.
4. *The Stoic Philosophy of Seneca*, p. 228.
5. Boethius, *The Consolation of Philosophy*, pp. 68–69.
6. Jean-Jacques Rousseau, *Discourse on the Origins of Inequality*, in, *First and Second Discourses*, p. 105.
7. Ibid., p. 110.
8. Ibid., p. 116.
9. See Carl Honoré, *In Praise of Slowness: How a Worldwide Movement Is Challenging the Cult of Speed* (San Francisco: Harper, 2004).
10. Diane Coyle, *The Economics of Enough* (Princeton, NJ: Princeton University Press, 2011), p. 22.
11. See Neil Irwin, "You Can't Feed a Family with G.D.P.," *New York Times*, September 16, 2014. The median household income figure is taken from Carmen DeNavas-Walt and Bernadette D. Proctor, *Income and Poverty in the United States: 2013*, US Census Bureau, September 2014.
12. For a succinct summary of the history of the debate over the connection between material and subjective well-being, see Justin Fox, "The Economics of Well-Being," *Harvard Business Review*, January 2012.
13. See, for instance, Dirk Philipsen, "Rethinking GDP: Why We Must Broaden Our Economic Measures of Success," *Nation*, June 8, 2011.
14. See Jon Gertner, "The Rise and Fall of the GDP," *New York Times*, May 13, 2010.
15. Coyle, *The Economics of Enough*, p. 51.
16. Richard Easterlin, "Does Money Buy Happiness?" *National Affairs*, no. 30 (Winter 1973).
17. Coyle, *The Economics of Enough*, pp. 23–24.
18. Richard A. Easterlin et al., "The Happiness-Income Paradox Revisited," *Proceedings of the National Academy of the Sciences of the United States of America* 107, no. 52 (October 2010): 22463–68.
19. Kahneman and Deaton, "High Income Improves Evaluation of Life but Not Emotional Well-Being."
20. See Robert H. Frank, *Luxury Fever: Why Money Fails to Satisfy in an Era of Success* (New York: Free Press, 1999), chaps. 8 and 9.
21. Paul Krugman, "Invest, Divest, and Prosper," *New York Times*, June 27, 2013.

22. Steve Crabtree, "In U.S., Depression Rates Higher for Long-Term Unemployed," *Gallup Well-Being*, June 9, 2014, http://www.gallup.com/poll/171044/depression-rates-higher-among-long-term-unemployed.aspx.

23. See Frank, *Luxury Fever*, pp. 105–6.

24. Dan Witters and Sangeeta Agrawi, "Smoking Linked to $278 Billion in Losses for U.S. Employers," *Gallup Well-Being*, September 26, 2013, http://www.gallup.com/poll/164651/smoking-linked-278-billion-losses-employers.aspx.

25. "Global Food—Waste Not, Want Not," Report by the Institution of Mechanical Engineers, 2013, http://www.imeche.org/docs/default-source/reports/Global_Food_Report.pdf.

26. Dana Gunders, "How America Is Losing up to 40 Percent of Its Food from Farm to Fork to Landfill," National Resources Defense Council Issue Paper, August 2012, http://www.nrdc.org/food/files/wasted-food-ip.pdf.

27. "'Simply Unacceptable': Homelessness and the Human Right to Housing in the United States 2011," A Report of the National Law Center on Homelessness & Poverty, http://www.nlchp.org/Simply_Unacceptable.

28. Tanuka Loha, "Housing: It's a Wonderful Right," Amnesty International Human Rights Now Blog, December 21, 2011, http://blog.amnestyusa.org/us/housing-its-a-wonderful-right/.

29. Mary Ellen Podmolik, "Average Home Size Sets New Record," *Chicago Tribune*, June 2, 2014; US Census Bureau data, https://www.census.gov/const/C25Ann/sftotalmedavgsqft.pdf.

30. See Schor, *The Overspent American*, pp. 169–73.

31. Anne Lowry, "The Wealth Gap in America Is Growing, Too," *New York Times*, April 2, 2014.

32. See, for instance, "Thirty-Five Hours of Misery: Europe Wakes Up to the Folly of Excessive Labour-Market Regulation," *Economist*, July 15, 2004.

33. Richard Venturi, "Busting the Myth of France's 35-Hour Workweek," *BBC Capital*, March 13, 2014, http://www.bbc.com/capital/story/20140312-frances-mythic-35-hour-week.

34. See Chris Matthews, "French Workers Aren't As Lazy As You Think," *Fortune*, August 28, 2014.

35. OECD StatExtracts, http://stats.oecd.org.

36. Cited in Peter Hawkins, "Nobel Winner Defends France, *Connexion*, December 2013.

37. Figures taken from *Federal Reserve Economic Data*, http://research.stlouisfed.org/fred2/. See also Anders Hayden's account of the progress made by the Work-Time Reduction movement in *Sharing the Work, Saving the Planet*.

38. Staffan Linder, *The Harried Leisure Class* (New York: Columbia University Press, 1970).
39. Skidelsky and Skidelsky, *How Much Is Enough?*.
40. Schor, *The Overworked American*.
41. Judith Lichtenberg, "Consuming Because Others Consume," *Social Theory and Practice* 22, no. 3 (Fall 1996): 273–97.

CHAPTER 7: THE ENVIRONMENTALIST CASE FOR SIMPLE LIVING

1. Genesis 1:28.
2. Aristotle, *Politics*, bk. 1, chap. 8, trans. Benjamin Jowett, in *Basic Works of Aristotle*, p. 1137.
3. Keith Thomas, *Man and the Natural World: Changing Attitudes in England 1500–1800* (Oxford: Oxford University Press, 1983), p. 91.
4. Ibid., p. 264.
5. De Graaf et al., *Affluenza*, p. 93.
6. Keith Heidorn, "The Art of Ecofrugality, *Living Gently Quarterly*, http://www.islandnet.com/~see/living/articles/frugal.htm.
7. "Corn Biofuels Worse Than Gasoline on Global Warming in Short Term—Study," *Guardian*, April 20, 2014, http://www.theguardian.com/environment/2014/apr/20/corn-biofuels-gasoline-global-warming.
8. Christina Nunez, "How Green Are Those Solar Panels, Really?" *National Geographic*, November 11, 2014.
9. "An Updated Lifecycle Assessment Study for Disposable and Reusable Nappies," publication of the Environmental Agency, 2008, https://www.gov.uk/government/uploads/system/uploads/attachment_data/file/291130/scho0808boir-e-e.pdf.
10. Richard Gray, "Greener by Miles, *Telegraph*, June 3, 2007.
11. David Owen, *Green Metropolis: Why Living Smaller, Living Closer, and Driving Less Are the Keys to Sustainability* (New York: Riverhead Books, 2009).
12. Lloyd Alter, "Is Burning Wood for Heat Really Green?" *Treehugger*, June 6, 2011.
13. Michael Pollan, *The Botany of Desire* (New York: Random House, 2002).
14. Michael Specter, "Big Foot," *New Yorker*, February 28, 2008.
15. See Owen, *Green Metropolis*, p. 300. See also Will Boisvert, "An Environmentalist on the Lie of Locavorism," *Observer*, April 16, 2013, http://observer.com/2013/04/the-lie-of-locavorism/4/.
16. Michael Munger, "Recycling: Can It Be Wrong When It Feels So Right?" *Cato Unbound*, June 3, 2013.
17. See Michael Braungart and William McDonough, *Cradle to Cradle: Remaking the Way We Make Things* (New York: North Point Press, 2002).

18. See Frank, *Luxury Fever*.
19. Numbers taken from National Priorities Project, https://www
    .nationalpriorities.org/budget-basics/federal-budget-101/spending/.

CONCLUSION

1. Marcus Aurelius, *Meditations*, VII, pp. 92–93.
2. United Nations Department of Economic and Social Affairs, "World
   Urbanization Prospects: The 2005 Revision," http://www.un.org
   /esa/population/publications/WUP2005/2005wup.htm.
3. Matthew B. Crawford, *Shop Class as Soulcraft: An Inquiry into the
   Value of Work* (New York: Penguin Press, 2009).
4. See Annie Lowrey, "Changed Life of the Poor: Better Off, but Far
   Behind," *New York Times*, April 30, 2014.
5. Jon Mooallem, "The Self-Storage Self," *New York Times*, September
   2, 2009.
6. Karl Marx and Friedrich Engels, *The German Ideology*, in Tucker,
   The Marx-Engels Reader, p. 160.
7. Cited in de Graaf et al., *Affluenza*, p. 184.
8. John Kenneth Galbraith, *The Affluent Society* (New York: Houghton
   Mifflin, 1958), p. 203.

Index